T0334109

"Both McMullen and Otteson are adept at navigating the ethical and moral arguments in the abstract, but each is willing to take seriously the problems of implementation and practical consequence. I enjoyed the discussion, and I expect that you will also."

Michael Munger, *Duke University*

Should Wealth Be Redistributed?

A central contested issue in contemporary economics and political philosophy is whether governments should redistribute wealth. In this book, a philosopher and an economist debate this question. James Otteson argues that respect for individual persons requires that the government should usually not alter the results of free exchanges, and so redistribution is usually wrong. Steven McMullen argues that governments should substantially redistribute wealth in order to ensure that all have a minimal opportunity to participate in economic life. Over the course of the exchange, the authors investigate a number of important questions. Is redistribution properly a question of justice, and what is the appropriate standard? Has the welfare state been effective at fighting poverty? Can we expect government intervention in the economy to be helpful or counterproductive? Are our obligations to help the poor best met through government action, or through private philanthropy and individual charity?

The book features clear statements of each argument, responses to counterarguments, in-text definitions, a glossary of key terms, and section summaries. Scholars and students alike will find it easy to follow the debate and learn the key concepts from philosophy, politics, and economics necessary to understand each position.

Key Features:

- Offers clear arguments written to be accessible to readers and students without a deep background in economics, philosophy, or political theory.
- Fosters a deep exchange of ideas with responses from each author to the main arguments.

- Provides in-text definitions and a glossary with definitions of key terms.
- Includes section summaries that give an overview of the main arguments and a comprehensive bibliography for further reading.

Steven McMullen is Associate Professor of Economics at Hope College and Executive Editor of the journal *Faith & Economics*. He is the author of *Animals and the Economy* (2016) and *Digital Life Together: The Challenge of Technology for Christian Schools* (2020).

James R. Otteson is John T. Ryan Jr. Professor of Business Ethics and Faculty Director of the Notre Dame Deloitte Center for Ethical Leadership, Business Honors Program, and Business Ethics and Society Program, at the University of Notre Dame. His most recent books are *Honorable Business* (2019) and *Seven Deadly Economic Sins* (2021).

Little Debates About Big Questions

About the series:

Philosophy asks questions about the fundamental nature of reality, our place in the world, and what we should do. Some of these questions are perennial: for example, *Do we have free will? What is morality?* Some are much newer: for example, *How far should free speech on campus extend? Are race, sex and gender social constructs?* But all of these are among the big questions in philosophy and they remain controversial.

Each book in the *Little Debates About Big Questions* series features two professors on opposite sides of a big question. Each author presents their own side, and the authors then exchange objections and replies. Short, lively, and accessible, these debates showcase diverse and deep answers. Pedagogical features include standard form arguments, section summaries, bolded key terms and principles, glossaries, and annotated reading lists.

The debate format is an ideal way to learn about controversial topics. Whereas the usual essay or book risks overlooking objections against its own proposition or misrepresenting the opposite side, in a debate each side can make their case at equal length, and then present objections the other side must consider. Debates have a more conversational and fun style too, and we selected particularly talented philosophers—in substance and style—for these kinds of encounters.

Debates can be combative—sometimes even descending into anger and animosity. But debates can also be cooperative. While our authors disagree strongly, they work together to help each other and the reader get clearer on the ideas, arguments, and objections. This is intellectual progress, and a much-needed model for civil and constructive disagreement.

The substance and style of the debates will captivate interested readers new to the questions. But there's enough to interest experts too. The debates will be especially useful for courses in philosophy and related subjects—whether as primary or secondary readings—and a few debates can be combined to make up the reading for an entire course.

We thank the authors for their help in constructing this series. We are honored to showcase their work. They are all preeminent scholars or rising-stars in their fields, and through these debates they share what's been discovered with a wider audience. This is a paradigm for public philosophy, and will impress upon students, scholars, and other interested readers the enduring importance of debating the big questions.

Tyron Goldschmidt, Fellow of the Rutgers Center for Philosophy of Religion, USA
Dustin Crummett, Ludwig Maximilian University of Munich, Germany

For more information about this series, please visit:
https://www.routledge.com/Little-Debates-about-Big-Questions/book-series/LDABQ

Should Wealth Be Redistributed?

A Debate

Steven McMullen and James R. Otteson

FOREWORD BY MICHAEL MUNGER

Routledge
Taylor & Francis Group

NEW YORK AND LONDON

Cover image: John Finney photography, via Getty Images

First published 2023
by Routledge
605 Third Avenue, New York, NY 10158

and by Routledge
4 Park Square, Milton Park, Abingdon, Oxon, OX14 4RN

Routledge is an imprint of the Taylor & Francis Group, an informa business

© 2023 Steven McMullen and James R. Otteson

ISBN: 978-0-367-42663-7 (hbk)
ISBN: 978-0-367-42662-0 (pbk)
ISBN: 978-0-367-85426-3 (ebk)

DOI: 10.4324/9780367854263

Typeset in Sabon
by codeMantra

Contents

Acknowledgments

Steven McMullen

This project has been a great intellectual experience and has given me the opportunity to carefully articulate ideas that I think about often, but that I too rarely subject to careful scrutiny. As such, my first thanks are to my collaborators in this project, most notably, Jim Otteson, who has been wonderful to work with, but also our editors Tyron Goldschmidt and Dustin Crummett. It is my belief that more books of this type should exist, and so I appreciate the work that Ty and Dustin are doing to edit this series, and the support they have received from Routledge.

Much of the time I spent on this book occurred during a sabbatical release offered by Hope College. I am thankful to be at an institution that supports me in this work, and for the unwavering support of my colleagues even when they disagree with me. As I was writing, I had my students and colleagues in mind as my audience, and I hope the book benefits them in some way.

The real unsung hero of all my writing is my wife Laura. There is no project I do that does not enlist her active support, and that has been especially true for this book.

Since many of the arguments I make in this book are things about which I have changed my mind over my career, I want to dedicate my portion of the book to my parents. They made it seem normal to carefully consider one's views, and be ready to learn and change through conversation with others.

James R. Otteson

I thank Tyron Goldschmidt for inviting and encouraging me to contribute to this volume, and for his various suggestions for improvement. I also thank Steven McMullen for writing it with me, for providing the opportunity to think this important issue through, and for challenging me to improve and reconsider my arguments.

I thank Routledge for publishing the volume. I also thank Dustin Crummett for helpful editorial advice.

For extensive help with and criticism of earlier versions of my contributions, I thank Gregory Robson and an anonymous reviewer. I have incorporated many of their suggestions, mostly silently, and my contributions are much improved for their considerable efforts. All remaining errors are mine alone.

I also thank my family—my beloved Katharine, Victoria, James, Joseph, and George—for their indulgence, understanding, and support. They are in this, as in all I do, my *sine qua non*.

I dedicate my contribution to this volume to my son James, whose unrelenting drive for excellence continues to inspire and amaze me.

Foreword

Michael Munger

In his famous short story, "Harrison Bergeron," Kurt Vonnegut imagined a future that took the moral imperative of social equality to its logical policy conclusions:

> The year was 2081, and everybody was finally equal. They weren't only equal before God and the law. They were equal every which way. Nobody was smarter than anybody else. Nobody was better looking than anybody else. Nobody was stronger or quicker than anybody else. All this equality was due to the 211th, 212th, and 213th Amendments to the Constitution, and to the unceasing vigilance of agents of the United States Handicapper General.

At the ballet, dancers who were more talented or athletic were obliged to wear heavy weights; people whose minds were faster or sharper had to wear helmets that delivered stupefying electric shocks; and news readers could not read out loud:

> The television program was suddenly interrupted for a news bulletin. It wasn't clear at first as to what the bulletin was about, since the announcer, like all announcers, had a serious speech impediment. For about half a minute, and in a state of high excitement, the announcer tried to say, "Ladies and Gentlemen."
> He finally gave up, handed the bulletin to a ballerina to read.
> "That's all right—" Hazel said of the announcer," he tried. That's the big thing. He tried to do the best he could with what God gave him. He should get a nice raise for trying so hard."

Of course, "Harrison Bergeron" is just fiction, and subversive fiction at that. No one (almost no one?) has proposed a society with equality of outcomes enforced by an intrusive national bureaucracy under the "Handicapper General." The standard of equality proposed in this book, and debated in a spirited fashion by Steven McMullen, of Hope College, and James Otteson, of the University of Notre Dame, is equality of *opportunity*, not outcome.

There are three large difficulties that any such discussion must address, of course. These are (1) the problem of innate differences; (2) the merits of the argument for forcible redistribution, where resources are taken at gunpoint from some and given to others; and (3) the "public choice" objections about the implementation and incentive effects of such a program, even if it is justified on the merits.

Innate differences: Pierre Omidyar, founder of eBay, famously said, "Everyone is born equally capable but lacks equal opportunity." Well, gosh; I'm not sure that's right. I might have tried for a decade to practice, but I still would not have the physical features required to play in the National Basketball Association in the United States, or to play on a Champions League European Soccer team. "Equal opportunity" would not have been enough; the only way I could have a fair chance to play in those sports is if the more physically gifted had to wear heavy weights, and possibly leg irons. I'm not very athletic, frankly.

The problem is that "innate differences" are not as obvious as they seem for most occupations and activities. Adam Smith, in his underappreciated parable of "The Philosopher and the Street Porter," shows how opportunity and experience may well be more important than many "superior" people might allow.

> The difference of natural talents in different men, is, in reality, much less than we are aware of; and the very different genius which appears to distinguish men of different professions, when grown up to maturity, is not upon many occasions so much the *cause*, as the *effect* of the division of labour. The difference between the most dissimilar characters, between a philosopher and a common street porter, for example, seems to arise not so much from nature, as from habit, custom, and education. When they came into the world, and for the first six or eight years of their existence, they were, perhaps, very much alike, and neither their parents nor playfellows could perceive

any remarkable difference. About that age, or soon after, *they come to be employed in very different occupations.* The difference of talents comes *then* to be taken notice of, and widens by degrees, till at last the vanity of the philosopher is willing to acknowledge scarce any resemblance. (Adam Smith, *Wealth of Nations*, Book I; emphasis added.)

The point is that the people who are *now* the philosopher and street porter were once very similar, and possibly nearly indistinguishable. One *developed* the talent of "being a philosopher," by being afforded chances to study and learn, and by being sheltered from an obligation to work to support herself and her family. The apparent differences, stark and dramatic to an observer when the two people are 40 years old, depended on a background system where others did all the other things—making food and clothing, providing housing and security, and so on—that made it possible for the philosopher to study for decades. Smith does not quite go as far as Pierre Omidyar, in saying that all differences in outcomes are due to differences in opportunities, but he is quite clear in saying that the innate differences are not nearly so large as "the vanity of the philosopher" would like to believe.

Smith's argument always reminds me of Jim Hightower's quip about a former U.S. President: "He's a man who was born on third base, and thinks he hit a triple." Innate merit is almost always *too* powerful an argument, because it "explains" too much: tall people play basketball; fast people play European football; geniuses follow Einstein or Picasso into theoretical physics or art. But innate merit fails to account for the fact that what appears to be profound differences in mature people may simply be the accretion over decades of differences in opportunity. Most "winners" in such a system think innate merit is the entire explanation for observed differences; most "losers" in such a system think denial of opportunity is the key factor.

The excessive determinism of the innate merit argument is simply unacceptable in a democratic society, where there are too many differences that are due to effort, and practice, and luck, to accept observed outcomes as "deserved," which brings us to the argument for, and against, coercive redistribution.

Redistribution: Steven McMullen takes up the banner of redistribution, partly as a corrective to unequal opportunities, and partly as a means of ensuring that future generations will have opportunities that, while not completely equal, are less disparate than the current situation of wild and undeserved difference. His argument has four parts:

- Distributive justice requires that each person has "the opportunity to participate in and contribute to economic life."
- With regard to basic economic opportunity, the United States is highly unequal, with differences attributable to differences in access to resources, differences in parental educational achievement and wealth, and the legacy of racial oppression.
- Some (at least) of the redistributive government programs that already exist would, if expanded further, increase the opportunities of those now excluded to participate and contribute to the economic life of the nation. This would have the moral benefit of affording greater opportunities for all, but it would also have the consequentialist benefit of expanding the size of the economy for all participants. As it stands, a substantial proportion of the U.S. population is neither able to support itself nor adequately supported by public programs. Increased opportunities would give many people the chance to realize their potential in ways that would actually reduce the burden on future generations.
- Therefore, according to McMullen, the U.S. government should expand the redistribution in those ways that will expand opportunity.

The response of James Otteson concedes at the outset that many, and perhaps most, of the goals of the McMullen program are uncontroversial. There are sound reasons to care about reducing historically and morally contingent barriers to equality of opportunity, and the exclusion of poor and minority citizens from basic chances to create flourishing lives for themselves and their families is one of the great shames of American history. But Otteson raises two questions, which he claims should be seen as lexically ordered in terms of their importance.

- Justice—Is the government morally authorized, and in fact obliged, to take resources away from some members of the society who have legally acquired those resources, and transfer those resources to other members of society? The claim that the recipients will benefit, and perhaps benefit more than the current possessors will lose, is a utilitarian claim; Otteson asks whether it is just to use coercion—actual law enforcement

armed with guns, threat of jail, and confiscation of property—
for the state to take the resources in the first place.

- Welfare—Is it true, in an actual system of government in which
  elected officials and bureaucrats have their own objectives,
  and in which organized interests play a significant role, that
  the net effect will be positive? That is, will the actual delivered resources, in terms of the benefits to those who will have
  increased opportunities, offset the harm to those who lose the
  resources?

Otteson grants that there are circumstances in which "the justice
question" can be answered in the affirmative, because of the legacy
of racism, discrimination, and manipulation of the means of creating and holding on to wealth. But those instances may be rarer than
the enthusiasts of redistribution might care to admit. The problem
is that it is never just to use a citizen, any citizen, simply as a means
for achieving ends desired by others. The fact that the wealthy have
money, and the poor need money, does not create even a *prima facie*
claim for redistribution. There would need to be a dispositive claim
that *this particular wealthy person* does not deserve, or have a just
claim to, the wealth that now is their property. All too often, the
argument for redistribution goes no further than expanding the Wil-
lie Sutton argument for robbing banks: rich people are the source of
funds for redistribution because "that's where the money is."

But, again, to be clear, Otteson does grant that there are circumstances where "the justice question" is answered "yes, redistribution
is morally allowed, and possibly obliged." The problem is that an
idealized conception of a benevolent, all-knowing unitary state is a
poor representation of the actual setting for redistributive policies.
McMullen argues that even many existing programs, if expanded
dramatically, would have proportionately dramatic effects on
increasing equality of opportunity. Otteson wonders whether it is
really true that the additional funds taken from the undeserving
wealthy would in fact be delivered in usable, and efficacious, form
to people who would then take advantage of the opportunities that
the resources afford them.

The arguments on both sides are formidable and challenging,
and readers will have to make up their own minds. Where do *I*
land? The advantage of McMullen's approach is that he focuses
primarily on changes in existing programs, both in the delivery of
improvements in the equality of opportunity and in the treatment

of wealth in nuts-and-bolts tax policy. He makes a persuasive case that the incentive effects of his proposals, far from being crippling, might actually be improvements. Ultimately, I think that McMullen effectively turns the tables on Otteson, in the sense that McMullen is arguing that it is precisely the deep incentive problems and pathological political atresia of the current system that provide his proposals with low-hanging fruit. It isn't that hard to do better. The current political system is far from ideal, so pointing out that politics has incentive problems is rather beside the point. McMullen's proposals have to be taken seriously because it is politics that has been the mechanism for reifying inequality in the first place. We can do better, and perhaps we should try.

That is the greatest benefit that I see into this congenial, but careful, dispute over the merits of redistribution as a means of fostering equality of opportunity. Both McMullen and Otteson are adept at navigating the ethical and moral arguments in the abstract, but each is willing to take seriously the problems of implementation and practical consequence. I enjoyed the discussion, and I expect that you will, also.

Opening Statements

Chapter 1

Redistribution to Expand Economic Opportunity

Steven McMullen

Contents

DOI: 10.4324/9780367854263-2

I   Introduction

One of the most pressing and difficult moral questions in ethics and in economics is the question of economic inequality. We live in a time in which there are vast differences between the standard of living of those who are wealthy and those who are poor. Moreover, despite rapid growth in global incomes, there are still populations that experience dire absolute poverty. This juxtaposition—wealth and poverty so close together—raises some important questions of justice. I will argue that, in such a situation as we find ourselves, justice demands that governments should redistribute material wealth from those who are relatively wealthy to those who are poor.

The structure of the argument that I offer here is simple. I start with three premises and offer a conclusion in the form of a policy proposal:

> **Premise 1:** To meet the demands of distributive justice we must work to build a legal and economic structure that grants each person the opportunity to participate in and contribute to economic life.
>
> **Premise 2:** In the contemporary United States, basic economic opportunity is limited by poverty, inequality, and a history of racial oppression.
>
> **Premise 3:** There are at least some redistributive government programs that, if expanded, would increase the opportunity to participate and contribute to economic life.
>
> **Conclusion:** The U.S. government should expand the redistribution in those ways that will expand opportunity.

Even among those who agree that poverty and inequality are a first-order problem, there is considerable debate about what kind of equality we should aim for. I offer here a fairly minimal egalitarian goal: every person should have the opportunity to fully participate in economic life. By this account, inequality alone does not necessarily require correction by the government. Neither do all types of inequality of opportunity. The injustice that I am concerned with occurs when poverty and inequality result in barriers to basic functioning and participation. Three such barriers to participation stand out. First, severe poverty, particularly for children, often prevents people from making the investments they need to participate in the economy. Second, inequality can increase the cost of participation in some parts of social life, further sidelining those who are poor. Finally, historic and current racial oppression and discrimination have a lasting legacy of economic marginalization.

In many cases, redistribution is justified solely on the basis of limiting the immediate harm of poverty. The social safety net in the United States has often been conceived in this way, and there is strong evidence that it has broadly been successful. The goal of distributive justice, however, should not be limited to poverty alleviation. It is important to make the investments in individual capabilities and institutions so that people have the ability to fully participate in a productive economic life. We have now accumulated a body of strong evidence that at least some redistributive government programs can be very effective at opening up these long-run economic opportunities. I argue that food assistance, health insurance, and preschool are all examples of these effective redistributive programs. I also propose a wealth-building program to decrease racial wealth differences. In order to fund these benefits, I propose increases in the estate tax, capital gains tax, and individual income tax.

Philosophers tend to argue in a particular way. They build arguments from a series of premises that they believe their reader will accept after some justification. They build these premises logically toward an interesting conclusion. Economists sometimes use this method, but we usually depend much more heavily on empirical evidence from experiments and studies to support premises and build to a conclusion. I will follow the style of my guild (I am an economist) and defend my second and third premises by appealing to the best empirical and experimental evidence that we have. This means that if I want to argue that education is an important egalitarian investment, I should justify it by appealing to data on student outcomes in a well-designed and well-executed study. This approach will not justify a once-and-for-all conclusion about the nature of justice (or education), however, and so our conclusions will always depend on the applicability of the evidence to the situation we find ourselves in.

I will build this argument in four parts, organized around the structure described above. In Section 1.2, I will describe the wide variety of strong arguments in favor of redistribution in principle, and argue that a number of these arguments are consistent with the "opportunity to participate" goal that I work with here. In Section 1.3, I provide evidence that poverty, inequality, and the legacy of racism all limit economic opportunities in the United States. In Section 1.4, I propose four specific ways in which **redistribution**[1] should be expanded and provide evidence that these types of government action can do a good job expanding economic opportunity. Finally, in Section 1.5, I will address some common economic objections to redistribution, particularly those regarding cost and adverse incentives.

Redistribution: when the government engages in public spending, either in cash benefits or the provision of services, to benefit a particular group of people, at the cost of others. Usually, redistribution intends to provide material resources to those who are poor using taxes paid by those who are wealthier.

Before moving on though, two notes are needed. First, the reader will see that I make the case for increased redistribution in the contemporary United States. This is not to minimize the importance of this same conversation in other countries. I focus on the United States because this is the country in which both James Otteson and I live and work. The United States, moreover, has been the site of high-quality academic research and data gathering regarding government programs and economic activity. As a result, it will be much easier to have a careful debate about the United States than about many other countries. More importantly, countries differ in state capacity, economic resources, culture, and history. As such, the debate will rightly take on a different form in each place. While I focus on domestic poverty and inequality, I do not want to minimize important questions about global inequality, global poverty, and redistribution across state borders. These questions are closely related philosophically, but in terms of institutions, policy, and law, they are too different to include here. For the sake of focus, we will have to put those questions to one side. Even with the conversation restricted to the contemporary United States, the debate is still expansive.

---

1. Terms in **bold** are defined in the "Glossary" at the end of the text.

2 What Does Justice Require of An Economic Order?

It is possible to argue in favor of redistribution on pragmatic grounds: promoting economic efficiency, human health, or democratic governance. This is a common approach for social scientists. This will not be my approach, however, at least not yet. Those pragmatic concerns will become important in later sections. Instead, I will start by making the case that redistribution is a matter of justice. In particular, this is a question of distributive justice.

Distributive Justice: is the domain of justice that pertains to the right distribution of material wealth across a population.

Colloquially, we often want to ask, "What is a just distribution of material wealth?" or perhaps "What is a just *way* to distribute material wealth?" To answer these kinds of questions, we must think about justice as a characteristic of a whole social system. It is not enough to note that it was a violation of justice when Bernard Madoff defrauded his customers of substantial wealth, though it definitely was. We must also be able to talk about whether a state of affairs is just even when people are following all of the rules. In other words, we have to interrogate the rules themselves, and the impact of those rules on people's lives.

For example, suppose there was a society in which one ruler had a legal claim to all of the wealth in society purely as a result of being the firstborn child of the right parents. Anything of value that anyone produces in this society immediately becomes the property of this ruler. There would, in such a society, be at least three distinct legitimate claims of injustice:

1. **It matters how wealth is gained:** The ruler did not earn their wealth through some morally deserving activity, and so their claim is suspect. Moreover, this imagined society would be one in which no one who produces wealth through work, risk-taking, or creativity is able to claim the rewards of their work.
2. **Human well-being matters:** The single ruler does not need their extreme wealth in order to meet any basic needs or to

participate in society. Other members of society, on the basis of their need, might have a stronger moral claim to at least some material wealth.

3.   **Opportunity matters:** There was no chance for anyone else in society to achieve a position where they could have any wealth. The rules of the game predetermined the extreme outcome at birth.

This example is crude, but thinking about *why* this rich ruler scenario is unjust gives a quick window into the kinds of concerns that animate some of the best thinking about distributive justice. While no society is as starkly unjust as the one described, we can ask the same questions about the distribution of wealth and power in our modern societies. Does the manner in which people gain wealth justify their claim to it? Are people able to meet their important needs as humans and as citizens? Is everyone given an opportunity to participate in the economic and political system the way that they should? Each of these questions could motivate a theory of distributive justice, and each could motivate an argument for the redistribution of wealth.

To build my argument for wealth redistribution, it is important to establish a basic vocabulary and to note the breadth of thinking about distributive justice that has taken place in recent years. There are many different ways of specifying the requirements of distributive justice, each built from different moral intuitions. These different accounts do not all hold together—indeed, philosophers are exceptionally good at pointing out the differences between their view and that of others—but each approach contains some useful intuitions about justice that can guide us in policy-making. In fact, I will argue that each of these broad ways of thinking about distributive justice can help build a strong case for redistribution. All of them are valuable. As an organizational device, moreover, I will use the three categories above to motivate this brief tour through the literature about distributive justice, with a focus on what both philosophers and economists have written.

2.1   *The Method in Which Wealth Is Obtained Matters*

The first way of thinking about justice and injustice focuses on the way in which wealth has been obtained. This is a good place to start, in part, because one of the biggest divides in popular thinking about distributive justice hinges on this question. When the Cato Institute polled people in 2019, they found that 60 percent of Americans thought that "most rich people in this country earned their wealth," whereas 39 percent believed that "most rich people in this country got rich by taking advantage of other people." Not surprisingly perhaps, those who were older, conservative, high income, or religious were more likely to agree with the first statement, whereas those who were young, left-leaning, low-income or not religious were more likely to agree with the second proposition. Those in the first group were less likely to support government redistribution of wealth; those in the second group more likely to do so (Ekins 2019). The stories we tell about the source of wealth are very important for our moral evaluation of inequality.

To make a judgment about the morality or immorality of wealth for a whole society, according to this way of thinking, we must have some understanding of the economic and legal system through which the wealth was obtained. As such, in the United States, people's evaluation of the morality of wealth ties closely to their evaluation of the morality of capitalism. The Cato study found that those with very favorable views of capitalism were more likely to believe that the rich have earned their money, while those with favorable views of socialism were more likely to believe that the rich had taken advantage of others.

Simple surveys such as this do not have too much value, but there is a close parallel in the conversation about distributive justice among scholars. Parfit (1997) helpfully divided **egalitarian** thinking into two camps: telic and deontic. **Telic egalitarians** are those who think that the fact of inequality is necessarily bad. These thinkers would reject inequalities without needing to know where they come from. **Deontic egalitarians** reject inequality only when those inequalities are the result of injustice. In this section, then, I am considering what Parfit called deontic egalitarian arguments.

2.1.1 Libertarian Theorists: Justly Obtained Wealth Should Not Be Redistributed

Libertarian thinkers often frame distributive justice primarily as a question of whether the means through which people obtain wealth are just or unjust. These scholars often also have favorable views of capitalism, arguing that the way markets distribute the gains from economic exchange is largely just. Libertarians are, accordingly, often suspicious of wealth redistribution by the government. There are some libertarians who favor redistribution (Zwolinski 2017), but that is a minority position. Nozick (1974) famously articulated this kind of view, and a number of other scholars have followed with complementary work. Nozick's starting place was a commitment to individual self-ownership, individual rights, and individual freedom. He argued that wealth is justly held if someone obtains their wealth through a free exchange with someone who themselves has a legitimate claim to it. In this way of thinking, property rights form the foundation of individual freedom, free markets in labor and goods are morally laudable, and wealth distributed through free markets is justly obtained. Some, following in Nozick's footsteps, argue that taxation and redistribution is often an illegitimate violation of individual rights to property (Huemer 2017).

Economists often adopt this approach to distributive justice. While they are famous for making consequentialist arguments, economists will often defend the current distribution of wealth as a result of a fair and efficient market process. Finis (1999), for example, argues that increases in inequality between 1970 and the late 1990s were, in large part, due to increasing rewards for skill and education, and are thus largely justified. Mankiw (2013) makes the argument that there have been increasing gains at the very top, but that this is unproblematic because it is due to entrepreneurship and innovation that benefits all of society. Following the pattern, both of these economists are skeptical of efforts at redistribution.

2.1.2 Wealth Tied to Historic Injustice

One of the complications of a libertarian theory like Nozick's is cases in which wealth is not justly obtained. Consider, for example, a white farm owner who obtained the farm only after violently driving away the previous black owners (Lewan and Barclay 2001). In cases like this, the resulting distribution of wealth is clearly not morally justified by libertarian principles, and justice requires some rectification. Nozick, in fact, notes that one cannot use his theory to justify any current distribution of wealth, or condemn redistribution, until after some rectification of this kind has been taken into account (Nozick 1974, p. 231). As I will document later, the actual history of economically significant injustice is substantial, and it has a lasting impact on the current distribution of wealth.

Under normal circumstances, if an injustice of this kind occurs, the best remedy is to restore what was stolen, and make individual restitution. In practice, this is difficult for many historic injustices, particularly those injustices committed legally. The immediate victims and perpetrators might not be alive or well-documented. As such, it can be difficult to identify who would be owed restitution for wide-scale property crimes one century prior. Alternatively, as in the case of "redlining" that prevented black Americans from obtaining home loans in many neighborhoods, it might be difficult to estimate the monetary value of the damage done. All of this makes pursuit of justice difficult.

That said, it is possible to acknowledge the injustice and enact second-best policies that remediate some of the harm. In the case of harms perpetrated by, or approved by the state, it is easy to point to the state as the appropriate body to make restitution. Furthermore, it is possible to target government responses to redress some of the long-term effects of the crimes, even if the specific impacts on individuals are not recorded. The more widespread the injustice, the greater the case for broad restitution.

2.1.3 Socialist Theorists: Wealth Accumulated in Capitalist Economies Is Normally Unjust

There are some scholars that accept a similar premise—that the way in which wealth is accumulated matters—but then argue that under normal conditions, capitalist accumulation is not just. This would mean that it is not just historic crimes or exceptional cases of unjust institutions that should warrant attention, but the whole economic system. Many who take this kind of position are working in a Marxist or socialist framework. Marxist and socialist theories offer other justifications for redistribution as well. For example, some argue that political equality demands economic equality and that distribution should be based on need. I want to focus here, though, on a fundamental part of this kind of leftist thinking: that there is injustice baked into the system of market exchange and capital accumulation.

The strongest forms of this argument follow the intuition, if not the strict logic, of Marx's theory of exploitation. Marx built his theory of exploitation on a labor theory of value that is now widely rejected. However, modern thinkers have proposed more sophisticated versions of many of Marx's ideas, and point to market exchange as a site of routine injustice. The market economy, Cohen argues (1995, chaps. 1 & 2), is a place where people are compelled to take involuntary risks just to survive. Roemer (1996, pp. 13–114), moreover, has argued that exploitation is endemic in market societies in multiple forms, all stemming from different kinds of market power.

Arguments of this kind abound well outside of socialist circles as well. Many economists are concerned with the implications of concentrated economic power (Stiglitz 2012). Employers can exert considerable power labor markets, particularly in concentrated industries. This can drive down the wages of workers. Labor unions, minimum wage laws, and other institutional mechanisms can act as a countervailing power that pushes up wages for those workers included in the market. The decline of unions and the erosion of the value of the minimum wage, for example, have been credited with part of the rise in inequality in the United States and the United Kingdom (Machin 1997; Card et al. 2004).

If market exchange is suspect, then so too are the accumulated distribution of wealth and the wage rates that contribute to it. A considerable amount of the debate about distributive justice proceeds on these terms. Critics of the current system point to accumulations that are the result of blatant injustice and/or the exercise of economic and political power. Defenders of market economies point to more benign causes of inequality and argue that market exchanges are fundamentally fair and thus just. I cannot wade deep into these debates here. I accept this as important intellectual ground and will argue in favor of redistribution for two related reasons. First, accumulated wealth and income almost inevitably result in reinforcing exclusionary economic power (Section 1.3.2) and that current and past injustices undermine the moral justification of current patterns of wealth, and justify restitution (Sections 1.3.3 and 1.4.4).

2.2   The Well-Being of People Matters

Distributive justice is not just a debate about the way wealth is accumulated. It is also a debate about the availability of goods that people need. Using Parfit's categories, we need to consider the telic egalitarian arguments: those who believe that the fact of inequality is bad, no matter what the source. These kinds of egalitarian theories often start with an intuition that in order to ascribe proper value to all persons, each person should share an equal consideration of a kind that has some material implications.

Some ethicists make material equality a foundational moral principle on par with other basic human rights. If equality of all persons before the law is a bedrock principle, as is equality in democratic deliberations and equality in the right to life, why not also an equal claim to material goods? Nielsen (1981, 1985) argued for a strict egalitarianism on these terms. In his view, an equal respect for persons required economic egalitarianism as well. Cohen (2009) makes a parallel argument, grounding his commitment to equality in the relationships of a community. Still others argue for limitarianism, the view that wealth itself is morally impermissible in a world with serious material problems (Robeyns 2019).

Most egalitarian theorists do not argue for the total redistribution or strict equality of Cohen and Nielsen. There are a variety of views about what it is that should be equalized, and why. Some, like John Rawls (1999), favor an equalization of resources; others favor an equality of welfare (Hardin 1990); many, though, support an equality of opportunity. I will leave the question of opportunity until the next section. For now, it is worth noting that there is a kind of consensus among many of these thinkers. In an unequal society, they will all agree, involuntary poverty is a first-order moral concern that warrants some kind of systemic response.

2.2.1 John Rawls and the Difference Principle

One of the most important figures in the 20th century to delve into questions of distributive justice was John Rawls. While he is certainly not the first to try to answer these questions, he is notable for having laid the groundwork for many egalitarian theorists with his seminal work, *A Theory of Justice* (1971). Rawls develops his account of justice by posing a thought experiment in which people are given the opportunity to make decisions about the economic system prior to finding out what place they would have in such a system, and before knowing any relevant details about themselves. From this neutral "original position," he posits, people's biases for particular people and communities would not be in play, and so people would be able to think objectively. In this situation, he thought that people would be likely to agree on some basic principles of justice.

Rawls thought that the starting point for political philosophy was equal respect for all persons, and that under his thought experiment, there would be a consensus of the following kind: (i) Each person is due equal basic liberties, and (ii) inequality should be tolerated only inasmuch as (a) the social position that grants an unequal share is open to all people under fair conditions, and (b) the inequality attending any social position results in the greatest benefit to those who are least well-off. While each of the elements of his theory is worth discussing at length, I would like to focus first on the final element, sometimes called the "difference principle." Rawls believed that there could be some kinds of inequality that would increase the well-being of the whole society, and only in these cases would inequality be justified. In other words, Rawls placed a very high priority on the absolute well-being of those who are materially poor.

Many have used Rawls as a starting point for their work in distributive justice, or have built similar arguments. Scanlon (2018) echoes Rawls, arguing that everyone has a right to be subject to procedures that no one could reasonably reject. He then argues, not as a requirement of rational consensus, but moral argument, to a conclusion very similar to the difference principle. Some interpretations of Rawls require pretty strict egalitarianism, implying that we should eliminate almost all inequalities, even at great cost, if doing so improved the lot of the poor by even a small amount. Rawls himself allowed for some inequality if it created positive incentives for people to be productive and thus ended up helping everyone. Others have interpreted Rawls's difference principle somewhat more generally as a statement of priority for those who are poor (Rothwell 2019).

For Rawls and his followers, the justification for the difference principle is both procedural and moral. It is procedural because Rawls believed that, behind a veil of ignorance, if people did not know whether they would be rich or poor, a rational person would choose a system that favored the least well-off. It is moral because Rawls thought that this principle was the way that basic respect for human dignity would be best translated into liberal democratic principles.

2.2.2 Consequentialist Theories

There are many other thinkers who share a set of moral principles that are similar to the difference principle, even if they do not agree with Rawls's approach. Those who subscribe to **utilitarianism**, for example, sometimes argue that the most moral system is the one that maximizes total welfare (or satisfies preferences). Utilitarian egalitarians will note that there is likely to be a diminishing marginal utility to wealth or consumption. If this is so, then each additional dollar that a person spends brings them less well-being. Intuitively, someone who is quite poor might be delighted to find a $10 bill on the ground, or to find out they are getting a $200 a year raise. A rich person, however, might pocket the $10 bill and forget about it, and might not even notice an additional $200 in wages. The utilitarian, then, notes that we could make the world a happier place if we take $10 from the rich person, and hand it to a poor person (Singer 2010). John Stuart Mill, a famous liberal and utilitarian, also described himself as a socialist, in part because his utilitarian logic led to egalitarian conclusions (McCabe 2021).

Some scholars are not willing to accept all of the conclusions of utilitarian egalitarianism, and note the difficulty of interpersonal utility comparison. Some have argued instead for a "prioritarian" justification for redistribution. The idea is that one should, when considering distributional policy, always give priority to those who are least well-off (Parfit 1997; Arneson 2000). Or alternatively, always give priority to those worst off, until they reach a basic level of well-being, after which other goals can prevail (Crisp 2003). In these accounts, we need not pursue equality at any cost, as might strict egalitarianism. As a rule of thumb, it closely follows Rawls's difference principle, but does so in a consequentialist framework similar to utilitarianism.

2.2.3 Justification for Redistribution

While there are many differences between the thinkers presented in this section, it should be clear that there are a wide variety of powerful arguments in favor of crafting a system that is tilted in favor of those who are least well-off. Whether they support redistribution as a basic reflection of human equality, in order to maximize well-being, or as a way of fulfilling a kind of minimalist consensus for a just system, many people place some kind of equality as a very high moral goal. To frame these conclusions clearly as a question of justice, it could be put this way: there is a broad consensus that involuntary poverty, as a regular part of a wealthy economic system, is a wrong imposed on the poor. This framing foregrounds one of the interesting elements of these theories. None of them ask the question, "Why is this person poor, and this other person rich?" This is because each theory gives an account of why a just system would include basic provision of goods, or at least access to a minimal standard of living, no matter what the cause of poverty.

While I will not defend a strong version of any of these views, because I am not interested in pursuing strict egalitarianism, it is worth pointing out an economic parallel to the work of these philosophers. The idea that some kinds of redistribution are warranted for all citizens, independent of their life choices, shows up in the way that economists often talk about public goods. **Public goods** are not "used up" when one benefits from them, and it is usually hard to keep people from benefiting from them once they are produced. These goods usually have wide public benefits. While economists rarely argue that there is a moral requirement for governments to provide public goods, because economists work hard to avoid normative language, it is common to argue that a well-run economy will include a functional government that efficiently provides public goods and subsidizes goods that have wide public benefit. Anti-poverty programs that have substantial spillover benefits to other people will sometimes be considered public goods.

Any provision of public goods in a system with a progressive tax code has the effect of redistributing wealth. If the government disproportionately collects tax revenue from those who are wealthy, and then subsidizes vaccinations against illnesses, the benefits are shared evenly across the population, even among those who pay very little in taxes. This is one of the most important ways in which wealth is redistributed in market societies, because government provision of, or funding for, universally available goods, creates a really important consumption floor for those the least well-off.

2.3 Economic Opportunity

I have ignored, up until this point, one of the most important concerns when thinking about distributive justice. What if people are poor because they have made unwise decisions, while others are wealthy because they have scrupulously saved their money? Shouldn't people's choices have a big impact on the distribution of income and wealth? Indeed, there is a long history of people dividing the poor into two groups: the "deserving" and "undeserving" poor (Geremek 1991). The deserving poor are usually those who are poor through no fault of their own: widows and orphans in ancient societies, those with disabilities that prevent them from working, or those subject to other considerable misfortune. The undeserving poor would include those who are able but unwilling to work, those who are capable but unwilling to complete their education, or others who seem culpable for their afflictions. It is easier to make the case for redistributing wealth toward those who are deemed deserving than for those who are considered undeserving. We could recast much political debate about redistribution, in fact, as arguments about whether we should place various groups of people into one category or the other.

This concern about who deserves redistribution on their behalf has two broad responses in the philosophy literature and a parallel argument in the economics literature. The philosophy literature includes a set of theories proposing an equality of opportunity rather than equality of resources or outcomes, and a closely related cluster of views sometimes labeled "luck egalitarian." On the economics side, there is a broad literature about government-provided insurance or safety-nets against misfortune. I will discuss each of these briefly. We will see that, even after considering that some people are poor because they have made poor decisions, there remains a strong case for redistribution, particularly, if this redistribution is targeted at expanding opportunities to participate productively in the economy.

2.3.1   Equality of Opportunity

Not all sources of inequality warrant correction. If Peter and Paul both earn the same amount of money, but Peter saves 15 percent each year while Paul spends and accumulates debt, Peter will be far richer than Paul. Taxing Peter's wealth to remedy Paul's poverty might even be unjust, depending on the circumstances. In a world in which this kind of scenario is possible, it is often argued that egalitarians should be more concerned with equalizing opportunities than with equalizing wealth or income. In this view, justice demands not that we are concerned with poverty or inequality per se, but instead that we only aim to make sure that each person has a fair shot at a decent life. A common metaphor describes the goal as creating a fair starting position in a race. For this reason, these arguments are sometimes referred to as starting-gate theories.

Starting-Gate Theories: An egalitarian theory that argues that a just system is one in which each person starts with the same opportunities for success. They sometimes adopt the metaphor of a fair race, in which everyone is starting from the same position.

As noted earlier, John Rawls's theory of justice started with the principle that, if there was inequality, the more advantageous positions should be accessible to everyone. This principle could be consistent with a meritocratic system and certainly would rule out discrimination on the basis of race or sex. It also serves as a baseline for establishing an equality of opportunity. Rawls himself was concerned that redistribution from Peter toward Paul would undermine the incentive of either of them to work hard, innovate, and save money. As a result, Rawls allowed that some inequality might be justified.

Following Rawls, Scanlon has a helpful formalization of the concept of equality of opportunity. Scanlon presents equality of opportunity arguments as a partial defense of some kinds of inequality (2018, p. 41). The defense has three parts. For inequality to be justified, it must be the case that: (1) it is necessary to have some social institution that generates unequal rewards, (2) the unequal rewards are a necessary part of this social institution, and (3) the favored positions in this institution must open to all who could fill the role. Such a framework would most obviously condemn a system with a hereditary aristocratic class where only those born into privileged families had a chance at positions with wealth or power. The injustice in this case, however, might not be the fact of the inequality, but instead the closed nature of the best life outcomes.

In contrast, this theory could justify inequality in a market system, with the logic that a well-functioning labor market uses differences in compensation to attract the best candidates into the jobs where their skills are the most valued, and to push job candidates out of jobs where their skills are not productive. Such a labor market system could result in substantial inequality, but that inequality would be allowed if everyone has a similar opportunity to develop the most valuable skills. The inequality would only be justified, however, if it could serve the general interest by ensuring a productive labor force and broadly shared prosperity.

2.3.2 Luck Egalitarians

If you take the logic of equality of opportunity seriously, you are forced to think, quite immediately, about the kinds of opportunity that should, ideally, be equal. Some scholars have proposed starting-gate theories that propose an equalization of any unchosen attribute that would influence success. Education should be equally available to all, in this view, while discrimination in labor markets and in education should be eliminated. People should be the recipients of redistribution not if they happen to be poor, but if they have unchosen characteristics that prevent them from having the same opportunities.

On this point, there is some controversy. There is a general consensus that one's race should not prevent someone from holding an executive position, and that those born into poverty should have some chance to build their skills and participate in high-reward professions. Both race and family are outside a person's control, and so some argue that people should not be punished for these characteristics. Applying this logic to other differences, however, pushes us well outside any normal public policy consensus. It is well-documented, for example, that tall people and physically attractive people earn more money than their short and less-attractive peers (Hamermesh and Biddle 1994; Mankiw and Weinzierl 2010). Do these unchosen differences warrant compensation? Most argue that they do not, but these debates reveal that it can be difficult to turn simple notions of opportunity into similarly simple policy.

Luck egalitarians argue that we should redistribute on the basis of personal characteristics or misfortune, though they disagree on the specifics (Anderson 1999). We do not have to believe that all luck needs to be equalized to recognize the importance of this logic. When economic success is the result of strategic risk-taking, hard work, frugal saving, or creativity, we celebrate it. But when wealth is the result of being lucky, the moral claim on that wealth is far weaker. Frank (2017) makes a convincing case that the economy is increasingly rewarding luck, not merit, and that a progressive consumption taxation would actually improve well-being. In a similar way, if poverty is caused by misfortune, the moral case for some collective remedy is stronger than if a person's poverty is due to poor choices.

2.3.3 Redistribution as Insurance

In contrast to the work of these philosophers, economists often argue for redistribution as insurance, or **social insurance**, against the uncertainty and misfortune that befalls people throughout life (Varian 1980). Thinking of redistribution as social insurance, or as a **safety net,** has a considerable intuitive appeal.

> **Social Insurance**: a way of thinking about government redistribution as protection against economic misfortune. In the United States, for example, there is unemployment insurance and disability insurance, which replace a portion of workers' wages if they are laid off or become unable to work.

For many, economic life is both highly uncertain and has high stakes. Unemployment, chronic illness, disability, and business failures can be difficult to predict, and they often result in poverty for those they strike. In an ideal world, perhaps, we would have insurance markets that cover all such misfortunes at reasonable prices. If this were the case, then private markets could protect people from serious risks without any government action. Many misfortunes are not insurable, however, or are covered only by insurance policies available to those who already are somewhat wealthy.

The most obvious kind of system-wide risk to individual well-being is the risk of unemployment. Even in good years, tens of millions of workers are laid off or fired in the United States, often with very little notice or severance compensation. Most workers face some degree of unemployment risk, though the risk is borne disproportionately by those with low skill levels and low incomes. For a number of different reasons, there is no way to run a profitable unemployment insurance business, and so without government action, individual households who are poor or young would have a difficult time preparing for the possibility of unemployment. When people become unemployed, moreover, it causes a ripple of economic and social ills that are shared by many others. It makes sense, then, that many governments provide unemployment compensation as a kind of safety net. The same could be said regarding the uncertainty in health care markets, and public health initiatives (Arrow 1963). General taxation to provide support for those who are the victims of economic misfortune, then, is a public service that can improve the ex-ante well-being of almost everyone.

2.4   Opportunity to Participate: A Minimal Framework for Economic Justice

While there is great disagreement between scholars on the specifics, it should be clear now that there are a variety of ways of thinking about distributive justice, many of which can motivate a strong case for some redistribution of wealth. A minimal version of the arguments presented so far gives us three cases that could warrant redistribution. Those are: (1) when there is a history of substantial economic injustice, (2) when individuals, particularly children, lack basic necessities, and (3) when redistribution is necessary to enable the opportunity to participate in economic life. These cases are conceptually independent, but in practice they are easily consolidated, and I will provide evidence, for example, that historic injustice and poverty have the result of limiting economic opportunity. I will elaborate on each in turn here, starting with the third, before turning to the argument that these cases describe economic reality for at least some people in contemporary United States.

While it is common for egalitarians to have expansive visions for the transformation of the economy, these larger visions are often not necessary to justify egalitarian redistribution. The more important claims of justice point us toward what Anderson (1999) calls "democratic" or "relational" equality. Our primary goal is to make sure people have the opportunity to participate in political and economic life. Doing so will often require that we come to terms with the way in which our social order excludes people from full participation. Sometimes these barriers are laws or practices that are discriminatory. When we eliminate these barriers, we are promoting **formal opportunity,** or fair procedures. Everyone must play by the same rules. In other cases, however, we must pay attention to cases in which people have no real chance to pursue their talents because they face material barriers. Eliminating these barriers is sometimes called the promotion of "substantive opportunity." This is close to what Rawls (1999, sec. 12) called "fair equality of opportunity."

Rawls's notion of a fair equality of opportunity is, however, too ambitious itself. Consider two families, each with children that are similarly talented and industrious. One family has twice the material wealth as the second and is able to afford private tutors that the second family cannot. These tutors give the wealthy kids an advantage in school admissions and future jobs. A difference of this kind would violate Rawls's fair equality of opportunity standard. And yet these kinds of differences are inevitable. A government that tried to stamp out such advantages would necessarily trample on freedom of association and limit the freedom of families and communities. Even trying to measure such inequalities could require dangerous government overreach, and stamping out these kinds of inequality would be impossible.

Thus, instead of pursuing an equality of opportunity, it makes more sense to pursue a guaranteed minimum level of opportunity for each person in the society. For this reason, I will write in favor of merely *ensuring the opportunity to participate*. This view is similar, in many ways, to what some philosophers have called "sufficientarianism," which is the view that we should make sure that each person has at least enough material wealth to reach some basic standard of living. Even this standard, once properly defined, would be a huge step toward a more just system for a country like the United States. There is a considerable amount of poverty that results from people being excluded from economic life, often starting at a very young age. Sen (2011) makes a very similar proposal when he argues for "basic capability equality," in which he defends universal access to the most basic functions of life, which he calls **capabilities**: the ability to move, basic nutrition, clothing, shelter, and access to social life. Anderson (1999) builds on Sen's work, fleshing out the participation in economic and political life as essential capabilities.

Amartya Sen is a Nobel prize-winning economist and philosopher. He developed, along with philosopher Martha Nussbaum, the "Capabilities" approach to thinking about economic justice and economic progress. Their ideas have been particularly influential in the area of international economic development.

Aiming for basic capabilities allows us to sidestep the problems that philosophers and economists run into with utility, needs, and desires. If we aimed to equalize utility, as many utilitarians and economists advocate, we inevitably run into the problem of separating needs and wants. Even if a particular person cannot be happy without avocado toast or 20 acres of pristine wilderness, society does not have an obligation to supply them with those particular things. In contrast, the person who has no opportunity to feed themselves is a more important moral concern. By outlining the basic capabilities that humans need to function and participate in society, we avoid the problem of applying moral weight to people's trivial preferences. Thinking in terms of capabilities, or basic functioning, also gives us a way to navigate the question of whether we should worry about

absolute poverty or **relative poverty**. Thinking in terms of participation requires us to be concerned with absolute poverty when we are concerned with basic needs, but also relative poverty in those cases that poverty is locking people out of economic participation.

Even if we ensure the opportunity to access basic capabilities and to participate in economic life, we may leave in place many inequalities. If one person works long hours and another prefers more vacation, it would not be unjust for the first person to be more wealthy. If one person chooses to take great risks in starting a small business that is very successful, and the other person chooses a more secure career with lower pay, again, there is no injustice that needs correcting. If a person is able to work, but chooses not to, and spends his days surfing on the beach, there is no reason to give that man a basic income.

However, this vision of distributive justice would result in substantial redistribution when that redistribution is required to ensure that people have the opportunity to obtain these capabilities. Most notably, wherever there are socially constructed barriers to participation in economic life, we have an obligation to act (Fishkin 2016, p. 124). This gives us an egalitarian ethic with a particular focus. First, education, training, and access to employment are among the most important entry points for economic life. As such, redistribution to fund education is central. Second, in a context where people face livelihood-threatening risks, many of which are impossible to address through savings, we provide access to insurance against unemployment, disability, illness, and chronic disease. Finally, it is too rarely recognized that participation in the economy should also involve entrepreneurship. A strong safety net can help this, by allowing people to take risks, but ensuring access to capital and financing is also important.

Redistribution is not the only policy arena important for creating an economy where everyone has these opportunities (Tanner 2018; Rothwell 2019). While this debate will focus less on these areas, it is also important to scrutinize licensing laws, zoning, and regulations that consolidate economic power. Anti-trust laws are an instrument of distributive justice as well, if they limit the ability of powerful firms to shut out new entrants and competition. Criminal justice, when not operating as it should, can clearly shut down economic opportunities for a lifetime, so policing and sentencing are areas of vital concern. Finally, as noted earlier, discrimination on the basis of sex, race, orientation, disability, or religion clearly violates these principles. For this reason, you will find egalitarian theorists working in all of these important areas.

It is also important to note that ensuring basic opportunities is deeply consistent with, and requires that we address, the first two cases for redistribution: historic injustice and meeting basic needs. If distributive justice requires the goal of eliminating socially imposed limits on basic participation, the history of economic oppression takes on a particular importance. From property crimes and political intimidation to the creation of subtle racial barriers, the economic effect of much of this oppression has been to keep racial minorities from fully participating in economic and political life. Over time, predatory institutions have a cumulative effect on wealth, social capital, and the formation of institutions, creating clear economic divisions between racial groups. While many of these offenses would warrant criminal punishment of individuals, we must also grapple with the economic consequences of this dark legacy.

The first place to start is to ensure that a history of oppression does not prevent people from participating in essential ways in the economy. If creating economic opportunity is an important goal for the population generally, it is even more important when four centuries of law and exclusionary institutions have marginalized whole communities of citizens. In short, a strong case could be made for economic restitution in the form of reparations (Darity and Mullen 2020). At a minimum, though, redistribution should limit the negative impact of having been pushed to the margins of the economy and should focus on rebuilding opportunities for economic independence. In this way, the goals of restitution for past injustice are complementary, though not identical, to the goals of ensuring the opportunity to participate in the economy.

This complementarity also extends to what is perhaps the simplest justification for the redistribution of wealth: that of meeting basic needs. When individuals, particularly children, do not have access to food, shelter, or medical care, they are not able to pursue any of the higher-order capabilities. A failure on the part of a wealthy society to provide opportunities to meet these basic needs is a violation of the respect for persons. If, for example, the United States chooses to subsidize fossil fuel industries (a questionable practice on its own) at a cost of tens of billions of dollars each year, before providing basic needs of citizens, we have a simple case of misplaced priorities. The revealed preference for cheap fuel over food and medicine cannot be considered simply an amoral technocratic concern. At a minimum, then, public health programs, food stamps, shelters, and housing subsidies all fit into a category of redistribution that could be worth investing in even if they were not needed to provide longer-term economic opportunities. There is strong evidence, however, that they are important for both reasons, and that these programs that provide children's needs open up life-long opportunities.

This section has shown that there are a variety of arguments for the redistribution of wealth that grow out of different conceptions of distributive justice. There are strong arguments for redistribution in response to past injustices, in order to meet basic needs and to provide economic opportunity. There is some important practical overlap, though, between these arguments. I argue here that the most compelling account of distributive justice is one that prioritizes the opportunity to participate in economic life and access basic capabilities.

3 Poverty, Inequality, and Opportunity in the United States

Most of the argument thus far has been abstract. Philosophers tend to argue about distributive justice in very broad terms, with relatively little reference to empirical evidence about wealth, income, poverty, or social institutions. This approach has its uses. The goal of these philosophers is often to understand the nature of justice apart from a particular historical time and place. Economists tend to take a very different approach. We spend far more time exploring and interrogating the best empirical evidence about the distribution of income and wealth and the implications for our major economic and political institutions. In order to make a complete argument in favor of redistribution, it is wise to dwell in both conversations. Having described an account of distributive justice, I will now turn to the task of documenting the current need to increase the redistribution of wealth from those who are relatively well-off toward those who are not. This part of the argument has three points, framed in terms of economic opportunity:

1. Poverty is significant enough to limit economic opportunity.
2. Growing inequality limits economic opportunity.
3. The legacy and current reality of economic injustice in the United States limits economic opportunity.

We have built an economy with extraordinary opportunities, but these opportunities are only formally accessible to everyone. In practice, many people are shut out of full participation in economic life. There remains a great degree of economic deprivation in the United States, some of which is due to socially imposed barriers. These barriers are unjust, and can be partially remedied by targeted redistribution.

3.1   Poverty Limits Opportunity

If a just economic system is one in which everyone has an opportunity to meet basic needs and participate in economic and political life, it might not be immediately obvious that poverty or inequality is a problem. We could have an economy with substantial inequality and still have every person meeting basic needs and participating fully. Similarly, as long as those in poverty were able to secure food, shelter, medical, care, and education, it might not be obvious that there is any need for egalitarian policies. However, we do not, in fact, have an economy in which everyone has the opportunity to meet basic needs, even with our current egalitarian policies. Even more, poverty and inequality have the effect of placing substantial limits on people's opportunities and make poverty and inequality more persistent. In this section, I will describe the nature of poverty in the United States, and then three broad ways in which that poverty limits economic upward mobility.

3.1.1   The Experience of Poverty in the United States

The official U.S. poverty rate has changed very little over the past 50 years, despite big changes in the U.S. economy and a substantial expansion of the welfare state. However, the official poverty statistics are very limited. They do not count income from government programs and do very little to account for changing patterns of household expenditures. To understand people's actual standard of living, therefore, we have to examine some better evidence. Fortunately, scholars have developed far more useful data that gives us a clearer picture.

First, some definitions are important. There are two different conceptual ways to think about poverty. **Absolute poverty** defines poverty as falling below a particular material standard of living. **Relative poverty** defines poverty in relation to the income of other people in society. There are good reasons to use each of these approaches. I think the most useful evidence comes from a recent study that develops absolute poverty measure, combined with detailed income information to estimate how poverty rates have changed, and why (Wimer et al. 2016). They estimate that this absolute poverty rate in the United States dropped from 25.6 percent to 16 percent of the population, a 40 percent decline, between 1968 and 2012. However, they find that this drop in poverty is almost entirely due to government policies, not increased market incomes. Absent government programs, their calculated poverty rate "would have been 30.7 percent in 1967 (instead of 25.6 percent) and 28.5 percent in 2012 (instead of 16 percent)." This conclusion is important. In 2012, real per capita GDP of the United States was 118 percent higher than it was in 1968, and yet the absolute poverty rate, after subtracting out government benefits, barely changed. There are a wide variety of explanations, of course, for why the well-being of the poor has not improved, but the descriptive fact is hard to dispute.

The experience of poverty in the United States is one of economic precarity. That is, poor people have a warranted concern that they do or will lack basic needs (food, shelter, health, care, transportation). For example, one study describes the hard choices people must make when facing unexpected expenses (Bhattacharya et al. 2003). When an unanticipated cold snap increases energy costs, families decrease food expenditures by the full amount of the additional costs. This precarity is borne disproportionately, moreover, by the young. Even at the peak of a historic economic expansion, in 2018, 16.2 percent of children lived in poverty, compared to only 11.8 percent of adults (Semega et al. 2019). This poverty takes the form of food insecurity for 20 percent of households with children, and nutrition deprivation for 5 percent of households with children (Schanzenbach et al. 2016). These numbers are remarkable, in part, because the food and nutrition safety-net programs are among the most comprehensive in the United States, and because 85 percent of food-insecure households are led by a working adult.

A second important part of life in poverty in the United States is the compounding environmental harms. Evans (2004) collects a variety of evidence about the lives of children in poverty, showing that these children face setbacks that are complicated and multifaceted. Poor families are more likely to experience turmoil, violence, household disruptions, instability, and separation. Parents in poverty are less able to invest in their children, either through emotional and social support or through help with school and early reading. The neighborhoods that poor people live in are very often more physically dangerous, because of neighborhood violence, and environmentally harmful, with poor utilities, air, and water pollution. Public services, tragically, are often of poorer quality than in more wealthy neighborhoods as well. While not all of these are proper targets of government redistribution, it is important to note that offering the same legal/formal social opportunities to children in poverty and those born in richer circumstances will not necessarily result in a substantive opportunity for the poor children to succeed.

A third element of the experience of being poor, however, comes from the particular changes in the cost of living over the past 50 years. While average prices have been stable since the 1980s, this stability masks a decrease in the prices of some goods and dramatic increases in the prices of others. The short version is this: manufactured goods have become cheaper, but other essential goods have become more expensive. This phenomenon is sometimes called the "cost disease" (Baumol and Bowen 1968). These changes have improved people's access to basic goods in some respects: food and clothing are far cheaper than they used to be, once you adjust for inflation, as is gasoline. The big institutionally mediated services, though, are much more expensive. This includes, most importantly, higher education (or private secondary education) and health care (including basic care like physical or maintenance medications). Housing, also, has become more expensive in many parts of the United States.

While there is a live debate about what is driving up prices in health care and education, in each of these markets, the most powerful explanations are twofold: relative productivity and lack of competition. The extraordinary productivity gains in manufacturing and food production have not been matched by similar gains in professional services and higher education. The health care industry, moreover, has seen strong technological innovation matched only by rampant institutionalized **rent-seeking**. The result is that, in relative terms, these essential economic institutions have become less and less affordable. The fact that they hold such an important role in the economy, moreover, has guaranteed them customers and cultural support, and the result has been favorable regulation, subsidies, and ballooning administrative costs. The end result is that poor people in the United States can afford all of the toys they ever wanted, but outside of public provision, health care, education, and housing are out of their reach.

3.1.2   Education

In too many ways, the poor find themselves shut out of the most productive parts of the economy where there are real opportunities. It is worth digging deeper into the ways in which this happens. The first place to start is in education. Schooling serves an important role in preparing people for productive and independent lives. If we want to have a system in which everyone has an opportunity to participate, education is one of the important places where investments can be made. However, despite spending very large amounts of money on education in the United States, we still have wildly different schooling experiences for different kids, and these differences have a long-term impact on the lives of those children (Rothwell and Massey 2015).

There can be dramatic disparities between the schools attended by the wealthy and the schools attended by the poor. The funding differences between wealthy suburban districts and poorer urban and rural schools can explain some of the differences in opportunities. Often, there is a three-to-one ratio in funding between the most- and least-funded schools within a single state (Darling-Hammond 2001). With some exceptions, we tend to fund schools more generously where there is less need. Moreover, we have a growing wealth of recent evidence that increasing funding to neglected schools can have substantial long-term impacts. Researchers followed the outcomes of students who attended schools that received court-ordered increases in funding and found that an increase in per-pupil funding resulted in higher rates of high-school graduation, greater college enrollment rates, higher wages, and lower poverty rates (Jackson et al. 2016; Hyman 2017).

It is not just funding differences that matter for education. Putnam (2016, chap. 4) documents the differences in the schools in great detail: schools in wealthy communities have better classroom environments and offer more sports and extracurricular opportunities. Even the curriculum differs: schools with more minority students focus less on complex thinking and more on basic skills and rote learning (Darling-Hammond 2001, pp. 210–11), and poorer schools are far less likely to offer advanced placement classes. Even ambitious and talented students in these schools will not be given the same opportunities to set themselves up for college success.

The biggest education disparities, however, seem to be connected to the quality of the teachers and the performance of peers. There is strong evidence that having good teachers can have a really big long-term impact. One prominent study found that replacing a poor teacher (lowest 5 percent in value added) with an average teacher would be worth $250,000 in discounted lifetime earnings (Chetty et al. 2014). Identifying the best teachers is sometimes difficult to do institutionally, but we know that schools in low-income neighborhoods are frequently staffed with teachers who have less experience and worse qualifications, and the teacher turnover there can be quite high.

Similarly, student's peers matter greatly. When a student moves from a low-performing school to a higher-performing school, there is a big impact on their performance. Students profoundly affect one another by setting the tone of the classroom environment, setting expectations for behavior and studying, and by sharing aspirations. For this reason, the practice of concentrating students with the most disadvantages in the same schools, and then offering those schools, on average, less funding and inexperienced staff, compounds barriers and disadvantages. Students entering this environment can learn, but they will fight much more of an uphill battle than a similar student in a better school.

For some minority students, moreover, race is another barrier to getting a good education. We have accumulated substantial evidence that black students are subject to lower expectations by teachers (Chin et al. 2020), are tracked into less demanding coursework (Diette 2012; Hippel and Cañedo 2020), and subject to harsher school discipline (Riddle and Sinclair 2019). Minority students are also far more likely to attend schools with lower levels of funding and support. Moreover, because schools are usually tied to neighborhoods, the long history of housing discrimination has its legacy, too often, in schooling as well.

These wide and well-documented disparities in educational opportunities are becoming more important over time. There is great evidence that schooling has the potential to be an equalizing force in the economy (Downey et al. 2004). In fact, however, the initial gaps between young people are too often exacerbated by the system. This results in life-long differences in opportunities in the job market. Economists have long measured the "return to education" as a way of tracking the increase in income that results from an additional year invested in schooling. This return has been increasing consistently for the past 40 years (Ashenfelter and Rouse 2000; Autor 2014). It is now far more important that a child graduate from high school and pursue a college degree. And yet college graduation has been increasing primarily among those whose families are relatively well-off. College education among children in the bottom half of households has increased only slightly, and many of them attend lower quality for-profit schools with lower rates of return (Putnam 2016, p. 187). The education gap thus tracks young people into very different parts of the economy. Those born into poverty have fewer opportunities to prepare for college, while those who excel in higher education have much better earnings and face far less economic uncertainty and volatility than their less-educated peers.

The institutional problems with education in the United States are daunting, and I would never claim that redistributing wealth, in the ways I propose, can fix all of these disparities. Nor can we attribute all educational problems to differences between schools. On the contrary, scholars are in wide agreement that the worst-performing schools are often fighting against family and community dysfunction. Nevertheless, we have a system that compounds the disadvantages that result from that dysfunction. If we care about economic opportunity, we must contend with the large population of young people who grow up in poverty and then are offered a substandard educational environment, and permanently diminished work opportunities.

Some might worry that these educational disparities are due to poor choices made by those who end up poor. However, this concern does not stand up under the scrutiny of our best evidence. Those "bad choices" are often endogenous. For example, one research team (Heckman et al. 2006) has spent years rigorously documenting the importance of various "non-cognitive" skills that determine many important educational and economic decisions.

These non-cognitive skills, often studied in terms of personality, in turn, are persistent over the long run, and they are impacted by good schooling programs and policy (Cunha and Heckman 2010; Almlund et al. 2011; Heckman et al. 2013). In a different policy environment, people would make very different choices. Income changes have a small but real effect (Blau 1999), good early schooling has a larger effect, and simply helping people move to a different location has a big effect on young people (Chetty et al. 2016).

Thus, there is a strong case to introduce more redistribution into educational funding. We know that the low incomes of the poor are, in aggregate, partially due to poor educational opportunities. Children from poor households often face substantial barriers to economic independence. Flipping the perspective, we also know that the relative wealth of those who are rich, in aggregate, is partially due to better educational opportunities. This mitigates (but does not eliminate) both the moral claim of the wealthy to their wealth, and the moral responsibility of the poor for their poverty. Even if we don't fully equalize opportunities or incomes, it is no more unjust to ask a wealthy household to contribute taxes for the improved schooling of their poor neighbors on the other side of the city line than it is to ask them to pay for the schooling of those within their city limits. Given the grim history of neighborhood segregation, it seems clear that the cause of justice lies on the side of broader financing of educational programs.

3.1.3   Health and Nutrition

Education is not the only part of modern life in which economic opportunities are limited for those who are poor. The health system in the United States is also an important guarantor of public participation, and yet it has proven inadequate to the task in some key ways. The most obvious failing is that too many face the risk of a serious medical expense, harming family finances. Too often people avoid spending money on health care, opting instead to head for an emergency room for problems that could have been treated earlier. It has been estimated that as many as 40 percent of serious injuries in children go untreated in families without insurance (Overpeck and Kotch 1995). In some cases, health expenses are the cause of bankruptcies. The most conservative study on this finds that 6 percent of bankruptcies among the uninsured and 4 percent of bankruptcies overall are likely due to expenses related to hospitalizations (Dobkin et al. 2018). Adding in the cost of other medical care and prescription drugs would push that percentage higher.

Poor health and poor access to health care can limit long-term economic opportunity. We can infer this by observing the economic benefits of providing people with insurance. When people receive health insurance, it improves their long-term health and productivity. Recent research has found that children who received coverage from Medicaid when it was introduced had better health outcomes throughout their life. They worked more, and were less likely to file for disability or use other government benefits. In fact, the government actually received an annual return between 2 and 7 percent just in reduced public benefits payments (Goodman-Bacon 2016). For this cohort of children, having insurance opened the door to a productive independent life.

The health-income-education-opportunity relationship goes far beyond unanticipated health expenses (Khullar and Chokshi 2018). Health, income, and education are all positively correlated for almost all measures of physical health. Wealthier people have better nutrition, live in less physically stressful environments, work in physically healthier environments, and have more convenient access to healthy food and health care. Those same people also prioritize healthy activities and make better decisions regarding smoking, nutrition, and exercise. With many empirical issues in health economics, causation often runs both ways for any raw demographic correlation, and so making the inferences that are important for concerns about economic justice can be difficult. And yet, we can see some accumulating evidence that being poor has a real causal impact on health, and through that, on economic opportunity. First, there is a strong connection between hunger, nutrition, and education performance. Food insecurity has been linked to hyperactivity, chronic absences, lower test scores, and behavioral problems (Murphy et al. 1998; Alaimo et al. 2001). The school lunch and school breakfast programs are intended to alleviate these concerns. Second, we have a large body of evidence, some documented later in this chapter, that alleviating poverty through government benefits has substantial positive impacts on health (Jones et al. 2003; Strully et al. 2010; Berkowitz et al. 2017; East 2020). We can infer from these findings that poverty has a reinforcing quality to it. It is not just the case that people who are poor have different preferences or make unhealthy choices. Being in poverty is actually bad for your health, and particularly bad for children's health. Alleviating child poverty, therefore, can have long-lasting returns.

3.1.4 Decision-Making

Poverty restricts economic opportunity in many ways. The arguments I have made about education and health are somewhat straightforward. The argument deepens, though, when you consider the implications of research on poverty and decision-making. This research is essential because it cuts right at the core of the judgments we make about the persistence of poverty. If people are poor because they have a preference for leisure, or because they lack some important virtues, then the poor person bears some moral responsibility for their poverty, and there is less of a duty to improve their lot beyond basic needs. If, however, the "culture of poverty," or the prevalence of poor decision-making is actually the result of poverty, then people who are poor could be stuck in a kind of poverty trap for which they are less culpable. This also bears on pragmatic arguments about poverty alleviation. If poverty creates incentives for rational people to make decisions that look, from the outside, like self-destructive habits, or if poverty prevents people from making the long-run rational decisions that would help them become self-sufficient (Karelis 2009), then it is more likely that anti-poverty programs can help people escape poverty.

In fact, there is a growing body of evidence that some of the poor decision-making by those who are poor is actually a result of the stress of poverty and inequality (Mullainathan and Shafir 2014; Payne 2017). While it is tempting to judge people's choices in the abstract, when people actually have to make the choice to defer spending or make a careful investment, they are doing so in a particular physiological state. It turns out that being in poverty, with all of the attending uncertainty and stress about basic needs, makes it far more difficult to make these important decisions. One study (Mani et al. 2013) finds that low-income people asked to think about expensive car repairs perform worse on spatial and reasoning tasks. In contrast, low-income people performed far better on those tasks if they were prompted to think about inexpensive car repairs, and more wealthy people performed similarly in both cases. Similar results were found studying farmers in India. People who are poor have to make high-stakes (but perhaps low dollar amount) financial decisions regularly, and are primed to think about financial stress far more often than higher-income people (Shah et al. 2018). The resulting mental load has significant impacts on the decision-making ability—amounting to 13–14 IQ points on reasoning tests—and substantially diminishes the ability to exhibit self-control (Haushofer and Fehr 2014; Mullainathan and Shafir 2014). In short, poverty makes it harder to make some kinds of decisions.

Delving further, one key part of economic decision-making is the ability to be patient, defer gratification, and make decisions based on long-term consequences. Economists talk about this in terms of **time preference**. It has often been noted that those who are poor exhibit a higher rate of time preference than wealthy people (meaning more preference for present rather than future consumption). This observation also plays an important role in the argument that poor people remain poor because of their own unwise choices. However, for poor people to be culpable for short-sighted behavior, it is usually assumed that causation works in just one direction: that poor people have a static rate of time preference that causes them to make poor choices and remain poor, and that they would behave similarly if they were not poor. If, however, causation runs the other way, and the conditions of poverty encourage short-term thinking, then the ethical implications of the argument are very different. In fact, we have a wealth of evidence that rates of time preference can change and depend on things like wealth, uncertainty, and other economic conditions (Becker and Mulligan 1997). Recent scholarship has provided strong evidence that poverty causes people to have a higher rate of time preference, and that this is related to the stress and riskiness of poverty (Haushofer and Fehr 2014).

A closely related issue is risk-taking. While some kinds of risk-taking are destructive to long-term wealth, some risk-taking is essential for innovation and investment. For reasons closely related to time discounting and other future-oriented decision-making, people in poverty are far more likely to be **risk-averse**. This is a learned psychological habit, but it is also a rational response to living in an environment with substantial environmental risks and limited access to credit (Haushofer and Fehr 2014). As an example, starting a small business could be an important step toward long-term financial independence, but doing so is highly risky, and often depends on substantial connections to those with specialized knowledge and access to good credit. Those in poverty, and those who come from households and communities in poverty, will be less able to bear the required risk, and so will be less able to use entrepreneurship as a ladder for upward mobility. Overall, there is a wealth of evidence that poverty can be psychologically reinforcing, so that those in poverty face substantial invisible barriers. Even more importantly, we cannot make a simple comparison of behaviors and judge that those who are poor are "undeserving."

3.2   Inequality Limits Opportunity

It is not just poverty that limits opportunities in the economy. Inequality also diminishes economic opportunities for those at the bottom in important ways. There are good reasons to be less worried about inequality than poverty (Frankfurt 2015), but in our current system, inequality has some effects that warrant concern. In particular, inequality has a reinforcing quality to it, as social and economic institutions are formed in the context of the unequal distribution of wealth and power. Over time, institutions that exclude the poor are built. The result is a decrease in economic opportunity and mobility.

3.2.1   Inequality, Power, and Mobility in the United States

There is substantial disagreement in the economics profession about how to measure economic inequality and what the most important causes are. In recent years, however, economists have done a much better job using rich administrative data to explore these questions. What has emerged is a broad consensus that inequality has increased since the 1960s, and that social mobility decreased over much of the 20th century. I will describe this consensus as three stylized facts:

First, income and wealth inequality have increased, particularly since the mid-1960s. Much of this growth in inequality has been concentrated in the top decile, with incomes growing much faster at the top, over recent decades, than those at the median or in the bottom deciles. The result is that the gap between the top 10 percent of earners and the median earner has grown. Even more, the gap between the top 1 percent and the top 10 percent has grown even faster. Debates about how to measure inequality matter for the magnitude of the increase, but not for the substantial trend (Piketty and Saez 2003; Goldin and Katz 2008; Kopczuk et al. 2010; Mechling et al. 2017).

Second, relative mobility, measured by correlation between the income rank of parents and children, has been relatively constant (Chetty et al. 2014). In order to allow comparison across time and space, we often measure social mobility as the probability that someone born in the middle quintile will end up reaching the top quintile of earners. Measures of this kind have been stable, at least since the 1970s. It appears that, buy this measure, mobility is lower in the United States than in more equal societies.

Third, absolute mobility, measured by the percentage of children who are better off than their parents in absolute terms, has fallen. In the first-half of the 20th century, the vast majority of children grew up to earn more than their parents. By the last third of the last century, less than half did. On average, children now end up with the same real income as their parents, or a bit less (Chetty et al. 2017). Given that there has been substantial real income growth in the United States, on average, how could this be true? It turns out that median incomes in the United States have been largely stagnant for quite some time, or at a minimum, have grown very slowly since the early 1980s (Katz and Krueger 2017). Meanwhile, the growth of incomes at the very top of the distribution has proceeded steadily. It is worth making a quick mathematical observation: if those top income gains were available across socioeconomic classes, then we would see higher absolute mobility, on average, even though median mobility might remain low. The average levels of mobility remain quite low, however, because those income gains are concentrated among not just the currently rich, but those whose parents were also wealthy. Inequality is growing, and the vast majority of those getting rich were also born wealthy.

The theory of distributive justice that I am working with does not condemn inequality outright. While some philosophers disagree, as discussed in Section 1.2, I believe it is much more important to ensure economic opportunity than pure equality. Nevertheless, inequality can still be unjust if it is the result of some other injustice, and it can cause injustice if it substantially limits the opportunities of others in the economy. Both of these seem to be true in some important cases. Broadly, though, inequality in the United States is not itself an injustice, nor the result of injustice. Most inequality in the United States is the result of a combination of structural changes in the economy. These structural changes are, at worst, the result of debatable public policy, but often the result of a changing mix of technology, demand for skill, schooling, and trade (Autor et al. 2008; Goldin and Katz 2008; Autor 2014).

There are two big exceptions to the general rule that inequality is not the result of injustice. The first is the obvious case of historic injustice toward minorities in the United States, which I will discuss in Section 1.3.3. The second is **rent-seeking** behavior, which, in this instance, refers to the practice of governments and businesses creating rules that benefit some at the expense of broader economy. Where the rules of the game can be changed by the participants, the rules almost always come to benefit those who have already been successful (Stiglitz 2012). This problem is an old one, and is not unique to market economies, but as our economies become more complex, it can be more difficult to see the ways in which power and regulation limit entrepreneurship and competition. When examining the system of regulations that limit competition in the United States, Lindsey and Teles (2017) describe it as a system of "upward redistribution" because of the many ways in which the system grants economic power and profits to those already wealthy.

Two examples of rent-seeking will suffice to illustrate the problem. First, consider the growth of occupational licensing. While only 5 percent of workers needed a license to do their job in the 1950s, by the end of the 20th century that had grown to 25 percent (Furman and Orszag 2018; Kleiner and Krueger 2013). The growth of these regulations can sometimes be warranted by consumer safety concerns, but they are, just as often, artificial barriers that require additional training or fees simply to limit entry and competition. The impact is clear: when you need a license, and usually additional training, to start in a profession, it is harder for the poor to move into those professions. Those occupations that have fared the best in the past 50 years, and those that occupy the bulk of the top third of income earners, are all heavily regulated and licensed. It is physicians, lawyers, and accountants that have the steepest entry barriers (often with an ugly racial history) and often face the least competition in the marketplace. Specialist doctors often run near-monopolies in local markets, employed by hospital systems that also face little competition, particularly when you consider the competitive barriers created by the insurance system (Rothwell 2019, chap. 9).

A second example of rent-seeking is the growing concentration of power and profits within industries. It is difficult to demonstrate conclusively that firms are taking advantage of **market power** to increase their profits at the expense of the rest of the economy. That said, all of the indicators point in this direction. Consider that in 12 of 13 of the broad industries we have data on, market concentration has increased over the past 20 years. We have seen rapid growth in inequality between firms and between industries, rather than within (Song et al. 2019). Over the period that we have seen rising inequality in the United States, job creation has decreased, job destruction has decreased, and firm entry has rapidly decreased, with entry rates in 2012 becoming half of what they were in 1975 (Furman 2016). Finally, corporate profits have increased steadily, even while productivity growth has declined. All of these clues point, in aggregate, to an increase in the market power and stability of firms, which has allowed those companies to profit beyond what their innovation and productivity warrant.

The implications of the rent-seeking argument are complicated. The obvious policy responses are to scrutinize regulation and engage in aggressive anti-trust action. These solutions are highly fraught, though, and are difficult to enact in an across-the-board manner. Moreover, there might be a natural move toward concentration in an increasingly global economy. Still, the growth in rent-seeking raises the possibility that better policy could hit a rare trifecta: increase productivity, increase economic dynamism, and decrease inequality. Scholars who have focused on these legal issues have a variety of helpful proposals that are beyond the scope of this argument (Furman 2016; Lindsey and Teles 2017; Tanner 2018, chap. 9). One implication for redistribution, however, is that taxation on these profits is unlikely to have a strong disincentive effect, since taxation of rents does not discourage creative activity. In other words, because of the growth in rent-seeking, higher progressive taxes and redistribution will not diminish economic activity or innovation as much as it might in a different economic environment.

Beyond the problems of rent-seeking, there is a reasonable amount of research that connects inequality and economic mobility (Andrews and Leigh 2009). It is worth exploring this connection in detail, because if inequality undermines economic mobility, then redistribution is worth pursuing for two reasons: (i) because it lifts up those at the bottom, and (ii) because the result is a more egalitarian society that might itself improve opportunities. To explore this, I will describe two broad ways in which inequality can undermine social mobility and economic opportunity.

3.2.2   Institutions That Reinforce Economic Hierarchy

I argued in Section 1.3.1 that poverty is accompanied by substantially lower economic opportunities. What remained unexplained, however, was the reason that vast differences in opportunities by school and neighborhood develop and persist. This is worth examining in some detail, because it is not random. Neighborhood differences in opportunity develop over time because of specific local histories. They also result from the demographic sorting that happens in a society with a high degree of inequality. We need to think carefully about the ways in which inequality, then, can impact opportunities to participate in economic life.

One of the most obvious ways that wealthy people can strategically spend their money is to make long-term investments in their communities and their children. This, of course, is often laudatory. In unequal societies, however, these investments can create exclusionary institutions (Reeves 2017). The exclusion of others is sometimes the point. We see this most clearly in country clubs and elite schools, where social capital is built among people who are at the top of the economic ladder and who expect their children to be there too. For much of the 20th century, these institutions have taken on the language and trappings of meritocracy, and rightly so. Nevertheless, that meritocratic language doesn't change the nature of the institutions. Our elite colleges and universities, where the rhetoric of meritocracy and diversity reign, still greatly favor students from the top 1 percent of the income distribution (Chetty et al. 2017).

Durlauf (1996) theorized that this kind of schooling selection would have the effect of reinforcing inequality. If wages become more and more dependent on location and schooling, then the relatively wealthy can segregate by income, giving their children a real advantage in the labor market and in access to elite institutions. This is what we see in the data, most thoroughly documented by Putnam (2000, 2016): we are living in a period of dramatically increased geographic sorting, at the same time that genuinely open public institutions and private associations are on the decline. This combination is particularly destructive to the cross-cutting civic institutions that served as unifying points for communities. The United States still has a thriving civil society, but these local institutions are too often segregated by income and race.

This sorting has too often had an obvious racial element. Moreover, racial segregation can persist for decades after explicit discrimination recedes because of economic barriers. A case study in the decline of public institutions that could create upward mobility can be found in U.S. schools, particularly in the South. When schools were desegregated by the courts, the result was not shared or integrated schools. Instead, in the aftermath of the legal change, there was an enormous rise in the support for, and enrollment in, private elementary and secondary schools, and decades of neighborhood sorting. The racially segregated schooling remains in many cities, with private schools and outer suburbs serving overwhelmingly white households, and minority households being served by public schools in cities. The segregation is imperfect, but it persists in the form of income segregation that has a racial element.

In many communities, the same dynamic results from economic inequality. Private secondary schools operate in every major U.S. city, charging high-enough tuition to guarantee that only the wealthy can afford to send their kids there. These schools then develop a pipeline to elite colleges and universities. Vast disparities of income in a small geographic area also have a sorting effect. School district lines running through neighborhoods can make a huge difference for housing prices, with wealthy people in one district and low-income families a few blocks away in a different district. This proximity does not result in opportunity, though, since residential zoning decisions and housing prices keep the school districts income-segregated.

This kind of income-based sorting into institutions often happens at the neighborhood level, since different neighborhoods can have access to vastly different public and private services. We now have great evidence that moving neighborhoods can have substantial long-term impacts, particularly on young people (Chetty and Hendren 2018). In the "Moving to Opportunity" experiments, families were given subsidies to move to a better neighborhood. The impact on adults and older children was limited to mental and physical health improvements, but the impact on young children was marked. Children in these families earned higher wages, were more likely to attend college, and less likely to be single parents. The value of the taxes collected on future wage increases, moreover, was larger than the cost of the moving subsidy, so there was a net positive return to taxpayers. Moreover, these neighborhood-related gains don't seem to be due only to schooling (Chetty et al. 2016).

While economists have focused their research on entrepreneurship, schooling, and neighborhoods, there is a wealth of evidence that the social sorting that accompanies inequality also diminishes the opportunities of the poor by limiting social connections. Sociologists refer to the value of interpersonal connections as **social capital**. These connections have proven to be really important for economic opportunity: intellectual development, schooling, employment, and even health (Cook 2014). For a number of interrelated reasons, there is a strong case that economic opportunity depends on having a pretty unified open set of cultural institutions and high-quality, open public services. The only times/places that the United States has experienced substantial upward mobility without that recipe has been when people could get very cheap or free farmland, or, in the case of the GI bill after the Second World War, when the government engaged in a massive investment in housing and education.

3.2.3 Community and Consumption

If inequality diminishes opportunity by sorting and polarizing the population, it is worth examining the cultural implications of this kind of change as well. It is difficult to run society-wide lab experiments on inequality, and so the associations are always complicated and uncertain. Nevertheless, we have a large body of research showing that more unequal societies have a diminished capacity to invest in each other. First, and most notably, perhaps, is the difference that emerges in trust. More inequality is associated with substantially less trust in a population (Wilkinson and Pickett 2011). This shows up at the macro and micro level. Trust surveys show a strong correlation, and we also see people far less likely to participate in or form local groups in more unequal communities (Alesina and La Ferrara 2000). In experiments, inequality diminishes people's willingness to contribute to public goods (Anderson et al. 2008). Similarly, there is some empirical evidence that increased inequality decreases charitable giving (Duquette 2018). Overall, it seems that inequality undermines local solidarity.

If inequality diminishes our propensity to trust and productively associate with those around us, it also impacts our consumption. The economist Robert Frank has spent much of his career documenting the ways in which our consumption depends on our peers. People who are surrounded by others who have one car will think a single car for a family is normal. Once a critical mass of people own two or three cars, expectations will change. Particularly for goods that signal status and relative position, inequality can push us to consume far more than we would otherwise (Frank 2005, 2010).

This **competitive consumption** or "trickle-down consumption" can even proceed when the additional consumption brings little pleasure to the consumers, and can crowd-out other uses for money, such as charity or savings (Schor 1999; Frank 2005).

This has an important implication for my argument. This kind peer-setting consumption can exclude people when the ever-increasing consumption levels get built into public life. The automobile was a luxury item for years, until it became a necessity. The switch occurred when neighborhoods were built in such a way that you could no longer transport yourself to any essential businesses or institutions without a car. In a city designed for cars, public transportation and biking become impractical, and so the basic cost of living increases (Stromberg 2015; Semuels 2016). The same has happened with communications technology, first telephones, then mobile phones, and the internet. Many routine acts of civic engagement and economic life now require the internet and a mobile phone to participate. For this reason, the cost of participation in society rises as consumer expectations rise. In an unequal society, the poorest members may be able to afford physical necessities, but still find them slowly priced out of civic and economic contributions.

The connections between inequality and opportunity are not immediate and direct, but the long-term results are still real. As income and wealth become less equal and mobility becomes limited, the culture becomes more stratified. The kinds of institutions that naturally build opportunity get hollowed out in those communities that need them the most. Redistribution by the government will not replace these institutions, but it can help create more equality and mobility, so that the process of stratification slows down.

3.3 Historic Racial Injustice

We cannot responsibly examine poverty and inequality in the United States without accounting for racial disparities in education, employment, income, and wealth. Furthermore, we cannot account for these racial disparities without taking a hard look at our history of theft, murder, exploitation, and oppression, and at the current evidence regarding racial discrimination. Our current distribution of property and wealth is the result of this history, and so the pattern of inequality and poverty has been partly caused by these injustices. In many cases, moreover, these injustices were encouraged or committed by the state, and so restitution of some kind, by the state, is appropriate.

3.3.1 Theft of Land from Native People

The history of interactions between European immigrants and native peoples is a violent one. As European people increased in numbers over the 18th and 19th centuries, they often settled on land that belonged, both by history and treaty, to native people. These conflicts often resulted in military action, followed by a new peace treaty. The structure of these treaties followed a pattern: native people would agree to move west or inhabit a small portion of land, giving up a much larger region. In return, the U.S. government would give some kind of monetary payment to the tribes and to some individuals. Under the right conditions, these agreements might seem just. However, no historian of the period argues that these treaties were generally entered into voluntarily. On the contrary, these agreements were part of a long campaign of violence. Furthermore, the U.S. government and European settlers repeatedly ignored the content of the treaties, even within the lifetime of the initial signatories, which resulted in new waves of settlers, new conflicts, and new coerced agreements (Prucha 1986). This pattern of events, moreover, was accompanied by mass murder, forced dislocation, and outright theft of land on numerous other occasions, enforced by the military of the United States.

The legacy of this violent history is bleak. Native people groups now can claim small fractions of the land they were promised. Their history and culture were subject to popular denigration and a campaign of erasure for 300 years. The economic legacy is similar. Having been systematically robbed, disenfranchised, and shut out of the economy, the remaining native communities have some of the highest rates of unemployment and poverty in the nation. Resolving this history through redistribution is probably impossible, but there is room to move in the direction of a more just future, by ameliorating some of the damage of that historic legacy.

3.3.2 Oppression of Black Americans

Even more close to the public eye, perhaps, is the injustice visited upon racial minorities, particularly black Americans. The damage done to those enslaved and brought to North America is incalculable. The systematic political and economic oppression that lasted well into the 20th century, moreover, has imposed a long-term economic cost on the black community. This legacy is continued in policies and practices that reinforce racism in systematic ways. For the purposes of this argument, I will focus on two implications of this history that are relevant for distributive justice. First, the racist institutions and actions that were normal for many years substantially limited the opportunity for black Americans to participate in economic life through schooling, work, savings, investment, and entrepreneurship. The legacy of this history is a stark gap in wealth between black and white families. Second, this racist legacy continues in labor market discrimination and differential schooling opportunities, so that black Americans continue to fight an uphill battle to engage in normal economic life in competition with other citizens. I will take each of these arguments in turn.

First, descriptions of the historic economic marginalization and oppression of black people have been made in great detail by a number of different scholars. I will only briefly survey the argument here. First, consider the accumulation of productive property. The opportunity of reconstruction, in which land was supposed to be granted to formerly enslaved people was never fully realized. In the years that followed the end of the Civil War, black Americans were subjected to a campaign of terror and theft, particularly in the South, that explicitly punished black households for savings, investments, and economic progress (Breed 2001; Lewan and Barclay 2001). Their job opportunities were sharply curtailed; they were excluded from unions and professional certifications and paid lower wages (Rothwell 2019). Moreover, the political and legal channels for restitution were blocked through voter suppression and legal and informal harassment. When black citizens moved to other parts of the United States seeking opportunities, they found barriers elsewhere too, including extractive banking institutions and explicit legal barriers keeping them out of many parts of economic life (Massey and Denton 1993; Coates 2014). I use the word oppression carefully, to denote instances where political power is used to systematically prevent people from exercising normal freedoms. For at least 100 years following slavery, the United States systematically oppressed black Americans in an explicit effort to limit their economic and political freedom. Moreover, too many of the vestiges of this oppression continue in our institutions.

The result of this history of economic and political oppression is a wide gap in wealth, social capital, and community institutions. Of these, the wealth gap is perhaps the most important for this argument. Despite achieving formal, or legal, equality in many arenas, we still see large gaps in wealth between black and white Americans. The median black household's net worth is one-tenth of the white median household's net worth (McIntosh et al. 2020). That gap cannot be explained simply by home ownership, or by behavioral differences. Darity and Mullen note that, after controlling for income, black households save at similar rates to white households, despite greater kin obligations. Nor can the difference be explained by family structure (the gap remains even among single parent households), or education (controlling for socioeconomic status, black youths get more education than white) (2020, pp. 32–3). Moreover, many white families built wealth for generations through gifts from the government, most notably the Homestead Act and the GI Bill, both of which were partially or completely unavailable to black households.

One reasonable explanation for the wealth gap is that there is an intergenerational element to wealth. Research shows strong ties between wealth of grandparents and their grandchildren, particularly the wealth of grandparents during the childhood of grandchildren. One reason for this is that inheritances and gifts matter more than you might expect. As much as 4 percent of all income earned in a year takes the form of an inheritance, and one study found that somewhere between 26 and 50 percent of an adult's wealth position is due to gifts and inheritances from their family (Feiveson and Sabelhaus 2019). Intergenerational transfers can take many forms, from paying for education, providing a down payment on a house, a loan during hard times, or help starting a business. Following families over generations, researchers found that white families gave six times as many gifts across generations as did black families (Darity and Mullen 2020, p. 36). Black households start with less wealth, and this has a direct impact on their children's ability to invest and deal with financial risk. The wealth gap is a lasting legacy of generations of economic exclusion and theft.

This history is exacerbated by current barriers to economic opportunity faced by racial minorities. While the degree of discrimination in the labor market has been long debated, a series of experimental studies have provided conclusive evidence of pervasive racial discrimination that has remained relatively constant for the past 30 years at least (Quillian et al. 2017). Scholars have sent identical resumes and job inquiries to employers, varying only the race, or the name of the applicant, and found that black applicants were far less likely to get calls for interviews than their identical white peers (Bertrand and Mullainathan 2004). Even white job candidates with criminal records had better results than black applicants without any such records (Pager 2007). Education does not eliminate these barriers, either. Black applicants from elite universities received the same number of calls from employers as white applicants from much less selective schools (Gaddis 2015). There is some evidence, in fact, that discrimination is greater in high-skill occupations. These differences do not seem to be due to productivity either. Where it can be observed, black worker productivity cannot explain the wage differential with white workers (Rothwell 2019, p. 96). Discrimination also shows up in other key parts of the economy, including education and the granting of loans, which are essential to economic success (Blanchflower et al. 2003).

The result of this historic disadvantage and current discrimination is that black Americans earn lower wages and are more likely to be unemployed. If you add in the considerable evidence that the justice system exhibits racism as well, it becomes hard to ignore the widespread limits to economic opportunity faced by black Americans. The implications for economic opportunity and mobility are not surprising: the children of high-income black families are far less likely to also be high income than other high-income families, and low-income black children are far less likely to move up. Social mobility in the United States varies greatly by race (Chetty et al. 2020).

3.3.3 Restitution for Injustice

There are two important implications of these injustices for the purposes of our debate. First, the long history of theft and exclusion undermines the moral legitimacy of the claim that other Americans have to their wealth. Family wealth originating in land that was expropriated is clearly suspect, but so too is some of the wealth that has grown from that land. The moral claim to these assets is not entirely eliminated, particularly since the passage of time has likely added the legitimate gains from labor, risk, and savings. Neither is it focused only on those with direct ties to the land, since many benefited directly from these historic crimes. However, theories of distributive justice that depend on the legitimacy of property claims must account for these past injustices.

The second implication we can draw from past and current injustice is that these victims are due some kind of restitution. The United States has not offered even formal/legal equality of opportunity for racial minorities in too many cases. There is a strong argument to be made for reparations for past injustices, particularly those that can be attributed directly to actions of the U.S. government. A number of scholars have made cases for reparations for specific wrongdoing (Coates 2014; Darity and Mullen 2020). Nevertheless, while I find these cases largely convincing, I will take a slightly different approach here. The kind of economic injustice described here is prevalent in history beyond the experience of black Americans and Native people. Identifying all similar victims and discerning the amount of restitution that they are due may be impossible. Identifying those who have benefited directly from past injustices is similarly difficult. While we can point with clarity to some victims and some beneficiaries, drawing the lines around these populations will inevitably be arbitrary. Even with discrimination happening today, it is far easier to identify the average effect than to identify specific cases of injustice. Finally, we do not have a consensus on the underlying ethics, much less the procedural elements that would be required for the administration of justice. You can think of this as a targeting problem. It does not mitigate the injustice; it merely makes restitution harder to administer.

It is partially for this reason, and partly for political reasons, that contemporary politicians have often proposed universal programs to remedy these injustices. The effect of the history of injustice has been to economically marginalize black Americans and Native people. As a second-best option, then, instead of targeted reparations, it makes sense to respond to these injustices by building just the kinds of wealth and opportunity that have been undermined by the past and current oppression. I follow Hamilton and Darity (2010) by arguing that a universal wealth policy, or "opportunity accounts," could be an appropriate, if partial, policy response.

This section provides evidence that poverty in the United States is serious enough to substantially limit the long-term economic opportunities of the poor. That is, the poor remain poor because they have access to lower quality education, less health care, and neighborhoods with less social capital and public services. In this environment, it is normal for those in poverty to make less productive choices that they could avoid if they were in a better material position. The growing inequality in the United States, moreover, further widens the opportunity gap by contributing to institutional barriers to economic life for the poor. Finally, the long history of racial injustice in the United States has severely undermined economic opportunity for minorities.

4   Redistribution for Economic Opportunity

The account of distributive justice and the economic evidence I have surveyed so far support an expansion of the welfare state. In the United States today, we still have numerous children lacking basic needs and with severely restricted economic opportunities. In order to defend the proposition that we should do more to rectify these problems, however, it is necessary to focus on specific policy changes. Without a proposal, it would be difficult to ascertain whether increased redistribution would be just or effective.

I am not interested in defending all kinds of redistribution, nor even all current egalitarian redistribution in the United States. There are, doubtless, some programs that are poorly designed and targeted. Overall, though, our best evidence points to a broad positive impact of the welfare state in the United States. As noted earlier, absolute poverty rates have declined substantially since the 1960s, and that decline is almost entirely due to government support (Wimer et al. 2016). Over time, the welfare state has actually gotten better at lifting people out of poverty (Trisi 2016). However, this still leaves open the question of which parts of the welfare state are effective and which might not be. It is important to examine the best evidence we have and craft policies that meet the most important needs in the most efficient manner. I believe that this would be best accomplished, broadly, through three expanded programs and one new policy:

1. Expanded food stamps (SNAP)
2. Health insurance coverage
3. Universal preschool
4. Opportunity Accounts

While I don't have space to justify or detail any of these changes in great depth, I will give each policy change a brief description, and then survey evidence that each policy will substantially improve economic opportunity. In the next section, I will address funding and some common economic objections to redistribution. The most important argument from this section is that, contrary to popular conceptions, there are at least some core welfare state programs that seem to result in improved economic productivity over the long term, and they do this by providing basic needs, reducing uncertainty, and investing in valuable skills.

The Supplemental Nutrition Assistance Program (SNAP) is funded and administered by the U.S. federal government in cooperation with each state. Formerly, and still popularly, known as "food stamps," the program gives low-income people the ability to buy food. The program started in 1964. In 2018, the program provided food aid to 40 million people, with the average participating household getting close to $127 worth of food a month.

4.1 Expand Nutrition Assistance

The **Supplemental Nutrition Assistance Program** (SNAP or food stamps) provides funds to families in poverty that can only be spent on food. Because of the targeted nature of the program, and its administrative simplicity, it is a particularly efficient form of redistribution. The program, like many others, is **means-tested,** so that only those with low incomes qualify for benefits. As a result, there is a labor supply disincentive for those on the margin of eligibility, and a slight disincentive for participants since the generosity of benefits decreases as people's income increases. This means that participants in the program might be somewhat less likely to work, or might work less, because of the program.

Labor Supply Disincentive (or work-disincentive): a side effect of some tax and redistribution policies, in which the policy reduces the benefit of working, either because the take-home income is reduced through taxes or because additional wages reduce the person's eligibility for government benefits.

SNAP is designed with a phase-out so that this effect is less dramatic than some other benefit programs, though that could be improved. Accordingly, the SNAP expansion that I would like to consider here is to diminish the rate at which benefits are "taxed" away as income increases, and adjust the formula to make the benefit more generous. In policy terms, this proposal would increase the earned income deduction. Compared to our current system, the policy would moderately encourage people to work more and move toward economic independence.

Part of the case for an expansion of the SNAP program rests on the evidence that the program is quite effective at achieving its goals. The first broad goal is to improve access to food among the poor. There is strong evidence that SNAP (or food stamps) has reduced hunger and improved nutrition. The formation of the food assistance programs, including the school lunch program and WIC, had a large impact on malnutrition in the poorest parts of the country (Currie 2006, chap. 3). Scholars have found that the program results in fewer food hardships (DePolt et al. 2009) and increases spending on food in amounts similar to income increases (Hoynes and Schanzenbach 2009). The overall health impacts are also well-documented, particularly for children and teens that participate in the program (lower obesity) and infants (higher birth weights) (Jones et al. 2003; Kreider et al. 2012; Almond et al. 2010; East 2020). Adult participants using SNAP were better able to manage diabetes, reported better health and fewer sick doctor visits (but more checkups), and had fewer days sick in bed away from work (Gregory and Deb 2015; Hoynes 2016).

The most powerful arguments in favor of SNAP stem from the long-run impacts of the program on health and economic independence. Scholars tracked the cohorts of people that first had access to the Food Stamps program over time, and observed a significant long-term reduction in heart disease, diabetes, and blood pressure. Women who grew up with access to the program also had greater self-sufficiency, earning higher wages and less reliance on public benefits (Hoynes et al. 2016). Another study similarly found that early participation in SNAP resulted in better education outcomes, greater economic independence, longer lifespans, better neighborhoods, and decreased crime (Bailey et al. 2020). These results run directly counter to some of the dangerous narratives that surround the food stamps program. In the long run, the program supports both health and economic independence.

4.2   Expand Health Insurance Coverage

Many of the biggest financial risks that people in poverty face are health related. Because of the high cost of routine care, those without insurance can face hard choices about whether to see a doctor. Some of those who are poor in the United States receive **Medicaid** (health insurance). Children whose parents do not qualify for Medicaid might still qualify for SCHIP (a similar program for children) and many others might get subsidized health care through an Affordable Care Act insurance exchange. The coverage of these health insurance programs has improved recently but is still not complete, and it varies greatly by state. The subsidies and availability of private plans is also highly variable. This patchwork of coverage ends up making health care finance a nightmare for hospitals and doctors, on the one hand, and highly uncertain for participants.

Too often, moreover, the administration of enrollment in these programs is a big problem. Currie describes the perverse system where some states have an incentive to push people off Medicaid rolls, even if many of them qualify. The result is very low uptake and frequent purges for minor administrative problems. Then, hospitals, looking to bill Medicaid for expenses, find it profitable to employ a separate company, at great expense, to work through the government bureaucracy on behalf of their patients. This is pure administrative waste (Currie 2006, chap. 2).

In health care, we could achieve near-universal coverage with a system of health insurance exchanges that included a public option

Medicaid is a U.S. federal public health insurance program for low-income families, children, and those with disabilities. The program was created in 1965 and expanded most recently in 2019. In 2020, over 77 million individuals received some amount of health insurance through Medicaid or related programs.

in which people are automatically enrolled if they do not choose a different provider. Health insurance would be subsidized for those with low incomes, with a slow reduction in subsidies as income increases. Universal coverage is particularly important for health insurance because those who are uninsured very often end up having medical services paid for by the government in emergency situations. Requiring coverage, moreover, fixes one of the biggest technical problems with insurance markets: the problem of adverse selection that can undermine risk pooling.

It is possible for poor administrative design to be an injustice in itself, and the U.S. health care system is a prime example. A well-designed public program could set standards for billing and pricing transparency that would cut through the obfuscation created by our current patchwork of funding mechanisms. Most importantly, though, it would tie funding directly to patients, and since coverage would be universal, the extraordinary health risk that people face, combined with uncertainty around financing, would be largely ameliorated.

I include health insurance in this proposal both because it is a way for our economy to meet people's basic needs and because it has long-run positive effects on health, income, and opportunity. One of the primary benefits we see from government-provided health insurance, like Medicaid, is through improvements in health. People with health insurance are more likely to get treatment for serious conditions, and to have those treatments come earlier, when treatment can be cheaper (Newhouse 1993; Currie 2006, chap. 2). Early doctor visits are far cheaper than emergency room visits, and good prenatal care is far cheaper than treating the conditions that it can prevent. Moreover, there is strong evidence that eligibility for Medicaid and the Children's Health Insurance Program improves health in the near and long term (Thompson 2017). Mortality among non-white children was reduced by 20 percent as a result of the program introduction

(Goodman-Bacon 2018) and infant mortality has been consistently reduced by Medicaid expansions (Currie and Gruber 1996).

Again, though, the most powerful argument for these programs comes from the substantial long-run benefits for recipients. The case that Medicaid, in particular, has been good for long-run economic opportunity has been made recently by scholars examining the life trajectories of people with different levels of exposure to health insurance, tracking state differences in eligibility and implementation. The results are encouraging: those with greater Medicaid eligibility have lower mortality, are more likely to attend college, and delay childbearing. Women were found to earn higher wages. The long-term budget implications are good too. Medicaid decreases benefits received from the Earned Income Tax Credit, and increases taxes paid, so that one study found the federal government actually gets back 58 cents of each dollar paid into the program (Brown et al. 2020). Another study followed people longer and found that Medicaid eligibility at young ages decreased life-long mortality, increased labor force participation, decreased disability claims, and reduced reliance on public health insurance up to 50 years later. This study found that the government actually earned a 2–7 percent return on their investment in Medicaid (Goodman-Bacon 2016).

Making sure people get preventative care and can pay for good care when health problems arise is a basic humanitarian goal, but it is also economically important. Lack of access to health insurance creates long-term problems for people, and lifting that barrier allows them to be more productive and independent members of society.

> **Head Start** is a federally funded preschool program for children of low-income families and those with special educational needs. The program was created in 1965, and substantially expanded in 1981. The program now serves around a million children each year.

4.3   Universal Preschool

The primary publicly funded early child education program is **Head Start,** which offers preschool to children with developmental delays and those in poverty. We have come to see that the program has less dramatic short-term academic effects than congress hoped, but more dramatic and positive long-term effects than anyone expected. Moreover, we now have a wealth of research that shows that investments in children have a bigger effect when they are younger, and that increased schooling reduces academic performance gaps. Most importantly, perhaps, education is the most important way we invest in the future productivity of citizens. Better educational investments at key developmental stages open up opportunities.

The most important schooling expansion we can deliver, therefore, is likely to be a universal preschool program for four-year-olds. Providing broadly accessible preschool is important for two reasons. First, there is ample evidence that integrated schooling with socioeconomic diversity simply works better. Second, the current income test leaves the children of many families without affordable preschool options, which, in turn, limits the ability of the parents to work. Right now, qualification for Head Start is far too limited. The schooling could greatly benefit many children whose family does not qualify, and given the volatility of incomes, any strict income test will exclude many people.

The case for universal preschool rests on the evidence that this kind of investment has strong long-term impacts. This policy area has been hampered by early studies of the Head Start program that found few academic gains that lasted more than a year or two. The program remains, but it has taken years for researchers to build a case for the real impact. Researchers have since found that the "fade-out" of test score gains is not a good indicator of long-term benefits. In fact, some of the populations that showed the quickest fade-out show the largest long-term gains in graduation rates (Deming 2009). The academic gains that do show up are encouraging: participants in Head Start, when compared to similar peers, are more likely to graduate from high school, attend college, and receive a degree (Deming 2009; Baur and Schanzenbach 2016). They also have higher earnings into their 1920s, and are less likely to commit crimes (Garces et al. 2002). Other studies have found health benefits, including decreased behavioral problems, fewer health problems, less obesity, and less depression (Carneiro and Ginja 2014).

The long-term benefits of Head Start seem to extend even further. Barr and Gibbs have found that the children of parents who attended Head Start have increased educational attainment, less teen pregnancy, and decreased crime rates (2019). The benefits of investing in the skills of these young people, thus, appear to be transferable across generations. This pattern of results make sense in the context of research that identifies early education as an important investment in non-cognitive skills that are likely to have high payoffs and be longer lasting than some strictly academic skills (Heckman 2007; Heckman et al. 2013).

Opportunity accounts, or "Baby Bonds," have been proposed in the United States, patterned after the Children's Development Accounts in the United Kingdom. These accounts would build, through means-tested deposits and management by the U.S. treasury, until the child reaches 18, at which point the recipient could use the funds for a limited set of purposes.

4.4 Opportunity Accounts

If wealth is self-reinforcing, and if inequality results in exclusionary social institutions and a less dynamic economy, then providing for basic needs can only partially address the problem of limited economic opportunity. Particularly in the context of a long history of exclusion and theft, and the context of current discrimination in employment and lending, a universal basic wealth policy makes sense. Wealth is one of the primary ways in which the economic advantages from the past accumulate and get passed on to children. A wealth-building policy that is progressive, rather than our current regressive asset-building programs, could have a big impact (Hamilton and Darity 2010).

The wealth-building proposal that I will consider for this argument has been recently proposed in congress as an "opportunity accounts" policy. The policy would establish a savings account for every child at birth, with an initial deposit of $1000. Each year, the government would add money to the account, but would add more money to the accounts of families with lower incomes: $2000 for the poorest children, and less for families as they move up income brackets. The children of the most wealthy families would only receive the initial $1000. The funds are managed by the treasury to earn a low-risk 3 percent annual return. When the child reaches the age of 18, the money in the account can be used, but only for college tuition, a down payment on a house or other property, a business startup, or the start of a retirement savings account (Kliff 2018).

The way the plan would work, children whose family was below the poverty line for all 18 years would have $46,000 in their account. Children from the wealthiest families would have only $1681. This kind of policy would ease borrowing constraints for poor children, immediately opening up college and property ownership. The egalitarian impact would not be immediate, but it would be substantial. The impact, moreover, would not only disproportionately help the poor, it would also disproportionately aid minority children. The proposal drafters estimate that the average white child would have an account of $15,790, based on the income of their parents while growing up. The average Hispanic child would have an account balance of $27,337, and the average black child would have $29,038.

Unlike the other policies discussed here, there is not a large body of empirical evidence on the impact of a policy like this, as it has not yet been attempted. However, asset-building policies have a long history in economic thinking about development, and so there is a larger literature that can help us understand how this kind of policy could work (Sherraden 1991; Plastrik et al. 2002). The broader logic of my argument implies a case for optimism. The consistent long-term positive effects that we see from redistribution programs imply that there are substantial barriers to economic success that depend only on access to material resources. Relieving these constraints, then does not just improve their short-term well-being. The beneficiaries of these programs live more productive lives, along multiple dimensions, because they are better set-up to participate (Boushey 2019). We could also think of this program as a parallel, in some ways, to the GI bill, which had economically and socially unifying effects, and was an engine of social mobility, though also a source of racial exclusion (Mettler 2002; Altschuler and Blumin 2009).

This section outlines four policies that would redistribute wealth in ways that target the most important barriers to full participation in economic life. There is strong evidence for substantial long-term positive effects from food assistance, preschool, public health insurance. Each of these programs increases the long-term likelihood that people will live economically independent lives.

5   Economic Objections to Redistribution

Redistribution is subject to a number of objections, some of which have been discussed already. I would like to address two of the most important objections here. The heart of each of these objections is the argument that there is a substantial unintended negative consequence of welfare state redistribution. The first and undoubtedly most important objection has to do with the cost of these kinds of programs, and the effects of the taxes that would be required to pay for them. The second objection is that welfare state programs have unfortunate incentive effects, most notably in discouraging employment. Each of these objections is worth considering carefully.

My argument in this section can be summarized in three broad points. First, the unfortunate side effects, while sometimes real, can be mitigated by good policy design. Second, some of the concerns about the welfare state do not stand up to scrutiny once the best empirical evidence has been taken into account. Finally, there are some real costs that attend government programs of this size, and these have to be weighed against the substantial benefits and ethical arguments in their favor.

5.1   The Cost of Redistribution

It would be easy, rhetorically, to argue that these programs would be beneficial, and then stop the argument there. In public policy, though, it is an important discipline to consider carefully the cost of each proposal. The increased redistribution that I have proposed is fairly expansive by U.S. standards, and so requires justification. I have estimated the annual increased government revenue that would be required to run all of these programs. The amounts cannot be precise, given the brief descriptions I provide here; many details would need to be worked out in the design of each program. In each case, I tried to collect a well-documented cost estimate for a similar policy from a reputable source. These rough figures allow the reader to think about the kind of taxation that would be necessary to sustainably fund each program (Table 1.1).

The estimated total cost of all of these changes together is $276 billion dollars each year, which amounts to 1.29 percent of GDP, 4 percent of federal government spending, or a quarter of what the U.S. federal government spent on Social Security benefits or National Defense in 2019. The funding mechanism for these

Table 1.1 Estimated Annual Cost of Each Proposal

Policy Proposal	Estimated Increased Annual Cost
Food stamps expansion	$12 billion[2]
Health insurance	$170 billion[3]
Subsidized preschool	$12 billion[4]
Opportunity accounts	$82 Billion[5]
Total	**$276 billion**

programs can be quite flexible. As long as they are not funded by a tax with a regressive impact, the overall redistributive effect of these programs will be preserved. For the purposes of this argument, I am not strongly wedded to any particular taxation strategy. I do offer a slate of tax increases here so that the reader can see the magnitude of the tax changes that would be needed.

There are a couple of broad principles of taxation that can aid in policy-making. The most important is that we should strive to treat similar or substitutable options similarly in the tax code. Most kinds of individual income are subject to the income tax, which has a progressive rate structure. This applies to income from salaries, wages, tips, income from self-employment, and interest earned on a bank account

2. Schanzenbach (2013) only gives incomplete cost estimates that are somewhat out of date, so I updated the details a bit. She cites the cost of the 13 percent increase from a previous reform, which is a bit more than half of the proposed reform by my calculations. Because SNAP expenditures vary greatly over the business cycle, this expansion would also vary in cost, and in a recession year it would likely be more expensive.

3. This is the cost of a health insurance reform, before budget offsets, from Vice President Biden or Pete Buttigieg's plans for expanding primary insurance proposed in 2019 during the democratic primary, which are the most similar to what I propose here. Cost estimates are from the Committee for a Responsible Federal Budget (Primary Care: Estimating Democratic Candidates' Health Plans 2020).

4. The Obama administration worked on a pre-K proposal that would cost $12 Billion, but the real cost here could be far lower. Brookings Institution scholars (Whitehurst and Klein 2015) argue that the Obama administration proposal wildly overstates the cost, estimating that we could get to universal pre-K for $2 to $4 Billion. What I propose would be somewhat more expansive, so I use the higher cost estimate.

5. There are a couple of different proposals for Baby Bonds or Opportunity Accounts. The most careful fiscal estimate of one of these proposals was by Zewde (2020), estimates an annual cost of $82 billion. While this plan differed somewhat from Senator Booker's proposal, and the one I offer here, the differences are not large.

balance. Income from property or financial assets that you trade or ownership of a company (capital gains and dividends), however, are taxed at a lower rate. The distinction between labor income, interest income, and capital gains is arbitrary enough that many have argued that the tax code should be simplified by treating these types of income similarly (Dolan 2020). However, this preferential tax is low for some good reasons, including the asymmetry of investment risk and that it encourages investment, and in turn, growth. The change I propose here would leave the preferential rate intact, but eliminate the step-up of the tax basis at death, which allows people to pass assets on to heirs who then do not have to pay taxes on the gains before they received it. This loophole allows investment wealth in financial markets to accumulate tax-free, and then be passed on to heirs without ever being taxed. No other source of income is treated this way, not even interest earned on bank account balances. Eliminating this change would limit inefficiency caused by the tax code that encourages people to hold on to investments longer than they would otherwise to avoid taxes. It would also increase annual government revenue by $85 Billion (Wamhoff 2019).

A second change that would raise substantial tax revenue would be to reform the estate tax, which is paid by those who receive inheritances. Currently all inheritances worth less than $11.5 million are exempt, and above that estates are taxed at a flat 40 percent rate. If we follow the details of the proposed Responsible Estate Tax Act, the tax would apply to far more estates (Phillips and Wamhoff 2018). This change would drop the exemption amount to $3.5 million, and then apply an increasing tax rate as the estates increase in value. The estate tax is the most progressive tax in U.S. law, and so the redistributive impact would be real. The argument for an aggressive estate tax is an old one, and can be traced at least as far back as the work of John Stuart Mill (Cappelen and Pedersen 2018). There are three broad elements of the argument for taxing estates. First, concentrations of wealth are behind some of the problems mentioned in Section 1.3.2. Second, the moral claim to inheritance income is less important than the moral claim to earned income. Third, the estate tax is subject to less problematic incentive effects than other taxes.

The last tax increase that would be needed to cover the proposed expenses would be an increase in the individual income tax. The change here would not need to be dramatic. A simple change would be to increase the income tax rate on all incomes by 1.5 percentage points. Assuming an $11 trillion tax base, this would result in close to $165 billion in annual revenue (Table 1.2).

Table 1.2 Tax Revenue

Tax Change	Increased Revenue
Increase estate tax	$24.6 billion
Capital gains tax reform	$85 billion
Individual income tax increases	$165 billion
Total	**$274.6 billion**

5.2 Behavioral Effects of Taxation

There is always a concern, when taxes are increased, that the tax will cause people to shift their behavior toward less productive activities and investments. For example, a high marginal income tax rate might decrease the incentive for people with high incomes to work harder. This could dampen the productivity of some of the most productive members of society. We have empirical evidence that this effect is real, but small. The sensitivity of work hours to tax rates among primary earners is small, though larger for secondary earners. Some have argued that the real margin is tax avoidance, not labor supply decisions, but the effect here also ends up being quite small (Chetty 2009).

The adverse behavioral costs to the estate tax will also be limited (Slemrod 2001). There is some evidence that the estate tax discourages savings, which could diminish the capital stock in the long run (Joulfaian 2006). This argument is undermined by the commitment of major central banks in recent decades to low-interest rates, however. Some have argued that the estate tax could discourage entrepreneurship, but scholars have not found clear evidence for this kind of effect (Burman et al. 2018). One strong behavioral effect of the estate tax is that it increases gifts to charity, since charitable giving is one of the easiest ways to decrease taxable estate wealth (Congressional Budget Office 2004). One can argue about the relative merits of larger inheritances compared to more charitable giving, but even critics will agree that this is usually a tradeoff between two good things.

The capital gains tax has been the subject of a large number of studies considering the timing of capital gains realization and also savings behavior. The policy proposed here is designed to minimize some of the worst capital gains behavioral effects and so would be an improvement on some margins. The largest concern is that savings and investment would decrease, but there is no strong evidence for this concern for the reform I am proposing, since the reform would close one of the tax-avoidance loopholes but the tax rate would not change. In particular, by limiting the incentive to hold on to assets to death, this would encourage the movement of money toward more productive uses.

Overall, the behavioral changes that result from these tax reforms should be small, with the exception that I would expect a large increase in charitable donations. As such, the real cost of these taxes will likely be the simple opportunity cost: the private activity that would have been funded by these taxes if not collected. A consequentialist justification of such taxes, then, would depend primarily on the positive impact of the spending that they fund.

5.3   Behavioral Effects of Redistribution Programs

One of the long-standing concerns about safety-net programs, particularly programs that are means-tested, is that they reduce the incentive to work. The argument is analogous to the labor supply argument made about income taxes. If a family is receiving food stamps, the amount that they receive in benefits declines as they earn more money. For Medicaid recipients, the disincentive can be even greater, particularly in states that did not expand Medicaid with the passage of the Affordable Care Act. If a person is considering starting a job, or taking a second part-time job, it may well be that the additional work will put them in an income category that makes them ineligible for their health insurance. If their employers do not offer insurance, and the cost of individual health insurance is too high, a person might rationally choose to work less, and earn less, in order to keep the Medicaid benefits. These problems can be exacerbated if there are multiple means-tested programs that have phase-out or income tests that overlap. For some families with unusual combinations of benefits, the effective marginal tax rate (in terms of lost benefits as a person earns money) can be as high as 80 percent.

New research gives us insight into the scale of this problem. A group of economists have used data on incomes, consumption habits, and program participation to calculate the combined disincentive effects that people actually face. They take into account all state and federal tax laws, all major safety-net programs, and even calculate the effect of taxation on savings over a lifetime (Altig et al.

2020). This project does not estimate the behavioral response to these incentives, but they bring us a few steps forward in understanding the prevalence of overlapping disincentives. Surprisingly, they find remarkably similar median effective marginal tax rates across all income levels. The disincentives faced by the average person are similar, whether they are poor, middle-income, or wealthy (Dolan 2020). More importantly, perhaps, they show that as many as a quarter of low-wage workers face effective marginal tax rates over 70 percent (Altig et al. 2020). On the other hand, workers in severe poverty face very low effective marginal tax rates, and some rates are negative. In particular, among families with children qualifying for SNAP, one study found a majority of households actually face negative marginal effective tax rates from federal law, in part because most families are not participating in multiple programs (Moffitt 2014). Overall, the distribution of effective marginal tax rates seems to place the biggest disincentives on those workers who have low-paying jobs and are above the poverty line. While these disincentives are concerning, they don't seem to be the reason people are not entering the labor force.

Most low-income workers and most people in poverty are not stuck in a poverty trap because of means-tested benefits. The immediate rewards from working are still quite high (Shapiro et al. 2016). The extent to which these disincentives result in people working substantially less, or choosing not to work, is hotly debated, but most find small labor supply effects (Moffitt 2002; Schanzenbach 2019). Low-wage workers have little power to choose the amount of hours they work, and are rarely well-informed enough to carefully track the relevant earnings margins. It is unlikely that a person would turn down a raise or promotion because of the cost in reduced benefits. Workers know that even if their immediate earnings increase less than the full amount because of benefit reductions, the career-long implications of advancement are worth pursuing.

Most importantly, while these concerns about work disincentives are interesting and important for the broader conversation, ultimately they do not undermine the proposal I offer here. Two of the changes I suggest would actually diminish the effective marginal tax rates faced by low-income households. The SNAP reform, by increasing the earned-income deduction, would diminish the benefit penalty when a person earns more on the job. Similarly, the health care proposal could radically diminish the degree to which the Medicaid earnings test creates a disincentive. By subsidizing insurance well above the Medicaid earnings cutoff, it would cover far more uninsured people and do so with a more consistent out-of-pocket price. No one would face a dramatic increase in health insurance costs if they started earning more money. Moreover, the health benefits of both of these proposals would encourage labor force participation.

The preschool proposal is also work-friendly, in part because it would decrease childcare expenses for families with young children. A large number of households near the poverty line include a single parent with children, and even two-parent families can find childcare prohibitively expensive. Education programs with earnings tests don't have the labor force impact that cash programs do, but even that would be diminished, moreover, by expanding the number of households that get federally funded preschool programs.

Finally, the opportunity accounts proposal, while means-tested, only imposes a higher effective marginal tax rate over a lifetime. There is no opportunity to immediately trade off these benefits for consumption. This time-lag will greatly diminish any work-disincentive. Even more, because the accounts are limited, and can only be used for school, home purchases, retirement, or entrepreneurship, the payoff is all well into the future. Anyone discouraged from working by the fear of losing this future benefit would, paradoxically, have to be operating with an extremely low discount rate (caring for the future) which is usually not the concern with those who are low-income and marginally attached to the labor force, since a low discount rate would generally also push the person toward work and saving.

This conversation about effective marginal tax rates and disincentive effects is somewhat technical, but the subject matter does not need to be. For two centuries, economists have made arguments that welfare state programs (even the most rudimentary) will encourage idleness and increase poverty. This seems not to have been true in 1834 (Clark and Page 2019), and need not be true now. As I have already noted, we have good evidence that publicly provided health care for the poor actually decreased dependence on the government in the long run, increased wages, increased education, and increased tax revenue (Goodman-Bacon 2018; Brown et al. 2020). Growing up with the SNAP program actually increased their chances of being economically independent over their lifetime, relying less on government benefits and earning higher wages (Hoynes et al. 2016; Bailey et al. 2020). Finally, publicly provided preschool has a well-documented impact on education, wages, crime rates, and health, and the behavioral benefits may even last into the next generation (Garces et al. 2002; Deming 2009; Baur and Schanzenbach 2016; Barr and Gibbs 2019). There is a concern about intergenerational persistence of poverty and social safety-net dependence, but, for numerous reasons, cause and effect are difficult to parse when looking at some of this evidence (Antel 1992; Gottschalk 1992; Pepper 1995). U.S. safety-net policy has become far more careful about these kinds of concerns, and there is strong evidence that points toward positive long-term effects.

> There are two important economic concerns with redistribution. The first is that the programs will undermine productivity and work. The second is that the cost, in terms of taxes and the effects of taxes, will be too high. I respond to each of these concerns, arguing that the policies I am proposing will have little effect on recipients' work choices, and that these programs can be paid for with a reasonable set of tax increases.

6   Conclusion

The United States is a wealthy country, but the opportunity to participate in and contribute to that prosperity is not universally shared. For 50 years now, the trend has been toward more inequality and lower social mobility. This is true for people born in the same city and for those with the same level of education, and for the same work ethic. Moreover, for white Americans, two generations ago, a high-school degree and a willingness to work consistently was enough to grant a relatively stable income sufficient to support a family in middle-class life. This has probably never been true for racial minorities on average, and is, today, not true for any demographic group (Putnam 2016). The requirements for upward mobility have become more stringent. In response, we as a society have not made sure that everyone has the opportunity to meet those requirements. Instead, the competition for good neighborhoods and access to the best schools has become an unsustainable race. The result for too many has been a life with few opportunities, poor health, poverty, and communities dominated by dysfunction.

This state of affairs is not just. Scholars have developed a number of strong arguments in favor of creating a more egalitarian economy. I offer an account of distributive justice that is far less radical than that of many other scholars, but this account still strongly supports additional redistribution. Each person should have access to a few fundamental good things in economic life: they should have the opportunity to feed and clothe themselves and have shelter. They should have access to health care, particularly catastrophic coverage that cannot be planned for. They should have the opportunity to develop the skills necessary to be productive members of the economy, and the ability to participate as entrepreneurs.

The legal freedom to go to school, form an association, own property, or start a business is essential. However, for a just society, it is not enough for people to merely have legal access to these things. These freedoms will not grant access to these basic capabilities in a society where getting a stable job or a business loan requires a $75,000 college education, a car, a phone, housing, clothes, and food. In the United States today, our inequality is driving up the cost of participation in society and leaving people behind. At the same time, poverty is dire enough for many that they never get the support they need to get started. And all of this is exacerbated by a history of staggering injustice toward racial minorities for whom success has been, too often, legally prohibited or dangerous.

The kind of egalitarianism I offer here does not require the redistribution of wealth merely because some people are rich. It does not require that people be granted a middle-class lifestyle if they could work but choose not to. It does not transfer cash, but favors in-kind benefits, because the goal is not to maximize libertarian choice. The point is that humans have a few specific basic needs that are prerequisites to economic opportunity. It does ask that we take care of the needs of children and invest in people in ways that open up long-run opportunities. The redistribution that I offer limits the damage of poverty and invests in people's ability to fully participate in economic life.

In another time or place, this argument would be different. The same principles of justice would apply, but the bar for full participation in economic life might be lower. In some places, the most important gains would depend not on redistribution, but on guaranteeing basic political and economic freedoms. In other places, there might be little for an egalitarian to critique. Nevertheless, the argument made here could be made in pretty similar ways in many countries around the world. Many economies are struggling with the same technological and historic challenges. In each place, however, the case for distributive justice and redistribution must be specific to the requirements that the society places on participation. It is not enough to redistribute wealth. We must do so in a way that will create opportunities.

Chapter 2

Justifying Wealth Redistribution

Can the High Burden Be Met?

James R. Otteson

Contents

I Introduction

Before evaluating alternative solutions to any problem, we first have to understand what the problem is that we wish to solve. The topic of this volume is the ethics of wealth redistribution. Thus, the question of how to engage in wealth redistribution ethically, or what the moral obligations are regarding wealth redistribution, is Question 1 of our discussion. Yet perhaps Question 0 is: What exactly is the problem that wealth redistribution is intended to

DOI: 10.4324/9780367854263-3

solve? There are, in fact, several possible problems it might be intended to solve, or at least address, but, though perhaps related, they are not the same, and hence the effectiveness of wealth redistribution to address them varies depending on which we wish to target. Erythromycin can be an effective treatment for a staph infection, for example, but it is useless against AIDS; if we want to evaluate erythromycin as a treatment, then we need to know what it is proposed as a treatment for. Similarly for wealth redistribution: we need to know what the problem is, exactly, for which it is proposed as a treatment.

It is also important to note at the outset that our discussion is not whether **socialism**[1] or **capitalism** is the preferable system of political economy. There is a great deal of popular and scholarly discussion of the relative merits of socialism and capitalism,[2] but that discussion is independent of the ethics of wealth redistribution. We could, for example, have a market-based economy that at the same time engages in wealth redistribution. The Scandinavian countries of Denmark, Norway, and Sweden are examples: they have largely free-market economies, and yet each of them also has a substantial system of wealth redistribution in the service of various centrally organized welfare and aid programs.[3] It is also possible to have a highly centralized or nationalized economy—that is, something approximating a socialist economy—while having little or no wealth redistribution, or at least not wealth redistribution to the poor. Cuba, Iran, North Korea, and Venezuela are examples of government-run economies in which citizens remain poor. However interesting the question of socialism vs. capitalism might be, then, that is not our question. We are interested instead in the ethics of wealth redistribution itself, whatever role it plays or might play in a larger system of political economy.

---

1. Terms in **bold** are defined in the "Glossary" at the end of the text.
2. For my own contribution to this discussion, see Otteson 2014. See also Cohen 2009, L. White 2012, and Niemietz 2019.
3. The Fraser Institute's most recent *Economic Freedom of the World Index* ranks Denmark, Norway, and Sweden respectively as the 11th, 43rd, and 46th freest economies in the world, out of 162 countries ranked (Gwartney et al. 2020). The Heritage Foundation's *2019 Index of Economic Freedom* ranks Denmark the 14th, Sweden the 19th, and Norway the 26th freest economy out of 180 countries ranked, all falling in its highest, or "mostly free," category (Miller et al. 2019).

1.1   How to Begin

How, then, should we begin an examination of the ethics of wealth redistribution? One might think we should start with an appeal to **natural law** and natural rights, but that would not get us far. We would immediately get bogged down in questions about what natural law is, what its implied rights are, and what their limits are, as well as whether it is dependent on some specific, and doubtless controversial, theological claims. Such questions are thorny and unlikely to be resolved—at least not here.[4] Similarly, a simple **utilitarian** analysis of what would lead to the greatest net increase in utility would face objections that some things that might lead to net increases in utility across populations could license practices—like slavery and forced labor, for example—that are immoral regardless of any utilitarian calculation. Finally, beginning the examination with a theoretical or *a priori* conception of property rights would likely also prove unproductive because it would depend on a prior conception of morality—perhaps indeed a conception of natural law or a commitment to a conception of utilitarianism—that would itself require defense and thus involve us in the same controversies noted above.

I therefore propose we start differently, by considering some main putative reasons for redistributing wealth, as well as the principal means at our disposal for effectuating wealth redistribution. By examining these reasons and the means available to us, and evaluating their strengths and weaknesses, we might be able to make some headway.

In what follows, I address three main reasons for, or goals hoped to be accomplished by, wealth redistribution: (1) to benefit the poor or enable poverty relief; (2) to punish for injustice or other wrongdoing; or (3) to realize, or more closely approximate, fairness, equality, or equity in society.[5] Regarding the means available

---

4. There is not even consensus regarding how we would settle them. An appeal to empirical evidence, for example, would not seem to suffice because it would risk the "naturalistic fallacy" of assuming that whatever is, is therefore good—that is, of fallaciously deriving normative "ought" statements from descriptive "is" statements. If human beings are naturally self-interested, for example, it would not follow that they ought to behave self-interestedly. For an overview of natural law theories and their controversies, see Duke and George 2017.

5. Other reasons for endorsing wealth redistribution include social harmony, stability, and peace. David Williams (2021) has recently argued that Thomas Hobbes

to accomplish wealth redistribution, there seem to be mainly two: targeted and general—that is, either by targeting specific individuals and redistributing their wealth to specific others, or by enacting more general redistribution through, say, income taxes whose rates increase with higher income levels.[6]

It is important to emphasize that our discussion does not concern *voluntary* wealth distribution, such as charity or philanthropy. People already voluntarily distribute a great deal of their wealth charitably. In the United States, for example, voluntary charitable giving totals hundreds of billions of dollars annually.[7] And the creation of wealth itself does not take place in an economic vacuum: in a market-based economy, it typically results from and is dependent on cooperation with others. If such transactions are mutually voluntary, then they tend to be **positive-sum** and productive of net increases in wealth or prosperity.

Positive-sum: an exchange or transaction in which both, or all, parties benefit; an increase in value to all parties entailing a positive net or overall benefit; contrasts with **zero-sum**, in which benefit to one party is offset by loss to another party, leading to zero net improvement.

The millions and billions of transactions in which people engage worldwide both create and distribute wealth, but according to individuals' own conceptions of value, given the constraints they face—not necessarily in directions that a philosopher or theorist might prefer or that we might prefer all things considered. And these allocations almost certainly will not fully comport with virtually

---

(1588–1679), for example, endorsed wealth redistribution on all three grounds. In the interest of space limitations, I will restrict my discussion to the three goals enumerated. I thank an anonymous reviewer for helpful discussion here.

6. Of course, one might advocate redistribution for a combination of these reasons, as well as endorse both of these means as vehicles.

7. According to Giving USA, Americans gave an all-time high of $428 billion to charitable causes in 2018. Per-capita giving was $1,300, and per-household giving was $3,289. See Giving USA 2019.

anyone's ideal aspirations about either individual or social benefit: each of us, as individuals, would no doubt prefer to have resources allocated differently to generate a positive effect in our own lives (we would likely all prefer to be paid more, for example), and if any of us took a snapshot look at society, we would doubtless prefer to reallocate at least some resources from where they are to other places or for other ends.

If any of us have surplus wealth beyond whatever we need to survive—above, for example, the level the United Nations defines as "**absolute poverty**"—then we are free to allocate some or all of that surplus to whatever places or to whichever persons we believe need or deserve it.[8]

> **Absolute poverty**: the condition of living on approximately \$2 per person per day or less.

Although such voluntary giving would constitute wealth *distribution*, it would not constitute wealth *re*distribution in the sense at issue here.

What we are considering instead is whether wealth should be *involuntarily* redistributed in ways or to recipients that are different from wherever people on their own want it to go. Our discussion hence pertains not to people making voluntary distributions based on their own private conceptions of their own or others' need, desert, and value, but, rather, using the apparatus of government to reallocate some wealth in directions other than whatever directions individuals already put it. Whether our aim is to benefit the poor, to punish transgressors, or to implement fairness, equality, or equity, the question with which we are concerned thus turns on whether

---

8. Peter Singer defines surplus wealth as any amount of wealth above the point of marginal utility, that is, the point at which the next dollar one would give would make one poorer than the poorest person to whom one might give it (Singer 2009, pp. 16–9; Singer 2015, chap. 3). If the U.N.'s standard of \$2 per person per day approximates the threshold above which one has surplus wealth, then approximately 100 percent of people in the United States today would qualify as having surplus wealth.

and when we are justified in using the nonvoluntary mechanisms that government employs to do so.

1.2 The High Justificatory Burden of Coercion

There are many uses of force that any civilized society must deploy if it wishes to survive—everything from punishing and potentially locking up violent criminals to enforcing voluntary contracts to protecting property to repelling invasion. Most of these uses are negative and defensive, however, not positive and offensive. That is, they are responses either to prior injury or possibly to the threat of injury with an eye toward protection of peaceful and cooperative life, rather than the initiation of force or the threat of force with an eye toward achieving a greater good or some other desired end. So, the question we face in our discussion is whether, and if so when, force may be initiated (or threatened) via involuntary redistribution of wealth to achieve a greater or important good, to exact justice, or to achieve fairness, equality, or equity in society.

This is an important if often overlooked point. All legal enactments either use or imply the use of force (Huemer 2013; Brennan 2016). This makes them fundamentally different from other kinds of human interactions. In a free or liberal society, a person may not mandate or command you to marry him, to work for him, to buy from or sell to him, to partner or transact with him, or to give your wealth or property to him. In a free society, each person retains what we might call an *opt-out option*.

Opt-Out Option: the right to say "no, thank you" to any proposal, offer, or demand and go elsewhere if the individual so chooses.[9]

But one may not say "no, thank you" to the Internal Revenue Service. If I do not like the terms you are offering me to work for your firm, I can decline and go elsewhere; if I do not like the terms the

---

9. See Otteson 2019a.

IRS is offering me, I must obey those terms regardless—at the risk, at the limit, of agents showing up at my door and taking me away.

It typically makes no practical difference whether I am given an opportunity to vote: the vast majority of agents, officials, and employees of the U.S. federal government occupy unelected positions—over 99 percent of them.[10] Even in those few cases in which I can vote, the successful candidate is rarely elected by a single-vote margin—which means my vote almost certainly made no difference. In the next U.S. presidential election, for example, the winner will, whether I voted for, voted against, or abstained from voting, still be my president. Similarly, if Congress enacts wealth redistribution policies, and empowers existing or creates new agencies to effectuate them, then neither you, I, nor any other individual citizen may "opt out" and decline to participate. If we choose to resist, eventually government agents will force us into compliance or punish us. Thus, in practice, the government will have its authorities and powers virtually regardless of anything I do or any other individual does. That means for substantially all Americans, there is no practical recourse or refuge—no "opt out" or exit opportunity—from government power.[11]

---

10. In 2018, there were 2,124,062 U.S. federal employees, not including military and Post Office employees (Congressional Research Service 2019). Of these, 537 are subject to election (435 members of the House of Representatives, 100 members of the Senate, the president, and the vice president). That means that approximately 99.97 percent are unelected. Because each individual adult citizen may vote for only two senatorial offices, one congressional office, the president, and the vice president, however, that means that approximately 99.9998 percent of all federal office holders are beyond the reach of the electoral authority any individual citizen has.

11. See Hirschman 1970 and Taylor 2017. One might respond that one has the right to leave one's country if one chooses. That is true in principle, but in practice is like saying, "you can vote them out." A theoretical right that has little or no practical import is largely an irrelevancy. A right to leave one's country, for example, is meaningful only (a) if one has the resources to do so (and can take them with one), and (b) if another country will accept one. Neither of these is given or certain. In any case, telling one to leave one's country seems to presume a rather extreme threshold. As David Hume wrote, "Can we seriously say, that a poor peasant or artisan has a free choice to leave his country, when he knows no foreign language or manners, and lives from day to day, by the small wages he acquires? We may as well assert, that a man, by remaining in a vessel, freely consents to the dominion of the master; though he was carried on board while asleep, and must leap into the ocean, and perish, the moment he leaves her" (Hume 1985 [1748], p. 475).

If we wish to evaluate wealth redistribution on its moral merits, therefore, it is important to keep in mind the nature of mandatory or government-enforced wealth redistribution: its judgment and authority are enforced by coercion or the threat of coercion. I contend that this raises the stakes of the discussion. If we are proposing to force people to do something that they otherwise would not do or would prefer not to do, then it is incumbent on us to have a compelling reason for doing so. The justificatory threshold, therefore, is high, as it should be.

1.3 Equal Moral Agency

Belief in the superiority of one person's or group's preferences to those of another person or group, or mere possibilities (as opposed to probabilities) of achieving net beneficial improvements, would not seem to meet this high justificatory threshold. I base this claim on what I will call the *equal moral agency* principle, which I believe should be the foundation of any morally justifiable system of political economy.

Equal Moral Agency Principle: based on the claim that all people have equal moral dignity, this principle holds that, except under extraordinary circumstances, everyone's agency and choices should be respected equally.

If all people are not just moral agents but equal in that agency to everyone else, then no one should extend her agency over, or substitute her will for that of, another without the latter's willing consent. If any person has the right to make free choices in her own case, then everyone does (or should); from a commitment to equal moral agency follows, therefore, a commitment to protecting and respecting each individual's maximal scope of individual liberty that is compatible with the same scope of liberty that everyone else enjoys. That means that a first principle of justice should be something like, as John Rawls (1921–2002) suggested: "Each person is to have an equal right to the most extensive total system of equal basic liberties compatible with a similar system of liberty for all" (1971, p. 302). Or, as Immanuel Kant (1724–1804) argued much earlier, "a necessary idea, which must be taken as fundamental not only in first projecting a constitution but in all its laws," is a "constitution allowing *the greatest possible human freedom* in accordance with laws by which *the freedom of each is made to be consistent with that of all others.*"[12]

Human life is complex, however, and rarely comports perfectly with any single moral or political principle. So, there will be reasonable exceptions to (nearly) any moral rule, arising from exigency or other peculiar facts of a given actual situation. A drowning person may make use of another's boat dock without asking permission; police may detain, forcibly if necessary, a suspected criminal; fire fighters may break apartment building windows to gain access; courts may require a deadbeat parent to support his or her children; and so on. But such exceptions prove the rule that, unless there are relevant exigent circumstances or other extraordinary reasons, we should respect and protect the sanctity of others' persons, property, and voluntary agreements. Uninvited third-party interposition into first-parties' persons or property, or into first- and second-parties' voluntary agreements, is therefore justifiable only when it can be demonstrated that an exception to the otherwise foundational premise of equal moral agency is warranted by sufficiently exceptional circumstances or by the weight of exceptionally compelling reasons.

So, now, finally, *the* question for our purposes: Do proposals for wealth redistribution rise to such a justificatory level? Let us consider this question by taking in turn the three potential purposes for wealth redistribution mentioned earlier: benefiting the poor, punishing transgressions, and instantiating fairness, equality, or equity.

> Evaluation of a proposed solution requires first a clear understanding of the problem it is intended to solve. If wealth redistribution is proposed as a means to address poverty relief, to punish for injustice, or to realize fairness, equality, or equity in society, then it should be evaluated on whether, and how effectively, it addresses these issues. Because government wealth redistribution involves involuntary

---

12. Kant 1929 (1781), 312 (B373); italics in the original. I note that denying this principle risks licensing morally objectionable behaviors like racism, sexism, xenophobia, and so on, which lends it at least strong prima facie support.

reallocations of people's wealth, and because people are equal moral agents, it must meet a high justificatory burden. Is wealth redistribution an effective means to achieve those ends, and does it meet that high justificatory burden?

2 Benefiting the Poor

We can distinguish two kinds of poverty in the world: *relative* and *absolute*.[13] The United Nations defines "absolute poverty" as living on approximately $2 per person per day or less, described as "a condition characterized by severe deprivation of basic human needs, including safe drinking water, sanitation facilities, health, shelter, education and information" (Mack 2016). There are currently approximately 650 million people on earth who live at or below that level. As large as that number is, it is less than nine percent of the world's population—the smallest proportion of humanity at or below that level in all human history (World Bank 2015). In 1900, approximately 90 percent of all people lived at or below today's equivalent of $2 per person per day; the dramatic decrease in that proportion since then, a decrease that has accelerated particularly in the past few decades to today's approximately 8.6 percent level, is historically unprecedented (Chandy and Gertz 2011; Follett 2015; Tupy 2017; McCloskey 2019, chap. 6; Bailey and Tupy 2020). In 1990, the number of people living in extreme poverty was approximately 1.9 billion; 30 years later, that number has fallen by almost two-thirds—despite an increase in global population of some 2.2 billion people (Roser and Ortiz-Ospina 2017). Consider just China: in 1980, an estimated 90 percent of all Chinese lived at the level of absolute poverty; today, less than ten percent do (Roser 2017). That means that over one billion Chinese alone have ascended from absolute poverty in just the past 40 years (Coase and Wang 2012; Donaldson 2017).

Throughout all human history for which we have been able to collect data—a period that now includes the past 12,000 years or so (though some economic historians, like Bradford DeLong (1998),

---

13. For discussion of relative vs. absolute income and wealth measures, see Milanovic 2016, 24–30.

believe we can make credible estimates going back a million years, to early hominins on the planet)—the average per-capita world product has been both remarkably consistent and remarkably low: around $2 per person per day in contemporary dollars, or approximately equivalent to the U.N.-defined level of "absolute poverty" (Landes 1999; Maddison 2007; Clark 2009). Today, however, the worldwide average is $48 per person per day (in constant dollars); in the United States, it has risen to $164 per person per day. This represents a 16-fold real increase worldwide, and a 55-fold real increase in the United States (Phelps 2013; McCloskey 2016, chaps. 1–5; Pinker 2018, chap. 8; Rosling et al. 2018; Davies 2019).

In some countries, the proportion of people living at "absolute poverty" has been virtually eliminated. In the United States, for example, the official federal poverty level is approximately equal to the *average* income worldwide.[14] And although there remain approximately 650 million people worldwide at humanity's historical levels of poverty—and there hence remains a great deal of work to be done—nonetheless, the good news is that nearly 7 billion people have been able to ascend out of that miserable historical norm. The even better news is that the proportion of people living at that low level is rapidly declining. In the not-too-distant future, we face, therefore, the stupendous prospect of, for the first time in human history, eradicating absolute poverty altogether from the world. This will be a crowning achievement of humankind, though, as Rosling et al. (2018) show, one that few seem to be aware of.

We have, therefore, made enormous, and historically unprecedented, progress addressing absolute poverty. One implication of this great news is that absolute poverty is today far less a problem worldwide, and particularly in places like the United States, than it has ever been—which means that it is far less a problem for wealth redistribution to address. It has not yet completely disappeared, but it soon should, which would suggest that the case for new large-scale efforts to marshal centralized wealth distribution to address it is weaker today than it has ever been before.

---

14. Milanovic 2010 calculated that the incomes of the poorest five percent of Americans would place them at the 68th percentile of the world income distribution (116–17). See also Whaples 2015.

2.1 Relative Poverty

But that addresses only *absolute* poverty; what about **relative** poverty? "Relative poverty" refers to some being poor relative to or in comparison to others—not necessarily absolutely poor, but simply poorer than at least some others. But relative poverty is a statistical artifact. In any distribution across a population—anything from height to BMI to income—there will be a bottom ten percent, a top ten percent, and so on. What the dramatic worldwide increase in overall wealth over the past two centuries portends is the prospect of the *relatively poor* becoming *absolutely rich*. The poorest ten percent of the population in Hong Kong, for example, are richer than the richest ten percent in Cuba (Monnery 2019). The bottom ten percent of a distribution of income in a country will, by definition, be poorer than the other 90 percent, but they might be—by absolute or historical standards—wealthy.

The poorest ten percent in the United States today enjoy a level of wealth that is far greater than that of much of the rest of the world, and they have access to resources that even other Americans from just a couple generations ago could only have imagined. Consider: over 90 percent of those making less than $30,000 per year today in the United States own a global communicator and supercomputer, enabling them to speak to virtually anyone on the planet and granting them instantaneous access to virtually the entirety of humankind's knowledge, and they carry it with them in their pockets or purses.[15] Their rates of access to food and potable water and electricity, their rates of literacy, their expected longevity, and the levels of peace they enjoy are similarly at unprecedented levels. And the improvements have accelerated in recent decades. As Tupy (2019) reports:

> The average time price (i.e., the amount of time that a person has to work in order to earn enough money to buy something) of everyday items relative to the hourly wages of unskilled workers declined [in the United States during the period of 1979 to 2019] by 72 percent. It declined by 75 percent for skilled workers and by 89 percent for upskilling workers (i.e., workers who started as unskilled workers in 1979 but ended

---

15. See Pew Research Center 2018. I note that a contemporary iPhone has approximately 100,000 times more computing power than did the lunar lander in the Apollo 11 mission of 1969 (Scott 2019).

up as skilled workers in 2019). That means that for the same amount of work that allowed an unskilled worker to purchase one item in our basket of everyday items in 1979, he or she could buy 3.56 items in 2019 (on average). A skilled worker's purchasing power increased from one to four and upskilling worker's purchasing power increased from one to nine.

Consider this from another angle. Andrew Carnegie (1834–1919), one of the richest Americans of all time—his wealth at its peak is estimated to have been some $310 billion in contemporary dollars—could not save his mother from dying from pneumonia. Despite his spectacular wealth, the antibiotics widely and inexpensively available today were simply not available to him—at any price (Krass 2002). In 1924, the then-U.S. president Calvin Coolidge's son, the 16-year-old Calvin Jr., was playing tennis with his brother when he got a blister on the third toe of his right foot; he developed a staph infection and was dead within a week—again, because the routine treatments available today did not exist then, even for the president (Shlaes 2014). One other example: Nathan Rothschild (1777–1836), likely the richest person in the world when he died, was felled by an infected abscess that today could be cured with a treatment costing only a few cents (Ferguson 1999). Examples like these give us some indication of, and perspective on, just how much wealthier we are today—not just in dollars, but in the goods and services available to us and the quality of life they enable even for our poorest—than even the wealthiest in the past.

These facts do not mean, of course, that the lives of the relatively poor are perfect, or that there are not still many problems to address. But it does mean that in a discussion of the ethics of wealth distribution, we should consider exactly what the problem is that we are trying to solve. If our wish is to solve *absolute* poverty, then that problem is already being solved, at a previously unrivaled rate—largely by the spread of protections of private property, legal access to markets, and encouragement of **cooperative** transactions, which are positive-sum, and discouragement of **extractive** behavior, which is **zero-sum**.[16] Given the speed with which absolute poverty

---

16. See Rose 2011 and 2019; Chandy and Gertz 2011; Acemoglu and Robinson 2012; Harari 2015; Oman 2016; and McCloskey 2019.

is already disappearing from the world, it is unclear how much more we could do. (And the mixed record of both governmental and private international aid would seem to caution us against having too much faith in their ability to help.)[17] That leaves us with *relative* poverty—but because that is a statistical artifact, unless we all have exactly equal holdings, by definition, it cannot go away. If the poorest ten percent in society (or in a country, or in the world) had average per person wealth of, say, $1 million, while the richest ten percent had average per person wealth of $1 billion, the former would have only 1/1,000th of the latter: they would therefore be extremely poor *relative to* the billionaires, but by *absolute* standards, they would be quite rich indeed.

Michael Jordan, whose net worth in 2019 was estimated to be approximately $1 billion, was extremely poor relative to Bill Gates, whose net worth was estimated to be just over $100 billion. Though Jordan thus enjoyed only 1/100th of Gates's wealth, Jordan was nevertheless extremely wealthy by any objective or absolute standard—and no one would suggest that because of the large 100-fold differential between them we should therefore redistribute some of Gates's wealth to Jordan. But consider even larger differentials. Are there people in the United States whose wealth is not 100 times, but 1,000 times greater than that of others? Yes. 10,000 times? Yes. 100,000 times? Yes. Double even that, however: a person whose net worth is only some 1/200,000th of Bill Gates's still has a net worth of $500,000, which is enough to have a big house, at least one car, and send her children to private schools and to college—let alone enough to have electricity, running water and flush toilets, and health care insurance. That level of wealth (and higher) comprises approximately 66 million people in the United States. Over 300 million people in the United States, or over 90 percent, have incomes that place them above the historical levels of absolute poverty. And if one looks at actual consumption of goods and services, rather than just income, the level of absolute poverty in the United States plummets effectively to *zero*.[18] Again, these are all historical landmarks.

---

17 See Schuck 2014. See also Coyne 2013 and Easterly 2013.
18. Chandy and Smith 2014 estimate this proportion to be 0.07 percent of the American population, or approximately 231,000 people—a number that is still

Jesus said, "The poor you always have with you" (John 12:8).[19] If Jesus meant the *relatively* poor, He was likely correct; if He meant the *absolutely* poor, however, that we seem to be well along in the process of refuting.

I suggest, then, that it is not clear that poverty is a problem that wealth redistribution, especially large-scale centrally organized wealth redistribution, is required to address. The spread of protections of private property and globalized markets are fast eliminating absolute poverty from the world, which suggests that there is little left of it for wealth redistribution even to address. And if the proportion of humanity that is the poorest, say, ten percent is rapidly becoming rich in absolute terms or compared with historical norms—the average income for the world's poorest ten percent today is approximately $4,625 in contemporary U.S. dollars, or over six times the United Nations' threshold of "absolute poverty" (Gwartney et al. 2019)—then, again, this increasingly looks like a solution in search of a problem.

That does not mean there are no problems in the world, of course, or that the even relatively poor do not face hardships that others do not face. It certainly also does not mean that wealth solves all problems. Indeed, however much wealth there is in the world, it will still be limited, and our needs and desires will doubtless always outstrip our resources and hence our ability to achieve all our goals, ends, and purposes. However much wealth any of us has, we still probably want more.[20] And of course wealth is not the only thing that matters in life. But what wealth can do is help us achieve what does matter to us. If I do not know whether I can eat today, or whether

---

too high, but within the statistical margin of error and thus rounding to zero. Meyer et al. 2019 argue that in the U.S., "our best estimate of the extreme poverty rate [defined as $2/person/day] is 0.24 percent among households and 0.11 percent among individuals" (1); strikingly, they find that "after implementing all adjustments, no SIPP-interviewed households with children have incomes below $2/person/day" (38)—meaning that there are effectively *no* children in absolute, or "extreme," poverty in the U.S. today. See also Meyer and Sullivan 2012, which uses consumption measures that include the impact of taxes, transfers, and corrections to the Consumer Price Index to argue that the real U.S. poverty rate had fallen to 3.6 percent.

19. Compare Deuteronomy 15:11: "For the poor shall never cease out of the land." I thank Tyron Goldschmidt for the pointer.
20. Though see Hirschfeld 2018, which denies that "individuals have unbounded desires" (62).

my children can eat today, then I am not thinking about writing the great American novel or where my children will go to college or whether I can afford a trip to Disney World this year: I am thinking about whether my children or I can eat today.

What wealth can do, then, is help us address our more immediate, pressing concerns—food, clothing, shelter, and so on—thereby enabling us to turn our attention progressively, or even incrementally, to the other matters that can fill out a life of meaning and purpose (Pinker 2018, chap. 18). Life will still be imperfect no matter how much wealth we have, but what we can hope for is continual real improvement. And that is exactly what we have seen over the past 200 years or so, and particularly over the past 40 years or so.

2.2 Wealth and Medicine

The historical reality of wealth creation and recent poverty reduction in the world suggests an analogy to medicine. Suppose there is a disease that has historically afflicted over 99 percent of our population, and the disease is often terminal. Suppose further that for centuries numerous experiments at alleviating this disease—including bloodletting—have been tried, but to little avail. But then suppose that in just the last 0.1 percent of our existence a new treatment was discovered—inoculation—that began to show promise. As that treatment spread, only slowly at first (partly because people were initially skeptical of it), those lucky enough to receive it began to improve their conditions. That led to more treatment for more people, leading to increasing rates of cure. Suppose the inoculation cure has been so successful, in fact, that our population has now grown several times over and yet over 90 percent of us have been cured, and we are fast in the process of getting the remaining less-than-ten percent cured even with our still increasing population. And suppose that in the meantime the first of those cured have gone on to vastly improved lives, enjoying levels of health (and perhaps prosperity) not only previously unknown to our population but significantly greater than that of the remaining unfortunate souls still afflicted by the disease.

Imagine, however, that someone now claims that the fact that some are cured and are enjoying extremely healthy lives (particularly relative to those still afflicted with the disease) constitutes an injustice, and hence proposes the earlier common but unsuccessful practice of bloodletting to improve the conditions of the remaining ten percent with the disease.

That approximates our situation with respect to perhaps the greatest afflicter of humanity, poverty. We have finally figured out how increasingly many people can rise out of humanity's historical norm of extreme poverty, and this method has proven spectacularly and unprecedentedly successful—to the point now where less than ten percent of humanity is still suffering at historical levels of poverty, and the proportion continues to decrease. Yet wealth redistribution has been tried many times before, but empirical study has discovered that it has had little, if any, effect; its benefit is at best temporary, and at worst it might actually have a negative effect on prosperity, particularly on that of the poor (Dollar and Kraay 2001; Brooks 2008; Scheidel 2017; Ingram and McArthur 2018). Voluntary charitable giving has a somewhat better record, but its effectiveness too is marginal in comparison to the effects of protections of private property and legalized access to markets (Easterly 2007; McCloskey 2016; Davies 2019). And governmental wealth redistribution has historically been plagued by waste, inefficiency, cronyism, corruption, extraction, and even intentional death (Rummel 1997; Courtois et al. 1999; Pinker 2011; M. White 2012)—which makes it analogous as a method of combatting poverty to using bloodletting to fight disease.

The first rule of medicine, as captured in its Hippocratic Oath, is "do no harm." I submit that as a first rule of political economy as well. If we have found something that has been extremely successful at reducing absolute poverty, that gives a strong reason not to depart from it when it is on the precipice of eliminating it altogether, especially by substituting another method that previous experiments have shown to be less effective or even counterproductive.

In the past 200 years, worldwide wealth has increased to unprecedented levels, and rates of absolute poverty have declined to unprecedented levels, largely due to the spread of protections of private property, access to markets, and encouragement of cooperative exchanges and discouragement of extractive exchanges. Relative poverty, however, continues, but even the relatively poor are becoming absolutely rich. As in medicine, improvements should be welcomed, even if not everyone yet has experienced as much improvement as we would like. Thus, government wealth redistribution is less necessary to address poverty now than it has ever been in human history.

3 Punishing Wrongdoing

A second potential reason to endorse wealth redistribution is to punish wrongdoers, and to compensate victims of the wrongdoers' crimes. Relevant crimes would include enslavement, conquest, theft, fraud, and breach of contract, as well as assault and trespass, and other *malum in se* crimes, such as libel and slander, which can be thought of as violations of one's property rights and one's reputation and good character. Further things such as nuisance and disturbing the peace might also count as actionable criminal or civil wrongs, though these can be more difficult to assess and adjudicate.

Whatever the final list ends up being, properly qualifying cases would seem to involve both of two key characteristics: (1) they inflicted harm or injury to, or they visited cost on, another; and (2) the harm, injury, or cost was uninvited, nonconsensual, or involuntary. While there are good-faith debates about what actually constitutes, or what should for the purposes of compensatory action count as, "harm," "injury," and "cost," as well as whether and when a person has or has not consented (what exactly constitutes having given consent, to what kinds of things a person can reasonably be considered to have consented, when a person is not or is no longer able to give consent, and so on); nevertheless, the principle seems sound that when there has been harm, injury, or cost that was inflicted without consent, punishment for the wrongdoer is required and, in at least some cases, compensation (including monetary compensation) is appropriate, even forcibly if necessary. To avoid complexities regarding hard or marginal cases, we might reframe this principle as: in cases where it is clear that one party imposed harm, injury, or cost on an innocent party without the latter's consent or over the latter's protest, then appropriate compensation is warranted.

Relate these considerations to the question of wealth redistribution. As mentioned earlier, there are two main ways of effectuating wealth redistribution—through either targeted or general measures. Targeted measures identify the wrongdoer(s) who committed an actionable offense and prevail upon them, using coercion if necessary, to compensate the victim(s). To justify a transfer of wealth on such grounds, there must be (1) an identifiable victim or victims, (2) an identifiable wrongdoer or wrongdoers who have been demonstrated through appropriately objective measures to have wronged the identified victim or victims, and (3) a reasonable way—within fairly broad guidelines—for the latter to make the former "whole" or to indemnify the former via compensation. These are default principles meant to capture the spirit of what constitutes wrongdoing and thus warranted compensation, not absolute or mechanical rules meant to infallibly produce the correct result in every case; as such, they are subject to exceptions and require judgment and interpretation to apply appropriately to any particular case. They will also be subject to good-faith disagreements about how they should apply to particular cases. Despite those inevitable difficulties, their sense seems clear and seems to capture both our moral intuitions and the core of our relevant legal principles.

If we have a case, then, that meets these criteria—that is, that reasonably meets criteria (1)–(3) above—is wealth redistribution justified? Yes, or at least arguably so. We might argue about the appropriate level, or even kind, of compensation required, but the general principle that in such a case compensation is indeed required seems sound. Although proper adjudication of particular cases will depend on their specific details, I endorse the general principle, as I suspect most people do. In any case, a system of criminal and tort law seems the appropriate place to seek redress from harm or injury, and in cases of tortious acts and civil wrongs, courts are the appropriate place to seek damages (Epstein 2017, part 3).

The problem for our purposes, however, is that such (properly identified) cases would license only targeted redistribution, not general. That is, if person A injured person B in relevant ways, then it is A who should, or should be made to, compensate B—not C, D, or anyone else. If you assault or steal from someone, then it is you who should be made to compensate your victim, not me. You were the one who broke the relevant rule of justice; you were the one who imposed an involuntary and uninvited cost, harm, or injury on another's person or property; you were the one who chose to visit, in Adam Smith's (1723–1790) words, "real positive evil" on another (Smith 1982 [1759], p. 78). Assuming you were not forced to do so by someone else, you exercised your agency in the violation of justice and thus you are properly held responsible for your actions. If you *were* forced into injustice by someone else, then that other person should be punished. In neither case, however, should any uninvolved third party be either punished or compensated. To punish someone uninvolved in the injustice would itself be to commit an injustice against that innocent person, by violating her person or property without warrant. And to compensate an uninvolved C in response to an injustice A committed against B would be to commit a double injustice: it would leave B as an undercompensated (or uncompensated) victim, and it would reward C with something to which C was not entitled.

General policies of wealth redistribution would involve, however, compensating people who do not deserve to be compensated, punishing people who do not deserve to be punished, or both. Consider the typically recommended mechanism for wealth redistribution: progressive taxation. Taxation rates that increase with income apply generally to all members of given income groups. So, for example, the U.S. federal government's 2018 income tax levels include rates of 10 percent for individuals earning up to $9,525 per year; 12 percent from $9,526 to $38,700; 22 percent from $38,701 to $82,500; 24 percent from $82,501 to $157,500; 32 percent from $157,501 to $200,000; 35 percent from $200,001 to $500,000; and 37 percent for over $500,000 (Berger 2017). There may be good reasons for these rates, or for a scheme of progressive taxation generally (I take no position here). But progressive taxation cannot be justified as a means to address punishment for wrongdoing or compensation for victims of wrongdoing because not all people in those income groups committed criminal or civil wrongs, and not all people who would be the beneficiaries of the collected wealth were victimized criminally or civilly.

Perhaps some in each group would indeed qualify—that is, some in those income groups have committed wrongs, and some among the beneficiaries were victimized—but not all of them were.[21] Indeed, the presence of even one person in the former group who is innocent and one person in the latter group who was not victimized makes the case. If we were to tax the former and benefit the latter regardless, we would hence end up punishing some (at least one) innocent person(s) and benefiting some (at least one) person(s) who is entitled to no benefit. In other words, we would be committing injustice against innocent parties and in favor of undeserving parties, and, in both cases, violating the equal moral agency principle.

The fact that one person is wealthier than another does not by itself suffice to show that the former committed any wrong or that

---

21. Even on the assumption that some in the groups were victimizers or others were victims, we would face the further difficult requirement of determining which of the former owe compensation to which of the latter.

the latter was wronged. Even if the former did commit a wrong or the latter was wronged, however, it would still remain to be shown that it was the particular former who wronged the particular latter. This would have to be demonstrated by due and proper procedures; in any case, it could not be merely inferred from the fact that one party is wealthier than another party. If one lives in a market-based commercial society, such an inference would be especially dubious, because in such a society, the principal—and only legally endorsed—way for people to gain is through mutually voluntary transactions. In such cases, the transactions that lead to relative levels of wealth are consistent with justice, and thus any differentials in wealth to which they lead would also be consistent with justice. Even great differentials in wealth might be innocent—and should be presumed innocent until it is shown that they resulted from extraction or other injustice by demonstration in particular cases. Hence, no conclusion about guilt or innocence could be inferred from the mere presence of a wealth differential.

We are already in possession of fairly well-established and well-understood system of **compensatory justice** that provides mechanisms of punishing criminal or civil wrongdoers, and of compensating victims.

> **Compensatory Justice**: a conception of justice relating primarily to a requirement to make an injured or harmed party whole; if A visited injury, harm, or cost on an unwilling or unwitting B, compensatory justice requires A to indemnify B through compensation.

It is not a perfect system, of course, but no such system is or can be perfect. But its principles are relatively clear and straightforward, and they comport with our settled moral intuitions about who is guilty, who is innocent, who should be made to compensate, and who should be compensated. All such determinations are targeted, however; meaning, they are indexed to the relevant individual agents. By contrast, imposing a general policy of punishment and benefit across populations in an effort to punish an unspecified subset of the former who might be guilty and to benefit an unspecified subset of the latter who might deserve compensation would entail punishing people who did no wrong and benefiting people owed no right.

> Wealth redistribution is an ineffective means of addressing injustice or punishing wrongdoers, because its indiscriminate application to groups is insufficiently sensitive to individuals within groups who are innocent or who were not wronged. Compensatory justice, though imperfect, is nevertheless an appropriate principle for identifying injustice and punishing wrongdoing.

4 Fairness, Equality, and Equity

Perhaps poverty relief is not, or soon will no longer be, sufficient justification for government wealth redistribution, and perhaps punishment for wrongdoing cannot be properly addressed through generalized wealth redistribution without involving commission of (further) injustice and violation of the equal moral agency principle. Nevertheless, one might hold that it is unfair that some people have so much while some have so relatively little. Perhaps there is some threshold beyond which further wealth differentials are unfair regardless of their sources or explanations, whether innocent or guilty. Is it fair that some have 100 times, 1,000 times, or even more wealth than others? Perhaps we might be willing to concede that, say, a 100-fold differential in wealth might be justifiable, but we believe that anything beyond that threshold so offends any reasonable sense of fairness, equity, or even justice—possibly *social justice* (Otteson 2017)—as to be no longer acceptable. *Reasonable* differentials in wealth, we might say, seem allowable, but *extreme* differentials seem to call out for redress.

It is difficult to assess such a claim, however, in part because the threshold, whatever it turns out to be or wherever we agree to place it, seems arbitrary. Why would, say, a 100-fold differential be allowable and not require wealth redistribution, while a 101-fold differential is not allowable and does require redistribution? People will, after all, have good-faith disagreements about this. Some might believe that considerably less than a 100-fold differential is already suspect, while others will believe that only a considerably higher differential (maybe indefinitely or even infinitely high) would be required. Settling on any one threshold would be not only practically difficult but would face the additional difficulty of requiring specific justification. If you propose that the 100-fold threshold (say) is the one we should use, then it would be incumbent on you to explain why a 99-fold differential is (or can be) morally acceptable but a 101-fold differential is morally unacceptable. Because whatever threshold you propose would entail coercive action in relation to those people above it, you would owe us an account explaining why the small marginal difference between just-below your threshold and just-above your threshold warrants such different moral action. It would be difficult to produce such an account that is not arbitrary, ad hoc, or both.

There is another problem, however, with attempting to implement a conception of fairness via wealth redistribution—namely, it might itself involve the creation of unfairness. Before explaining how, let us first consider how to define fairness.

4.1   Defining and Applying Fairness

John Rawls (1921–2002) was long-time Harvard philosophy professor and author of *A Theory of Justice* (1971). He argued for understanding justice as "fairness," which could be determined by asking what basic rules rational choosers would select in an "original position" from behind a "veil of ignorance" that prevented them from knowing what position in society they themselves would subsequently occupy.

People define fairness in different ways. For Adam Smith, the opposite of fair was not unfair but foul, meaning outside of or inconsistent with the rules—a sense of "fairness" still used in, for example, baseball, where a ball hit outside the lines is "foul." Another sense of fairness comes from John Rawls, who argued that a procedure, rule, or result is fair if it would be endorsed by properly deliberative and objective rational choosers. If a decision procedure would be endorsed by appropriately situated people behind a "veil of ignorance," then the procedure and its results would be fair (Rawls 1971, pp. 136–50). A third sense of fair is accurate, reasonable, or properly proportioned. A "fair estimate" or "fair judgment," for example, would be one that is reasonable given the circumstances. A fourth is connected with treating similar cases similarly, or giving each his or her due; this definition of fairness is sometimes called "equity." If my colleague received a 2.5 percent raise this year and my own accomplishments are relevantly similar to hers, then it is fair (or equitable) that I should get a 2.5 percent raise as well.

A standard of fairness that might capture parts of all these senses is Rawls's, namely, the standard of an imagined "**veil of ignorance.**" Fairness is whatever would be endorsed by us if we did not know what position each of us would subsequently occupy in the distribution. A procedure, distribution, or partnership to which each of us would voluntarily agree from behind this veil of ignorance is prima facie fair because by hypothesis, none of us is able to rig the procedure or results in his own favor. Because we do not know what position we would occupy once we emerge from behind the veil of ignorance and live under the principles to which we agreed, we are therefore incentivized to devise a procedure and agree to principles that would be fair to all.[22]

Perhaps we can draw on Rawls to adopt an uncontroversial, or relatively less controversial, conception of fairness and to use what seems a reasonable standard by which to judge it: *fairness* is due proportion and proper desert, and a good way to determine it is by asking what we would endorse behind a *veil of ignorance*, or without knowledge of which particular position each of us individually would occupy in any subsequent distribution scheme.

Given this standard and method for adjudicating specific cases, let us apply it to the question of wealth redistribution. What unfairness might wealth redistribution plausibly address? One candidate is sufficiently large inequality in income or wealth. In other words, inequality in income or wealth that is greater than a specified threshold is unfair. Let us put aside for the moment the difficulties with establishing or settling on any particular threshold, and stipulate that such a threshold has been identified

---

22. Parents often hit upon a procedure in the spirit of Rawls's suggestion for their children. If there is one piece of cake left, but two children who want it, one child divides the cake and the other makes the first selection. Such a procedure has obvious benefits.

and agreed upon. Let us further stipulate that there exists in our community (country, world) inequality in income or wealth that exceeds this established threshold, thus would be rejected by a person behind a veil of ignorance, and is thus unfair. Given these starting points, I argue that addressing this unfairness by using the vehicle of wealth redistribution would itself be unfair. Let me give an example to illustrate why.

Suppose you are a pie baker, and alone you can make ten pies per day. I am also a pie baker, but alone I make seven pies per day. If we voluntarily decide to partner and join our efforts, then, owing to the gains from division of labor, together we can make not 17 pies but (say) 24.[23] Suppose further that each of us works the same amount of time, but you are more skilled and efficient, which is why you are able to make more pies than I can. Nevertheless, when we partner, we both gain because the total output—and hence, let us assume, our total profit—increases.

Now, consider: What is the proper, or fair, distribution of our profit between us? What would we both have agreed to behind a "veil of ignorance" as a fair distribution, if we knew going into it that one of us would be responsible for approximately two-thirds of the total output and the other would be responsible for approximately one-third, but we did not know which of us was which? It would seem plausible that we would agree to a two-thirds to one-third split, even if we did not know which of us would get two-thirds and which of us would get one-third. We would endorse it because either way, it would lead to a gain for us over what we would have gotten on our own: two-thirds of 24, or 16, is more than the ten one of us (remember, we do not know who is who) can make on his or her own; one-third of 24, or eight, is more than the seven the other of us can make on his or her own. If we considered instead an equal split—each of us gets 12—that, too, would constitute a gain for each of us, and is hence a plausible ex ante candidate principle of distribution. But an equal split would undervalue the contribution of one of us and overvalue the contribution of the other. For that reason, I suggest that it is implausible that we would

---

23. These numbers could be changed to reflect differences that would satisfy stipulated thresholds of unacceptable inequalities.

both agree to it in advance; it would not be fair, in the sense of accurate or properly proportioned, to either of us.[24]

A two-thirds to one-third split would, over time, lead to a growing disparity in our respective incomes and (presumably) wealth. Suppose we are able to net a profit of $4 per pie, so our 24 pies lead to a daily $96 profit: a two-thirds/one-third split means that you get a profit of $64 per day, while I get a profit of $32 per day; each week, then, you get $320 and I get $160, and each month you get $1,280, and I get $640. If we each work 50 weeks per year, that means your annual profit is $16,000, while mine is $8,000. That is a substantial difference, and a substantial inequality—your annual profit is double that of mine. Yet it would seem to have resulted from a fair split and allowed by a fair procedure. It should also be endorsed by each of us behind a veil of ignorance because (a) it would represent a gain to each of us that is greater than what we would otherwise have had on our own, and (b) it is proportional to our respective contributions. One of us would profit $64 per day ($320 per week and $16,000 per year), as opposed to $40 per day ($200 per week and $8,000 per year); the other would profit $32 per day ($160 per week and $32,000 per year), as opposed to $24 per day ($120 per week and $6,000 per year). Regardless of which position we turned out to occupy, we would each be substantially better off, and hence each of us has clear reason to agree to the distribution.

Suppose, however, that, instead of considering the fair process that led to this inequality, we looked only at the final unequal result, judged that it was unfair, and hence decided to engage in wealth redistribution from you to me to reduce the inequality. This would generate several problems. First, it would likely not be endorsed by either of us behind the veil of ignorance because it would jeopardize our respective abilities to gain more from the partnership than what we could have gained on our own. We likely would not have agreed to the partnership if we knew that a redistribution benefiting one of us at the others' expense would take place. If you and I did not know which position we would occupy once the veil of ignorance is lifted and we began our partnership, we would not

---

24. If we were family or friends, we might, out of love or charity, agree to an equal split despite its inconsistency with our respective production levels. But the principles of association behind the veil of ignorance assume we do not know who will be associating with whom.

know whether we would be the one who would benefit or the one at whose expense the other benefited. Hence, if we knew that such a redistribution would take place later on, we would judge the proposed arrangement to be unfair. Neither of us would likely agree to the partnership or, therefore, the redistribution procedure in the first place. So, the partnership would not have gotten off the ground.

In addition, a later redistribution of the profit resulting from our joined efforts would disregard our respective contributions. If you actually contributed two-thirds of the output and I actually contributed only one-third, redistributing more than my third to me by taking it from you would constitute a failure to recognize and respect *both* of our actual contributions. That would constitute a violation of fairness understood as respecting due and proper proportion. It would be to pretend that my contribution was greater than it actually was, and to pretend that your contribution was less than it actually was. If fairness is giving each his or her due, or rewarding each according to his or her desert, then such a redistribution violates fairness. We might wish to support an after-the-fact redistribution on grounds of, say, charity, but that is independent of justice understood as fairness. In advance and from behind the veil of ignorance, there would presumably be no objection to allowing voluntary charitable giving outside the veil of ignorance. A proposed provision for an after-the-fact mandatory redistribution, however, would again jeopardize agents' reasonable willingness to agree in the first place.

These concerns are not eliminated or dissolved by taking a higher-order, or macro, perspective. We might think that if instead of looking at individuals and their person-to-person arrangements we look at society overall, the inequalities we might discover between the wealth of some classes or groups and that of others could justify a redistribution on fairness grounds. Putting aside cases of specific injustice—such as when a person or group engages in extractive behavior at others' expense, thereby warranting compensation on grounds of justice—the differentials in wealth that remain arise from voluntary transactions and partnerships. If, as Rawls argued, the point of entering into society with others, and the goal of the principles of justice-as-fairness that we would endorse behind a veil of ignorance, is to enable "a mutually advantageous cooperative venture according to rules" (1971, p. 112), then endorsing after-the-fact redistribution of wealth would violate that because it constitutes visiting costs on some innocents to provide benefits to some unwronged others. If none of us knew which side of that divide we would occupy in society—if we truly believed that we could just as likely be among those being forced to pay as among those benefiting—then, few of us would endorse such principles of redistribution behind the veil of ignorance. Instituting after-the-fact redistribution would violate the fair procedures we would have endorsed ex ante.

On a standard, or at least widely influential, conception of fairness, wealth redistribution is therefore unfair. It would not respect a criterion of due proportion or desert, and it would contradict what we would be likely to endorse behind a veil of ignorance.

Perhaps we would wish to put aside a mechanical or principles-based conception of fairness, however. Perhaps we simply believe it unfair that some have so much while others have so little. Perhaps we believe that great wealth inequality in society can disrupt social harmony or endanger community (Cohen 2009). Or perhaps we are concerned that the wealthy can use their wealth to curry favor with politicians or regulators, to insulate themselves from facing the consequences of their own bad decisions or actions, or to purchase other advantages or exemptions, including legal exemptions, that are out of the reach of poorer citizens.

These are all real concerns, and the last, especially, not only has gone on but continues to go on in many countries in the world today. Assessing the effects of inequality on social harmony and community would require comparing them to the effects of various attempts to reduce inequality and seeing which are relatively better or worse—a difficult and complex investigation that would go beyond the scope of our discussion. And our discussion offers only limited means to address the special favors that the wealthy can use their wealth to command, in part because this is an ancient problem that seems to be an enduring aspect of human sociality: people use whatever wealth they have to purchase advantages for themselves and those they care about. Our argument against extraction, and in favor of public institutions that prohibit or punish extraction, provides some means to address this problem, but they are imperfect and provide no guarantees. But this problem recurs in every human society, and no society seems to have been or to be immune from it. Perhaps limiting the mechanisms available to the wealthy to use their wealth to secure special advantages to themselves by allowing only cooperative transactions can prove relatively better at addressing it. The increasing prosperity of the poor in countries that more closely approximate the institutional requirements of protecting person, property, and promise might also supply some measure of protection against the cronyism and favoritism otherwise possible in alternative systems of political economy.

A virtuous life requires not only that we be secure in our own persons, property, and agreements, but also that we should distribute our surplus wealth in ways that benefit others or society generally. We can and should undertake to use our own surplus wealth and deploy it to benefit those we believe need or deserve it. We can hire them; we can partner with them; we can give charitably to them of our time, skills, or money. We can also seek to convince others to join us in our efforts, pooling our resources so that we have greater opportunity or resources to hire, partner with, or give to them. We can, as Adam Smith suggests, distribute our surplus "to those purposes either of charity or generosity, to which it is most suitable, in our situation, that it should be applied" (Smith 1982 [1759], p. 270). Such efforts would constitute wealth distribution, though voluntarily and not by force of law. Helping others in such ways would thus enable us to fulfill our obligations of virtue and would enjoy the additional benefit of respecting fairness.

> People define fairness differently, but one reasonable definition is Rawls's, whereby a distribution is fair if it would be agreed to by rational choosers from behind a veil of ignorance. Based on this criterion, after-the-fact redistribution is likely to be unfair, as it entails disregarding individuals' varied contributions and actual outputs. It would thus likely not be agreed upon by free rational agents in a Rawlsian original position. Voluntary partnerships, transactions, and charity can have beneficial effects, and virtue requires us to use our wealth in ways that lead to genuine mutual benefit.

5   Social Insurance

A final argument supporting wealth redistribution is based on the idea of social insurance.[25] The argument makes the following claims. First, although unanticipated and undesired negative outcomes

---

25. See Munger 2015 and Thoma 2015. I thank Adam Hyde for discussions of this argument.

from behaviors and choices, as well as unforeseen and unforesee-able chance occurrences (including luck), happen in everyone's life, they are especially worrisome in the lives of the poor because the poor have fewer resources to marshal to accommodate and address them. The wealthier one is, the more likely one is to have reserve resources on which to draw in times of need, including unforeseen need; the poorer one is, the less likely is one to have such reserves. Second, the knowledge that one has reserve resources on which to draw when necessary seems likely to play a role in how motivated one would be to take risks. If one has reserve resources, one is likelier to be willing to take risks; if one has little such reserves, by contrast, one is likelier to be risk-averse. And third, risk-taking is necessary not only for the increase in society's prosperity generally—it is the hallmark of entrepreneurs and thus a fount of innovation[26]—but it is likely also the key to discovering ways to improve one's own situation and thus to taking the steps that are likely to actually improve one's situation.

Putting the claims together, the argument is that without some reserve wealth, or perhaps insurance, too many people—and dispro-portionately the poor—will be averse to taking the risks that might improve their own situations or lead to the generation of value for society. This, then, might be a role for government, and a purpose of wealth redistribution: creating a system of **social insurance** that can level out the vicissitudes of risk in people's lives—vicissitudes that can be more detrimental the poorer one is—so that everyone, including especially the poor, feels secure enough to risk undertaking the entrepreneurial steps that might alleviate his or her poverty or improve his or her situation. Although wealth redistribution for the purpose of social insurance would likely be financed through a gen-eral mechanism like a progressive tax, it might be justified not only for the beneficial effects it is likely to have on the poor but also for the beneficial effects it is likely to have on society's overall prosperity by enabling more people to enter into the productive economy.

This argument does not depend on identifying any particular wrongdoers, which as I argued earlier is unlikely to be successful, and it does not depend on any particular notion of fairness, which as I also argued is likely to create its own unintended unfairness.

---

26. See Isaacson 2014 and Ridley 2020.

Instead, it addresses what seems like a real feature both of human psychology and of the nature of poverty: the poorer one is, the more risk-averse one is, and poverty makes one less able (even unable) to deal with the unpredictable but yet inevitable vagaries of life. This argument would thus fall into the first category outlined at the outset, benefiting the poor, though it portends—via an Adam Smithian "**invisible hand**"—ancillary benefits for the rest of society as well. For what might be a relatively small level of wealth redistribution, the government could provide social insurance for the poor, sufficient to give them the security they need to take the risks, especially the entrepreneurial risks, required to discover and pursue ways to improve their lives. And as they discover these ways, they will, by an "invisible hand," thereby also contribute to the prosperity of society generally.

I take this argument to be one of the strongest defenses of wealth redistribution. Nevertheless, it too faces questions about both its practicability and its effectiveness. They principally concern what economists call **moral hazard**, and the difficulty the government faces in getting either the level or price of the social insurance right.

Take these two concerns in turn.

Moral Hazard: when a policy of compensating people for loss, or protecting them against loss, unintentionally leads people to engage in more, not less, of a risky behavior.

5.1 Moral Hazard

The general purpose of insurance is to spread the cost of unpredictable negative results of accidents and of individuals' choices or behaviors, and to distribute the risk of individual actions, among many parties to reduce the costs and risks to any individual member of the pool in the event that an accident eventuates or an action fails. As related to wealth redistribution, the main purpose of "social insurance" would be to provide citizens, particularly those with little reserve resources but who face unforeseeable or unlucky eventualities, the security they need to engage in the risk-taking that would, or might, improve their lives enabled by the knowledge that should things turn out badly they do not face ruin. For people living close to the margin, even a small risk of a negative outcome could be disastrous; hence, their natural and reasonable conclusion might be not to venture any such risks at all. If they knew, however, that there was an insurance against ruin—say, an economic minimum below which the government would not let them fall—this knowledge might give them both the psychological and financial security they need to venture even modest risks of entrepreneurial action to improve their situations, as well as that of their families and communities. Such actions might include quitting a bad or ill-fitting job and seeking a new, better one; taking the time to engage in job or new skills training; getting an educational degree or certification, or an occupational license; or changing jobs or moving without fear of losing healthcare or other benefits.

Beyond the moral claim that this seems a humane way to treat the least-advantaged in society, there is also the economic argument that this might incentivize more citizens to engage productively in the economy, thereby generating benefits to the rest of society as well. If prosperity depends on economic production, and if production depends on the number of people engaging in productive economic activity, then the more people involved in such activity the better—for everyone. Social insurance can hence address the moral concern of humanely treating society's most vulnerable and the economic concern of encouraging yet greater creation of both individual and overall prosperity.

There is a potential moral hazard problem, however. A controversial finding of psychology is what is known as *homeostasis*, or the propensity of people to adjust their behavior to their perceptions of risk (Wilde 1998; Peltzman 2004). If people believe that the risk of accident, injury, or cost involved with an activity is high, they will, other things equal, tend to engage less in it; if they believe the risk is low, they will, again other things equal, tend to engage in it more. Note that the key is not the actual risk involved. What matters instead is what the *perceived* risk is—and people routinely misestimate risk.

Consider, for example, the paradoxical empirical result that the increased use of bicycle helmets has not reduced the number of injuries and deaths while bicycling. The reason, apparently, is that when riders wear helmets, they tend to take greater risks while bicycling. And people around them—car, truck, and bus drivers, for example—also adjust their behavior, passing helmeted bicycle riders with narrower margins and at higher speeds. The result is that there are more accidents, and when accidents occur, they tend to be more serious, counteracting whatever protection and benefit the helmet otherwise could have provided.[27] A similar paradoxical finding has resulted from the increased use of helmets while skiing and snowboarding. Despite the greatly increased numbers of people wearing helmets when engaging in such activities, the number of serious accidents and injuries has not decreased—apparently because people wearing helmets feel invulnerable and hence take far greater risks, like skiing or snowboarding on cliffs, at elevated speeds, or otherwise beyond their abilities.[28]

Finally, the worldwide increase in wearing seatbelts while driving cars has similarly not resulted in the anticipated reduction in vehicular deaths. Apparently, wearing a seatbelt—especially when combined with knowledge that one's vehicle has other safety features like antilock brakes and airbags—leads people to speed, take corners too fast, tailgate, and feel safe as they use their cell phones while driving, thereby increasing accidents and counteracting the benefits of the seatbelt and other safety features. According to one British study, "after the passage of the [1983 British mandatory] seat-belt law more pedestrians and cyclists were killed as a consequence of belted motorists driving less carefully. And after seat belts became compulsory for children in rear seats, the number of children killed while travelling in rear seats increased, again almost certainly as a result of the false sense of security induced in the parent/driver." According to one researcher, "There is no country in the world that has passed a seat belt law that can demonstrate that it has saved lives."[29] These are surprising, even depressing, findings, but they seem to be explained by homeostasis.

Similar adjustments in behavior, often unconscious, take place in other areas of life. If people come to believe that risks are decreased, they will take greater risks. And it is, or can be, perfectly rational behavior. Imagine I said to you: "Gambling is morally wrong, and you shouldn't do it. But if you do gamble, I will cover any of your

---

27. For a review of a number of related studies, see Cook 2004. See also Robinson 2006.
28. See, for example, Shealy et al. 2009.
29. See Adams 2011 for this and the preceding quotation.

losses." What would you do? If you believed me, you would take the next flight to Las Vegas. If the potential benefits of an activity are concentrated in, or redound to, me, but any potential costs or losses are paid by you (or distributed among many other people), then the logic is as clear as it is sinister: concentrated benefits and dispersed costs encourage and inevitably lead to risky behavior.

Now apply this reasoning to the idea of social insurance. If I know that losses resulting from bad decisions I make, or even unforeseeable bad outcomes from prudential decisions I make, will be paid for by someone else—the government, say—then that, *by design*, encourages me to take more risks. This can have the beneficial effect noted earlier of more entrepreneurial innovation and improvement, but because of homeostasis, it might also lead me to take unreasonable risks and make imprudent choices as well. When negative outcomes ensue, the losses are paid by others—which would fail to give me the feedback I need not to make similarly imprudent choices again in the future. If, for example, my health care bills are, or would be, primarily paid by someone other than me, then I might at least marginally be less averse to: leading a sedentary lifestyle, smoking, becoming obese, declining preventive or regular maintenance medicine, taking vaccines, or avoiding simple precautions that would prevent me from getting sick or injured. Similarly with, say, investing for my retirement. If I know that someone else will maintain me in my retirement if I lose everything or have saved nothing, then what incentive do I have to invest wisely or to save? If I am guaranteed a certain minimum regardless of what I do, then I might (rationally) conclude that I should take greater risks with my investments or spend and consume my resources now without concern for providing for myself for retirement.

Such policies create moral hazard. A laudable intention of protecting people from or securing them against bad, even catastrophic, eventualities can counterproductively and perhaps counterintuitively result in incentivizing them to engage in behaviors they should not and otherwise would not. This is neither an indictment of their character nor a suggestion that they are irrational. The claim is based only on the assumption that people respond to incentives, both negative and positive, as part of the calculus in which they engage when deciding to act. If the downside risk of any potentially beneficial action or behavior has been mitigated, or is perceived to have been mitigated, then people are likelier to engage in that risky behavior. Protection from potential negative outcomes can lead them to perceive a behavior as less risky than it might in fact be, with the likely if unintended result that people engage in more of precisely the risky behavior that we had antecedently hoped they would avoid.

Such social insurance can, then, run two significant risks. First, it can lead to increased engagement in risky behavior, with a predictable increase in negative outcomes. Second, it can blunt the feedback people need to develop good judgment. Judgment is a skill, and, like other skills, it must be used to be sharp and effective. But to develop one's judgment in good directions, one needs both the opportunity to exercise it and, crucially, the feedback—negative or positive, as the case may be—from its use to make better use of it in the future (Otteson 2006). Without that feedback, judgment either does not develop, or does not develop in good directions. The blunting of feedback can compound the likelihood of bad or imprudent decisions in the future.

5.2   The Tragic but Instructive Case of Madoff

> Disgraced financier Bernie Madoff (1938–2021) led a decades-long fraudulent "Ponzi," or pyramid, scheme that cost investors some $65 billion.

A connected risk of moral hazard arising from homeostasis is that it can incline people to be less anxious to scrutinize risk than they otherwise would be, potentially enabling them to be more susceptible to scams and cons. Consider the case of Bernie Madoff.

On December 11, 2008, federal authorities arrested Bernard Madoff on allegations of securities fraud.[30] They were acting on information from his sons, who alleged that Madoff was, through his company Bernard L. Madoff Investment Securities, LLC, operating a multi-billion-dollar "Ponzi scheme" in which he falsified reports of gains and drew from principal to pay out alleged returns. On March 12, 2009, Madoff pleaded guilty to 11 felonies, and he

---

30. For further details, see Otteson 2014, pp. 171–4.

was sentenced to 150 years in prison. The total wealth lost through Madoff's Ponzi scheme was estimated at $65 billion, involving some 13,500 investors.

Perhaps people should have known something was amiss. Madoff's reported returns averaged over ten percent per year—every single year for decades, regardless of what the market did. No one has returns like that. Indeed, some people did believe something was amiss. Harry Markopolos, for example, who was working for a rival investment firm, warned the Securities and Exchange Commission in 1999 and again in 2005 that Madoff could not actually have achieved the results he claimed—at least not legally. He also approached the *Wall Street Journal* in 2005, but the SEC declined to act on his allegations and the WSJ declined to go forward with the story.

Many very smart people lost a lot of money with Madoff. Nobel Peace Prize winner and Holocaust survivor Elie Wiesel lost not only the endowment of his charity but also his personal life's savings. Other investors who lost money with Madoff include people like Steven Spielberg and Larry King, as well as institutions like the Royal Bank of Scotland and HSBC. Madoff reportedly cultivated a "Wizard of Oz" personality: he often refused to meet personally with investors; some people's money he mysteriously refused to take; and he boasted that his investment strategies were too complicated for most people to understand. Still, should it have taken a stock market crash or high-level statistical analysis to know that something suspicious was going on—that there was no real wizard behind the curtain? In retrospect, it is hard not to wonder why so many people failed to exercise skepticism. How could even highly educated people and sophisticated institutions like worldwide banking groups fall for such a seemingly obvious fraud?

Part of the answer might lie in homeostasis and moral hazard. As we have seen, the more that people believe risks are minimized, the more likely they are to engage in dangerous or foolish behavior. Similarly, if they believe risks are heightened, they are more cautious than they otherwise would be. The consequence of the phenomenon of risk compensation most relevant here is that if third parties undertake to protect people from the undesirable consequences of their own bad decisions, it can give them the mental ammunition they need to *keep making bad decisions.*

Why would people fall for schemes like Madoff's? No doubt many factors played roles, but perhaps part of the explanation is as a consequence of their knowledge that there were numerous government agencies whose purpose is to prevent, discover, and punish frauds. People might have reasonably believed that they were protected and hence relaxed their scrutiny and attention. The people defrauded by Madoff might have thought he was above suspicion because he operated in what is, after all, one of the most extensively and tightly regulated industries in the world. The U.S. Securities and Exchange Commission monitored and required filing and reporting on every transaction in which Madoff's company engaged; moreover, Madoff's activities also fall under the supervisory jurisdiction of several other governmental agencies, including the Federal Bureau of Investigation and the New York State's Attorney. Together, these agencies employ thousands of people and have annual budgets totaling billions of dollars. Would it not be reasonable for people to believe that they were protected by these agencies—that, surely, no one could get away with malfeasance as flagrant as a decades-long multi-billion-dollar fraud? If they did have such a seemingly reasonable belief, homeostasis might have led them to relax the scrutiny and skepticism that good judgment might otherwise have indicated.

No one wants what Madoff did to happen again. But creating another government agency—or indeed many of them—whose purported job is to take care of the risks to investors might be precisely the *wrong* thing to do. The phenomenon of risk compensation suggests that doing so might encourage people to be less scrutinizing and less skeptical, and thus fitter targets for frauds. Imagine if what we said to people instead was: "You are on your own. If you invest foolishly and lose your money, too bad for you. So, you'd better invest wisely." What would their response be? Perhaps people would ask their brokers and advisers probing questions; perhaps they might shop their money around and bring market pressures to bear on investment advisers; perhaps they would become more suspicious of claims of profit guarantees or get-rich-quick schemes; and so on. In short, they might become far more careful with their money—which would decrease the chances of their becoming subject to fraud attempts, increase the chances of early detection of such attempts, or both.

These examples suggest concerns about the potentially negative effects on people's judgment of social insurance. To whatever extent people are relieved of facing the consequences of their decisions, they will tend to relax their attention and focus their scrutiny elsewhere. The desire to protect people from the negative consequences of not exercising, or not exercising well, their judgment is understandable and admirable. It is, after all, what good parents try to do for their children. But being a good parent also entails gradually releasing children from protection as they grow into adults. Except in extraordinary cases of actual incapacity, at some point, a good parent sets his children entirely free—for good or ill. Doing otherwise is to imperil an essential part of their humanity—namely, judgment—and thus to disrespect what gives them dignity—namely, moral agency and accountability. Not holding people accountable, therefore, not only disrespects their agency but also jeopardizes the conditions under which they can develop the judgment that is essential to their full humanity—and that encourages them to become harder targets for prospective con artists.

5.3 Getting the Price Right

The other principal problem facing the social insurance argument for wealth redistribution is that the government is ill-positioned to know what the proper level of insurance is to provide people. Private insurers face competitive pressures to make disciplined, good-faith estimates of risk and to figure out what the contributing and confounding elements are of risky behavior. They must do this to stay in business, because if they pay too much or not enough, they experience losses—which no firm can do for long and hope to survive. So, they are constantly reevaluating their levels of payouts and prices to ensure not only that they can attract customers with their coverage offerings but also that they pay out enough (but not too much or too little) so that they neither jeopardize their solvency nor lose customers. But government-provided social insurance faces none of these disciplining factors—and, in fact, is incentivized in only one, potentially counterproductive, direction.

If everyone is provided and legally entitled to social insurance by the government, then the government enjoys the position of a monopoly, with the attendant potentially negative consequences we would expect from a private firm in a market that enjoyed a legal monopoly. Those consequences include raising prices, offering an inferior product, and failing to innovate or improve services. There would be little or no incentive to keep costs down, for example, because the social insurance monopoly would face little or no competition due to its captive audience. Similarly, it would face little incentive to innovate or improve its services, or engage in careful, time-consuming risk assessment, again because its guaranteed customers can go nowhere else. Even if people were allowed to also buy private insurance, if they were, nevertheless, still required to pay for the social insurance through their taxes, then the disciplining features that market competition imposes would remain minimal for the government social insurance. What we should then expect is that the costs of the program would rise regardless of the quality or level of service, because the people working in the agency would, like anyone else in a monopolistic situation, have the natural incentive to seek higher return to themselves. One principal way to do so is to simply increase their budgets.

This is what we have seen with Medicare and Medicaid, for example: costs have gone up dramatically, far beyond what their proposers initially claimed, and the recurring complaints about their inefficiency and waste, as well as their spiraling costs, have become as predictable as they are unfortunate.[31] Think also of the Veterans Administration hospital system, the Post Office, Departments of Motor Vehicles, and so on. The point these examples make is that these are entirely predictable outcomes that should be expected. Their inefficiency and the disappointing quality of their services are explained not by assuming that their employees are immoral or irrational, but by simply assuming that they are responding to the incentives they face. This indeed suggests a general caution: there is no guarantee that a program that has been carefully crafted in theory will be executed flawlessly, or even effectively, in practice. On the contrary, we must consider the likely confounding factor

---

31. After the first year of the creation of Medicare and Medicaid in 1964, their spending rose to 0.5 percent of U.S. gross domestic product each, or approximately $7.4 billion total. By 2018, their spending had risen to approximately three percent of U.S. gross domestic product each, or approximately $1.2 trillion total—a nearly 200-fold nominal increase in expenditures, or approximately a 30-fold real (inflation adjusted) increase in expenditures. (For context, the population in the U.S. increased during that time only 1.67-fold.) See Chantrill 2019a and 2019b.

that the people staffing any government agency we empower to implement our vision will have motives and purposes of their own, which may not be what we wanted, imagined, or anticipated—and thus might compromise the success of our envisioned program, produce unintended negative consequences, or even be counterproductive.[32] Thus, we should expect similar results from social insurance as well—which similarly vitiates the benefits we should expect from social insurance.

Consider also the difficult issue of payouts. How much should a government-administered social insurance program pay? To whom should it pay? What eventualities should it cover? How much should the people staffing the agency get paid? In a monopoly setting, it is difficult if not impossible to know. Because they are not operating in a market in which there is competition and risk of loss, they would not have prices or other information to give them proper signals that they are allocating their resources appropriately, given people's needs and desires. In a market, people's choices give rise to prices that reflect their hierarchy of value under the constraints of scarcity they face. Such prices can then guide both suppliers and consumers to increasingly appropriate allocations of their respective scarce resources— "appropriate" meaning consistent with their hierarchy of values given their constraints. In a monopoly setting, by contrast, these information signals are diminished or absent, reducing people's ability to know how to allocate their resources. This leads them to make guesses more or less in the dark, which inevitably leads to oversupplies and shortages—in other words, to inefficiency and waste. Because our resources remain limited, we cannot meet every need or desire at the same time. Thus, choices entailing tradeoffs must always be made. Prices arising from the choices people make can give signals about what the most pressing desires and needs are, and hence where our scarce resources should be devoted first, then second, then third, and so on. Because the signals from prices would be muted in a monopoly

---

32. For statements of this principle, and thus statements of the foundations of the field of economics known as "public choice," see Buchanan 1979 (1999) and 2003.

situation, however, we would not know where the resources are most needed. Misallocations would thus ensue.

What we could predict in the case of a government monopoly, however, is that the answer to questions about resources, coverages, and payouts would always be "more," in part because they would be decided by political, not economic considerations. If the politicians making broad decisions about overall levels of funding and the workers administering the program are spending others' money, and if they do not face the potential risk of losing their own money (or getting fired or going out of business) if they engage in wasteful, unproductive, or counterproductive spending, then all the incentives are in one direction—spend more. And if the program were administered by a government that, like that of the United States, is increasingly accustomed to financing its programs by issuing debt, there might be little effective check on the spending levels—no ceiling, or no ceiling in sight, on the "more."

It is not that a government-run social insurance program funded by wealth redistribution could not in principle get the payouts, the beneficiaries, the costs, the incentives, and the levels and types of service correct. It is instead that it is exceedingly unlikely that those making decisions about funding the program, setting its policies, making its payouts, and determining and delivering its products and services would get it correct, because they would have neither the information nor the incentive to do so. Moreover, if their incentives might be such that they are rewarded simply for increasing everything—both their own funding and their payouts—then the program would, in addition to running the substantial risk of ever-increasing costs, also run the risk of engendering even more moral hazard among its beneficiaries. It would progress from protecting against only unforeseeable catastrophic loss, which would doubtless be how it would be described at its inception, to covering ever more people and ever more negative outcomes (requiring ever more employees to administer and ever-rising costs). As its range and scope of coverage increased, it could predictably lead to the negative unintended consequence of encouraging more of the behavior it sought to protect against—hence further compromising its ability to solve the problems it was intended to address and providing incentives for further increases in costs.

Perhaps the strongest argument for wealth redistribution is to provide social insurance, or protection against unforeseen emergency and a floor below which we do not want our fellow citizens to fall. Government-administered social insurance programs run, however, two substantial risks. First, they can lead to moral hazard, because insuring people against negative outcomes incentivizes them, owing to homeostasis, to engage in more risky behavior, not less. The crimes of Bernie Madoff seem a case in point. Second, such government programs operate as monopolies, which diminishes their incentives to get prices right, economize on resources, or provide effective services.

6 A Better Way

Given these considerable difficulties facing arguments favoring wealth redistribution, is there a better way of helping the poor, punishing wrongdoers, or instantiating fairness, equality, or equity? I suggest that the political-economic framework that Adam Smith set out can address and even promote all three of these putative aims of wealth redistribution, while avoiding many of the problems that governmental wealth redistribution itself faces. In this final section, I sketch the Smithian framework and then suggest how it might plausibly address poverty, punishment of wrongdoing, and fairness, equality, or equity.

Adam Smith (1723–1790) was the author of *The Theory of Moral Sentiments* (1759) and *An Inquiry into the Nature and Causes of the Wealth of Nations* (1776). Smith was a key figure in the Scottish Enlightenment, and is considered by many as the founder of the discipline of economics.

Smith argues for a conception of justice that is "negative," that is, that comprises restraint from taking action that would harm others—namely, action that would, in his words, visit "real positive evil" or "positive hurt" on another (Smith 1982 [1759], pp. 82–3). On his account, acting justly toward others requires refraining from causing such positive evil or hurt to others in three principal respects: their persons, their property, and their promises. That is, we cause positive evil or hurt to another, and hence act unjustly, when we harm their *persons* by killing, assaulting, or enslaving them; when we harm their *property* or possessions by stealing, trespassing upon, destroying, despoiling, or rendering them unusable; or when we defraud others or break our voluntary contracts or *promises* with them (Smith 1982 [1759], p. 84). The third aspect of justice, promises, has the further implication of debarring third parties from intervening uninvited into the voluntary partnerships and associations others make. Importantly, it would thus forbid someone from intervening to prevent, for example, businesses from serving willing customers or hiring employees from historically disfavored groups.

Smith contrasts the "negative" virtue of justice with all of our positive moral obligations, which he puts under the general heading of "beneficence," defined as taking positive action to improve another's situation. Smith writes: "Beneficence is always free, it cannot be extorted by force, the mere want of it exposes to no punishment; because the mere want of beneficence tends to do no real positive evil" (Smith 1982 [1759], p. 78). Note Smith's claim that a "want," or lack, of beneficence does no positive evil: if I fail to provide you a benefit, I do not harm you; I leave you exactly in the position you were. Because injustice does involve visiting another with harm, however, Smith argues that the state is justified in preventing or punishing it, by force if necessary. By contrast, beneficence "is always free" and "cannot be extorted by force"—meaning that the power of the state should not be employed to force people against their wishes to provide benefit to others. If one is forced to help another, even a deserving other, one's lack of free choice to do so robs one of any moral credit. Since free choice is required for moral agency, and hence virtue, mandating or coercing benefit eliminates it as an act of virtue. Smith argues that, to count as a virtue, beneficence should be left to the consciences of private individuals and private associations, and we should use the power of moral suasion, not legal coercion, to encourage people to engage in "proper beneficence" (Smith 1982 [1759], p. 270).

What political institutions are consistent with, or follow from, this conception of justice? Smith argues that the government should have three principal duties. The first two are: "first, the duty of protecting the society from the violence and invasion of other independent societies; secondly, the duty of protecting, as far as possible, every member of society from the injustice or oppression of every other member of it, or the duty of establishing an exact administration of justice" (1981 [1776], p. 687). The first duty would require a military for national defense, and the second duty would require police and courts; both fall under Smith's definition of "justice" as preventing or punishing harm against others' persons, property, and contracts or promises, whether from foreign or domestic aggressors.

The final duty of government according to Smith is: "thirdly, the duty of erecting and maintaining certain publick works and certain publick institutions, which it can never be for any individual, or small number of individuals, to erect and maintain; because the profit could never repay the expense to any individual or small number of individuals, though it may frequently much more than repay it to a great society" (Smith 1981 [1776], pp. 687–8). This third duty goes beyond the "negative," defensive-only conception of justice he had articulated, but as Smith goes on to clarify, what would qualify as a good or service that should be provided by the government must meet both of the two criteria intimated in the above quotation—namely, it would have to be something that (1) would benefit substantially everyone in society, not merely one person or one group at the expense of another; and (2) it would have to be unable to be provided by private enterprise, either for-profit or not-for-profit. The first criterion is to prevent injustice—namely, the injustice of extractively benefiting one person or group at the expense of another person or group. The second criterion enables us to address collective action problems in ways that are what economists call **Pareto-improving.**

Pareto-improvement: when a proposed policy or course of action results in a benefit or improvement to at least one member of a group without any other members thereby suffering a loss.

The union of those two criteria constitutes a high bar to cross, and Smith's argument shifts the burden of proof to the proposer: if you wish for the government to provide some good or service, then you need to demonstrate that it meets both criteria.[33]

Would Smith's conception of justice and the public institutions he argues it entails address the aims of wealth redistribution we have considered? Start with the most straightforward case, the second aim of punishment for wrongdoing. Smith's conception of justice gives us clear and plausible criteria for punishment. If one has injured another in her person, property, or voluntary promises and associations, then one has committed an injustice, and the state is therefore justified in demanding compensation: the "observance" of justice "may be extorted by force" (Smith 1982 [1759], p. 79).

The third aim we discussed, fairness, is also addressed by Smith's principles: "In the race for wealth, and honours, and preferments, he may run as hard as he can, and strain every nerve and every muscle, in order to outstrip his competitors. But if he should justle, or throw down any of them, the indulgence of the spectators is entirely at an end. It is a violation of fair play, which they cannot admit of" (Smith 1982 [1759], p. 83). This use of "fair" relates to the following of the proper rules, which for Smith is recognizing that all other people are "in every respect, as good as" oneself, and thus deserve the same respect and recognition that everyone else does (ibid.). We can extend this claim to hold that each person is as deserving of respect as any other, and thus entitled to the same consideration—no more, no less—as everyone else. Relating this claim to our case of unequal contributions to a joint product (pie-making, for example), this would mean that fairness requires that individuals be compensated properly according to their respective contributions to the output. If their outputs are unequal, then their compensation should be as well.

Smith's argument also endorses an equality—though a moral equality of agency, not an equality of wealth. Each person is

---

33. Smith himself considers three main goods or services that might meet his criteria: the administration of justice, such as courts and police; infrastructure, such as roads and bridges; and primary education that aims to teach every citizen to "read, write, and account" (Smith 1976 [1776], p. 785). In all three cases, however, he offers reasons why private provision is sometimes superior to public provision; in the case of education, he argues that it should be "partly, but not wholly paid by the publick" (ibid.).

accorded an "opt-out option," or the right to say "no, thank you" to any offer, proposal, or demand. In this way, each person's agency is respected equally, and people meet each other as moral peers, regardless of any differences in wealth or social status they have. If you can decline any offer I might make to you, then the scope of our respective decision-making authority, which is limited to our own person, property, and promises, is equal.

Finally, the first aim of wealth redistribution we discussed, poverty relief, is also addressed by Smith's framework. Smith's prediction was that countries that adopted his recommended public institutions would see their prosperity increase for all members, including especially for their poorest. Subsequent history suggests that Smith was right. Those countries that have most closely adopted Smithian recommendations of private property, markets, trade, and liberty for all citizens have generated far more wealth, including far more wealth for their poor, than countries with other systems of political economy. Indeed, the contest has not been close. The countries today that rank in the highest quartile on the Fraser Institute's *Economic Freedom of the World Index*, for example, have created on average eight times more real wealth than those countries in the lowest quartile; and the poorest tenth of citizens of the former countries enjoy an average annual income some ten times as high as the poorest tenth of the latter countries (Gwartney et al. 2019). By contrast, countries whose governments intervene more heavily into their economies, including by redistributing wealth, enjoy comparatively less overall prosperity. And their redistributive programs are difficult to sustain, as shown by the recent examples of Scandinavian countries like Sweden and Denmark, which not only required market-based economies to generate the wealth they redistributed but have or are now in the process of scaling back their redistributive schemes as they proved counterproductive and their costs proved unsustainable (Otteson 2014, pp. 85–6; Gronholt-Pedersen 2019).

Adam Smith's conception of justice is "negative," and provides for government protection of people's persons, property, and voluntary promises. It provides effective means to prevent or punish injustice, to address unfairness, and, as Smith predicted, and as subsequent economic history has corroborated, to enable the alleviation of poverty.

7 Conclusion

Alleviating poverty, punishing for wrongdoing, and instituting fairness, equality, and equity are worthy goals of any society that can be morally justified. Government-mandated and government-administered wealth redistribution is, however, ill-suited to accomplish these ends. By contrast, what can, and what has, made substantial and historically unprecedented progress toward all three of these goals is the set of governmental institutions that respects the person, property, and voluntary promises of each individual, and an economy in which, as Adam Smith put it, "Every man, as long as he does not violate the laws of justice, is left perfectly free to pursue his own interest his own way, and to bring both his industry and capital into competition with those of any other man, or order of men" (Smith 1981 [1776], p. 687).

In other words, what is required is, first, the removal of formal or legal restrictions placed on any individuals, or groups, that limit their ability to use the resources available to them to achieve a flourishing life as they themselves understand it; and second, endorsement of political and economic policy that rewards people for engaging in mutually voluntary cooperative behavior and partnerships that provide benefit and value to others as well as to themselves, and that hence punish or disincentivize behavior that extractively benefits one person or group at the expense of others. A liberal political regime that protects the widest scope of liberty of all its citizens that is compatible with the equal liberty of everyone else seems a plausible way to accomplish, or at least work toward, the first of these goals; a properly functioning market economy seems a plausible way to accomplish the second. And as the now large and still growing body of empirical evidence attests, these prescriptions have in fact enabled substantial progress on both these goals.

The other benefit of such a set of political-economic institutions, which Smith calls "the obvious and simple system of natural liberty" (Smith 1981 [1776], p. 687), is the moral equality it both reflects and presumes. It allows material inequality, but by protecting everyone's persons, property, and promises, it disallows transactions, exchanges, partnerships, and associations on any grounds other than by mutually voluntary choice. It thus respects each person's "opt-out option." If each of us can decline any proposal, offer, or demand anyone makes to or of us, then the only way we can benefit ourselves is by simultaneously benefiting others—according to others' own schedules of value. That means that however much wealth anyone has, or however much more wealth another has than we do, if we can say "no, thank you" if we choose, then our respective agencies are leveled. We meet each other as peers, as moral equals, and we are bound not only by the public institutions but by our own interests to respect others' goals and values.

The liberal system of political economy, then, along with the market economy it entails, offers, in addition to the benefits of alleviating poverty, providing protection against injustice, and instituting fairness in society, the additional benefit of respecting each person's equal moral agency. It does not propose perfection or a solution to all problems—as Smith acknowledged, perfection is not on offer for "so imperfect a creature as man" (Smith 1982 [1759], p. 25)—but it does propose allowing individuals to generate ever more resources enabling them to address ever more problems. Not perfection, then, but steady improvement, while respecting the moral dignity of ever more people. Thus, peace, prosperity, and equal moral agency: that is a conception of political economy worth defending morally.

First Round of Replies

Chapter 3

Poverty, Moral Hazard, and the State

Reply to James R. Otteson

Steven McMullen

Contents

I would like to thank James Otteson for his thoughtful opening statement. There is much here that I agree with and appreciate. There is much here I disagree with, of course, and for the purposes of our debate, I will try to outline those things in more detail. Otteson argues that redistribution is unnecessary, ineffectual, and unjust. Each of these is important. The claim that redistribution is unnecessary hinges on how we think about and measure poverty.

DOI: 10.4324/9780367854263-5

The claim that redistribution is ineffectual requires us to consider whether state programs actually achieve their goals. Finally, the claim that redistribution is unjust requires some reflection about the nature of justice and respect. I will use these different kinds of claims to organize my response, which has four parts. First, I will offer three broad observations about Otteson's argument—two points of agreement and two disagreements. Second, I will address his argument about poverty. What is the nature of poverty in the United States? Can we expect it to go away without redistribution? Third, I will focus on his claims about the effectiveness of the welfare state. Can we expect government action to be effective? How serious are the unintended negative consequences from the government action? Finally, I will address the part of his argument that is more purely philosophical. Is redistribution unjust? What kind of economic justice should we aim for?

The main thesis of this response is that Otteson's argument against redistribution pushes a number of arguments just one step too far. Poverty is declining, but not for everyone, and mostly because of government action. The moral hazard problem is real, but the effect is not large. Economic freedom is important, but there is no reason to believe that we have to choose between a market economy and having a real safety net. Most fundamentally, it is entirely reasonable and just to expect that everyone contribute to the funding of welfare programs.

Right from the start, however, I would note for readers that Otteson's arguments are reasonable and worth considering in depth. There are too many who argue that their political and intellectual opponents are wrong because they don't even want to pursue the good, or that they don't make arguments in good faith, or that if they disagree, it must be because they don't understand the real issues at stake. None of these are true in this case. Otteson and I agree about many of the main ends that we seek from our economic system: respect for individual dignity and widely shared material well-being. However, intelligent and well-meaning scholars still disagree about many of these hard questions, as we might expect, because they are hard. In this case, it looks like we disagree about how different elements of the good should be prioritized when in conflict, and we also disagree about how to best pursue those good ends. This is a debate worth having on its merits, and I am pleased to be participating.

1 Three Opening Observations

Sometimes it is helpful to first consider the broad scope of an argument before delving into the specifics. There are two broad points of agreement I want to emphasize, and then two considerable difficulties with his position.

1.1 Global Poverty, Economic Freedom, and Market Exchange

Otteson rightly starts with an argument that I neglected in my own first essay: the dramatic decline in global poverty over the past 30 years and the importance of economic freedom for ensuring broad prosperity. I do not want to give the impression that market economies produce only poverty and inequality, or that poverty and inequality can only be corrected by government action. It is true that the global percentage of people in extreme poverty has fallen considerably, and global inequality has even declined somewhat. While people can vary in their degrees of optimism, it now seems reasonable to imagine a future in which extreme poverty, at least by the $2/day standard, is only a problem for people in cases of extreme social breakdown or natural disasters.

There is a strong case to be made, moreover, that the extraordinary rise in living standards worldwide, and the declines in poverty, are due to increased access to stable market institutions, wide trade, and the ability to invest in education and capital. As a general rule of thumb, those who remain poor, worldwide, are those who are excluded from the market, not those most exposed to it. In all of this, Otteson and I agree. Where we disagree, however, is whether this broad positive trend also describes what is happening with poverty in the United States.

We also agree that simple market exchanges are basically just. As long as our legal system and economic institutions are working properly, there are few cases in which we should second-guess free exchanges. Even in the case in which a person makes an obviously poor choice, our respect for that person requires that we only interfere if we have a very good reason. This is at the heart of Otteson's principle of equal moral agency. On this, I agree, as should all who accept the basic liberal principles that undergird market economies and democratic government.

However, unlike Otteson, I am concerned that in a wealthy society, the cost of participation becomes fairly high, so that negative freedom, or procedural legal equality, is not enough to ensure that a person actually has economic opportunity. We do not disagree about whether a system of free exchange is good. Where we disagree is whether that system of free exchange requires a minimal state focused on protecting property rights or a more expansive state that ensures basic needs and invests in people's ability to participate.

1.2   The Possibility of Welfare Capitalism

Our agreements, I believe, are substantial. But so are our disagreements. The first, and perhaps most obvious, is that Otteson poses a choice between: (1) a system that respects individual moral agency, protects property, discourages extractive institutions, and decreases poverty, or (2) a system that engages in coerced government redistribution. If we actually had to choose between these two, I would agree with Otteson that the first is preferable. There is, however, an intermediate option. We can have the benefits of economic freedom and also engage in redistribution. Even the countries that rank highest in economic freedom, for example, have substantial government funding for health care.

Moreover, Otteson agrees that taxation and government are necessary, and that government should supply some public goods that have a wide benefit. The heart of my argument is that that list of government-provided goods should be larger, and that there are more good reasons for government action than Otteson provides. That is, we don't have to choose between a market economy and a welfare state. We can have both, and I believe the market is enriched, not diminished by a strong safety net. We should be clear that wherever you land in this debate, there will be taxes, there will be government-provided services, and the bulk of the economy will be private parties engaged in free exchange. As Otteson notes, this is not a debate about economic systems broadly, but about what policies we should pursue in our market system.

1.3   A World Without Redistribution?

Despite our areas of agreement, I find it striking how little government action is warranted in Otteson's argument. There is no allowance for any redistribution, even if minimal, except in providing true public goods. Compared with our current system, this would be a major change. Here is a quick tour of the government functions that would not make the cut: (1) public funding for education, (2) public health insurance, including Medicare, Medicaid, and subsidies for hospitals, (3) social insurance programs like Social Security, food stamps, unemployment insurance, housing vouchers, Temporary Assistance for Needy Families, and the Earned Income Tax Credit. None of these offer pareto-improving universal benefits that cannot be offered by private actors in a marketplace.

If we actually eliminated all these programs, there would be a lot of suffering. In the best-case scenario we would implement a slow, controlled phase-out of these programs. This would allow commercial enterprises and nonprofit organizations to enter the market to provide education, food security, and expanded private health insurance. The resulting tax system would boost many people's incomes and spending power, but decrease the income of the poor. Even after all those adjustments, though, there is no reason to believe that secondary schooling would be financially available to all children. Certainly education would not be free. Millions of people would end up going without health insurance and health care. Many already do, and the number of uninsured would expand to include those who are very poor. Even further, when a homeless person is brought to an emergency room for acute care in the United States, the state ends up paying for that care through broad subsidies to hospitals. Under Otteson's proposal, it seems unlikely that this would be the case. We could only hope for sufficient private donations to cover health care for everyone in dire need. I am skeptical that this would materialize in any universal way. Some communities would establish funds for health care for those who are poor, but many communities could never afford to do so.

The broad concern is this: commercial enterprise and private donations will address some of the need if we had no welfare state, but many more would go without. There is a reason that countries all over the world have public provision of some of these goods. Public funding just makes sense for schooling, to make sure it is universally accessible, and for health care, because catastrophic care is really hard to fund through savings, particularly for the poor. Even food security, which can be provided locally, can be done fairly efficiently through government action, and such a system has a lot of practical advantages.

Some might still see Otteson's alternative system—capitalism without a welfare state, public education, or health care—as an improvement, but I don't think most people would choose to live in that world. Some things would work better, but many things would be much worse. Particularly in those parts of the country with high concentrations of poverty, real standards of living would substantially drop. With worse education and health care, real economic opportunities would diminish as well. It is one thing to argue that redistribution programs are inefficient; it is another matter entirely to argue that they are so inefficient or unjust that we are better off not having them at all. In a world in which many people are already facing huge barriers to material security, I am unwilling to call that world just. As such, it behooves us to explore principles of justice that value individual freedom and also support investments in human capital and in a public safety net without framing it as an arbitrary compromise between incompatible goals.

This section makes three opening arguments. First, economic growth and voluntary market exchange are central to economic progress and justice. Second, there need not be a conflict between economic freedom and a generous social safety net. Third, the minimal liberal order that Otteson outlines would, if implemented consistently, rule out a wide swath of helpful government programs currently in place in the United States, with serious consequences.

2   Pragmatic Objections to Redistribution

I would like to address some of Otteson's pragmatic objections to redistribution before I move to his broader conception of justice. His pragmatic concerns are numerous, but I will focus on three. First, he argues that real material poverty, by global and historical standards, is not a large problem in the United States, and that it is most likely to be solved by a firmer commitment to his classical liberal economic order. Second, he argues that efforts to redistribute wealth are largely not effective at improving the lot of those in need. Redistribution moderates the consequences of bad choices, resulting in worse behavior. Finally, he argues that redistribution programs are prone to waste, both through a lack of accountability and a lack of important information. I think there is good empirical evidence that his first two arguments are unfounded, and enough good reasons to reject the third as well.

2.1 Poverty Is Real, and It Does Not Seem To Be Going Away

One of the first arguments that Otteson makes is very important. He argues that poverty rates are falling, that absolute extreme poverty has already plummeted "effectively to zero" in the United States (p. 16), and that the poor are, on average, quite well off by international standards. This, he argues, undermines the need to redistribute wealth to aid the poor. I will consider each of his claims about poverty here.

The first issue we must confront is how we should measure poverty. If we want to talk about people's actual standard of living, and see how it has changed over time, it is important to look at absolute poverty, not relative poverty. On this, Otteson and I agree. The measure of extreme poverty that Otteson references in part of his argument, however, is the lowest poverty line that is used by international organizations: the share of people living on less than $2 a day. The main point he makes is that global poverty is falling, and this is true. However, this $2 a day standard is not a realistic threshold for defining poverty in contemporary United States. Even a person living on $3 or $4 a day might be able to consume adequate food, but if they did so, they would certainly be homeless and without transportation, medicine, or access to any other goods or services.

We need, therefore, a better measure of absolute poverty if we want to measure trends in real material deprivation. Any line that we choose is somewhat arbitrary. In my argument, I favor the anchored supplemental poverty measure published by the U.S. Census Bureau. Wimer et al. (2016) use this to track how many people are living below the 1967 poverty line in terms of their absolute standard of living, adjusted for inflation. In contrast, Otteson draws on the work of Meyer and Sullivan (2012) who measure poverty through consumption (rather than income). Using either of these approaches, you see similar results: poverty rates have fallen somewhat since the 1970s. The amount of poverty reduction depends a bit on the measure, but not substantially. So on this, Otteson and I are at least starting with similar data.

There are, however, three broad ways in which I think we should disagree with the story Otteson tells about poverty. The first and most important is a simple one. We must ask why absolute poverty rates have fallen. Wimer et al. show that the declines in poverty are due to the increasing effect of government redistributive programs. The decline, moreover, is almost entirely concentrated among the elderly, due to the increasing value of more generous Medicare benefits. In fact, these scholars find that without the welfare state, poverty rates would be at least 10 percentage points higher. Furthermore, if you eliminate tax changes that give breaks/refunds to the poor, absolute poverty before government benefits would have actually increased since 1967. On average, there has been no progress in fighting poverty if we subtract the influence of redistribution, despite quite dramatic material progress for the country overall. If this is right, then it is incorrect to say that poverty rates are declining as a result of a general trend in material progress. It is even more problematic to attribute those decreases in poverty to a victory of free exchange over and against government redistribution. The exact opposite seems to be true. Poverty has been slightly increasing prior to government intervention, and that intervention has been successfully driving poverty rates down.

The second problem with Otteson's story about poverty reduction is that he moves from decreases in global poverty to decreases in domestic poverty easily, without noting the important differences. In fact, the same broad forces that have lifted so many out of extreme poverty around the world have failed to push up incomes for the poor in rich countries. Milanovic describes this phenomenon, noting that "the great winners have been the Asian poor and middle classes; the great losers, the lower middle classes of the rich world" (2016, p. 20). It may be that in the long run, a global market system will indeed lift up those in poverty in rich countries, but that has not yet happened. The data point to stagnant incomes for the bottom half of U.S. households as globalization and technology usher in dramatic increases in productive efficiency, but also increased competition for workers in wealthy countries. There is no reason to believe that this trend will not continue.

The final place where we disagree about poverty is in the measurement of the cost of living. Otteson observes, correctly, that consumers in the United States have access to cheap goods that previous generations could not imagine. He quotes Tupy (2019), who notes that even unskilled workers need to work fewer hours to afford the now quite cheap basic goods. There is a reason, however, that our poverty data don't show this dramatic improvement. These price reductions are only half the story. Tupy examines only the goods whose prices have fallen in recent years, including most manufactured goods and most food items, but he ignores the increased cost of education, which is far more important in the labor market than it used to be, and ignores the cost of health care and housing. Helland and Tabarrok (2019) explain this phenomenon best. They note that between 1980 and 2010 the cost of higher education has doubled, and the average amount spent on health care has more than doubled. These industries depend heavily on the cost of skilled labor far more than manufactured goods, and these changes in the cost of labor are the best explanation for the increases in relative prices.

The implications of this pattern of price changes are important. If we only examine the cost of manufactured goods, then the poor in rich countries really do look well off. But if we examine goods like housing, education, and health care, it looks like the poor are losing ground every year. The truth is that we must pay attention to all of the above. So while we should celebrate the newfound ease with which people can access phone service, we cannot therefore conclude that poverty is being eliminated. I argue that, regardless of how you measure poverty in the data, if there are people that don't have the opportunity to access to something essential for productive participation in social life, then those people are, in a real sense, impoverished. If our economic and political system introduces barriers that prevent people from meeting those needs, then there is something unjust about that system.

In short, I don't believe that Otteson's broad argument about poverty withstands scrutiny. Poverty has declined in the United States, but largely due to more effective government redistribution. Those in poverty in the United States do face real economic hardship, not because they lack access to cheap clothes and electronics, but because they lack access to education, health care, and affordable housing. Given the increasing importance of education for economic independence, the headwinds caused by automation and trade, and social barriers created by decades of inequality, it is not a surprise that economic mobility seems to be at a low point, at least for recent U.S. history. There are real needs in the economy, and they are not going away. The question before us is whether redistribution can make a difference.

2.2 Redistribution Works to Alleviate Poverty

The second part of Otteson's argument that is empirical or pragmatic in nature is his contention that redistribution just doesn't
work. He argues that: (i) redistributive programs don't really help
those who are poor, (ii) they create moral hazard problems, and (iii)
they may crowd out private sector solutions to the same problems.
If a redistributive program ends up hurting those it is trying to help
more than it helps them, I would agree that it is a bad program and
should be eliminated. Our dilemma is that we have a long list of
programs that do a lot of good, and also have some unfortunate
side effects. We are rarely given an unmitigated success or failure.
Given this, we need to carefully evaluate and weigh which programs
are working well, and in what ways, in order to craft good policy.

First, we should consider whether welfare state programs actually work to help those that they are intended to help. Otteson
writes that

> ...wealth redistribution has been tried many times before, but
> empirical study has discovered that it has little, if any, effect;
> its benefit is at best temporary, and at worst it might actually
> have a negative effect on prosperity, particularly on that of
> the poor.
>
> (p. 84)

This is a strong claim that demands evidence. Even in the list of
scholarly works that he offers with this claim, however, Otteson
does not provide any examples of U.S. welfare state programs that
fit this description. My read of the evidence is that welfare state
programs in the United States usually achieve their primary goals.
Social security provides income stability for the elderly, unemployment insurance provides short-term income replacement for those
who lose their jobs, Supplemental Nutrition Assistance Program
(SNAP) diminishes hunger and nutritional deficiencies, Medicaid
provides access to health care to a population that would be largely
uninsured without it.

I provide a summary of the evidence about a few of these programs in my opening argument (SNAP, Medicaid, and Head Start).
Each of these programs have demonstrated really substantial
long-term benefits. Let me turn here to a different example: the
Section 8 housing voucher program. Housing vouchers are not the

crown jewel of the American welfare state, and I would not support a huge expansion of the program without some reform (Semuels 2015). There are likely to be some adverse labor market effects that should be considered as well (Carlson et al. 2009). Nevertheless, the program does make great progress in overcoming the primary harm it is intended to combat: homelessness and home insecurity among the poor. There is in fact, wide evidence that the program has real positive effects, particularly on young children (Fischer 2015). Wood, Turnham, and Mills (2008) find that housing vouchers had a substantial positive impact on home stability, decreasing homeless, crowding, and frequent moves. That is to say, the program is flawed, but not because it does not do what it was intended to do.

The same can be said for most government welfare programs—on balance they lift the standard of living of the poor substantially. This raises the question, why do critics argue that the welfare state has been a failure? One reason is that the bar is just set too high. Robert Rector (2014), for example, argues that welfare programs fail because they do not result in long-term economic independence. The war on poverty, he notes, has not defeated poverty. By this thinking, the goal of the welfare state should be that fewer people need the welfare state. I am sympathetic to this argument; I do believe that economic mobility should be an explicit goal. I also believe, however, that some welfare state programs are worth supporting even if their impact is only to provide important needs. That does not eliminate our need to create economic opportunity, but the welfare state is only part of the infrastructure needed to achieve that goal. Even more importantly, we must consider the possibility that the welfare state really is working to lift people to independence, but that the vicissitudes of life and the market economy also result in a ready influx of people in need.

Much of the debate about redistribution, however, surrounds a slightly different question: does government redistribution change people's behavior for the worse? Otteson rightly frames this as a moral hazard problem: if the government takes away the risk of poverty, people may not work as hard to avoid poverty. In my opening chapter, I write about this as an incentive problem: the reward from working diminishes if your new job causes you to lose some valuable government benefit. The underlying problem, though, is basically the same. The concern is that people who receive SNAP, TANF, or other means-tested benefits will be less likely to seek full-time jobs, education, marriage, and business ownership because their financial stability is already secured, and they don't want to lose those benefits. I will try to address this objection in three parts. First, I will argue that there is a tension between support for market-oriented systems and opposition to safety-net programs on these terms. Second, studies show that these moral hazard problems don't seem to have big impacts on people's willingness to work. Finally, in the next section, I will address the broader moral hazard concern that Otteson raises. Overall, I will argue, it is difficult to conclude that a moral hazard response is morally significant enough to outweigh the benefits of safety-net policies.

We have to start a discussion of social insurance (or safety net) policy by thinking about risk. There is a substantial amount of riskiness in life that is difficult to avoid. Health problems strike the virtuous and vicious alike, and even the most healthy choices we can make can only mitigate, and not eliminate, the threat of disease and disability. Similarly, everyone faces some risk of losing their job. Those who earn the least, unfortunately, also face the highest risk of layoffs and longer-term unemployment. This risk is an inescapable feature of a market system. We want an economy that has constant innovation, competition, and creative destruction. That process, however, creates uncertainty, particularly for those who are young or poor and have not been able to save for hard times. There is a tension, then, between supporting a market economy and opposing all safety-net programs. The market system is only working well when there is a substantial amount of market risk for participants.

Moreover, this risk seems to have increased in recent years. Scholars have found that income volatility has increased since the 1970s up to the great recession, despite the fact that the pre-2009 period was relatively stable (Dynan et al. 2012). The increased risk was concentrated among those with high and low incomes. We would expect this in an economy facing increased global competition and a rising share of non-wage income at the top. The dynamism of the global market economy and technological advances create risk. Perhaps that risk is worth the benefits, but we should then contend with the fact that this risk is often borne by those with low incomes, whose earnings have grown the slowest. I argue that it is reasonable for some of that risk to be shared with the wider population that is gaining from the increased returns in the global economy.

Just as earnings risk seems to be slowly rising, health risk is also becoming more costly. Standard treatments for all kinds of health problems are becoming more expensive. The reasons for this are complicated, but at a minimum, it is fair to say that the problem would continue with or without the Medicaid and Medicare programs. It is getting harder for people to afford health insurance or health care treatments out of pocket. This should motivate two reactions: we need to figure out how to structure our health care markets to orient them toward cost-saving innovations, and we need to expand, not restrict, support for wider health insurance coverage.

Furthermore, it is at least worth considering that many of the risks people in poverty face are not fundamentally the result of poor choices. Otteson is concerned with policy encouraging people to make choices that increase risk. If most of the risk managed by Medicaid was the result of human choices, this would make sense. In fact, health is one of those domains where people do have some control, but even here, most health problems are not predictable and easily preventable through wise decision-making. Otteson's argument against social insurance needs to confront the problem of increasing market-based risk that is largely outside of people's control.

The second important point I want to make is that we can measure some types of moral hazard responses, and they seem to be small. First, consider the concern that social programs discourage people from working. There is a wealth of evidence that this problem exists, but that same evidence shows that the effect is smaller than has often been feared. Moffitt (2002) reviews a number of studies and concludes that there is only a modest decrease in employment due to safety net programs. Moreover, when you look at specific programs, the record is quite mixed. The Earned Income Tax Credit actually increases employment among those who are in poverty, because of the wage subsidy. Medicaid seems to discourage work among some populations, and increase it in other cases (Strumpf 2011; Hamersma 2013; Dague et al. 2017).

Beyond this, there are three broad points that are important to make about work and the social safety net. First, the incentive to work less is actually less of a problem among the very poor and is a bigger problem among those who are already working. This is just because we have built our welfare state to encourage work by creating slow benefit phase-out schedules and the wage subsidy built into the Earned Income Tax Credit.

> **Earned Income Tax Credit**: A refundable tax credit that offers a tax reduction for those who have low incomes and offers a cash rebate for the working poor. It is structured to encourage entry into the labor market and phase out slowly.

Second, it is possible to redistribute wealth in ways that avoid or mitigate the moral hazard concern. The proposal I offer in my opening chapter takes this concern seriously, as I note in the final section, and it would actually diminish the adverse incentives for each program that I propose expanding. Third, as I describe extensively in my opening argument, there is emerging evidence that in the long run the effects of some important safety-net programs, on average, actually increase labor market productivity and diminish reliance on government support. That is, for Medicaid, Food stamps, and Head Start, positive behaviors in the long run—increased labor force participation, decreased crime, and decreased reliance on public programs seem to partially or completely offset the cost of these programs.

The best reading of the empirical literature is that these programs have complicated effects: some people work less, some people work more, on average the change is small, and in the long run, some programs actually do lift people into lives of independence. This raises a question that is difficult to answer: how many people need to stop working, as a result of receiving public assistance, in order to conclude that the program is not worth pursuing? Since these programs demonstrably decrease real poverty, and increase access to essential food, health care, and education, I would argue that we need to see a substantial negative side effect to consider eliminating the programs. Instead, those concerned with moral hazard should do as I propose, and try to focus on altering the programs to minimize the dramatic benefit cutoff levels that would induce someone to work less to preserve their benefits.

2.3 Thinking Broadly about Moral Hazard

A careful reader will note that my response to Otteson's moral hazard argument has not, thus far, been right on target. Otteson does not actually seem overly concerned with the labor supply response.

This is, however, the most common concern of economists and policymakers. My response is, therefore, somewhat opportunistic: I have responded to the question that we have an answer to, and the question others often ask, not the challenge Otteson poses. Let me now turn to the somewhat harder question that Otteson raises. Otteson worries that social insurance programs blunt the consequences of poor choices. He is concerned that people will be deprived of the opportunity to practice exercising good judgment because they are protected from the consequences of their actions. People might save less, be less likely to marry, might take risks with their health, or otherwise act impulsively.

My broad response to this concern has five parts. The first three will be brief, as they draw heavily on arguments I have already made. The first is, perhaps the most important. Note that Otteson's argument assumes that the risks that are insured against, in a social insurance program, are the result of poor choices. This needs to be examined closely. It is certainly the case that plenty of people make really bad choices in life, and that these choices impact their economic livelihood. Most of the risks that we protect against with social insurance programs, however, are not the result of poor choices. People are not eligible for unemployment benefits if they are fired for bad behavior. Most health insurance expenses cannot be attributed to poor choices, and those that can (diet, exercise, and smoking, for example) tend to be conditions that private insurers gladly treat as well. Providing pre-school to children does not reward poor choices on the part of the child, certainly, and they are the ones that get the bulk of the benefit. Moreover, even when programs do provide benefits to people who are culpable for their poverty, the benefits are minimal. In the United States, a single impoverished adult without children is often eligible only for some very basic health care and food from the state.

Second, moral decision-making in economic life requires opportunities. Otteson's simple framework assumes that moral character is at least partially developed by a person, faced with real choices, choosing well or poorly and then reaping the rewards or the pain that results. However, many don't have access to stable education, employment, and safety, and so there is a real sense in which people don't face the same opportunities to make wise choices. Certainly, virtue is not only available to the wealthy, but sometimes the positive outcomes from making the right choices are. As much as Otteson worries that government intervention trains people that they will not face the consequences of poor choices, I worry that we have an economy in which people will not earn the rewards from good choices.

Third, it is worth noting that the description that Otteson gives of this character formation rests on the idea that good and bad choices are made as rational decisions. As I describe in my opening argument, there is a wealth of psychology indicating that the conditions of poverty make it far more difficult for people to make long-term forward-looking decisions. Instead, life in poverty tends to push people to focus on the more immediate needs to the exclusion of long-term thinking. This particularly impacts the domains of risk-taking, saving, and weighing costs and benefits across time. If this psychological account is correct, then the welfare state would actually free people up to make those positive character-forming decisions.

Fourth, Otteson argues for a world in which people are not protected from the consequences of their choices by the government, so that there will be fewer moral hazard concerns. What he does not consider in this part of his argument is that different people already face very different consequences for the same choices. The poor often face much harsher consequences for the same bad choices. If a household with a stable above-median income throws away $10,000 in a wild gambling spree, they have to face the consequence of being $10,000 poorer. If a relatively poor person makes the same mistake, they are more likely to lose their house, their car, or have to go without food. Neither of these cases involve injustice, since both consequences are the clear result of the same bad choice. Neither would be bailed out by any welfare state. At the same time, the stakes for the poor person are far higher.

Now extend that argument into all of the domains of life that the welfare state does cover. If a wealthy person makes poor health choices, they will be covered by their employer's health insurance, with all the same moral hazard implications. For a poor person without Medicaid, they are more likely to simply suffer from untreated illness or injury. Given the nature of our labor market, if a high-skilled person makes a mistake at work, and loses their job, the probability that they will get a new job quickly is fairly high. For a person with minimal education and a low skill job, finding new work can be far harder. Given this, it seems reasonable to ask: what kind of consequences for bad choices are appropriate and just? Should a person's poor performance on a job limit their earnings? Probably. Should it limit their ability to eat? Perhaps not. Should it limit their children's ability to eat, receive health care, or go to college? I would hope not. And it is these draconian opportunity-limiting consequences that I believe we should target with redistribution. In short, it is not enough to advocate a system in which people face the consequences for their actions. We must also consider whether those consequences are already dramatically unequal, and whether they are appropriate in severity for the nature of the action.

Finally, I think Otteson's moral concern about moral hazard, and the implications of government action for people's character, actually opens a much larger and thorny set of questions. When should we be concerned about the effects of an economic system on people's character? If we are worried about the moral hazard consequences of a social insurance system run by the government, should we not also be concerned about the same consequences from a private health insurance system? Should we be concerned about the risk-pooling characteristics of a limited-liability corporation? Should we eliminate bankruptcy law? Private health insurance, the structure of corporations, and bankruptcy law are all elements of our market system that allow people to limit the material consequences of risky choices. They should have an analogous impact on people's character as the welfare state.

Pushing the question just a bit further, I would argue that we should also be concerned with the sometimes problematic incentives created by market competition. There are cases in which competition drives out higher-cost ethical producers in favor of lower-cost unethical producers (Shleifer 2004; McMullen 2021). These questions bring us into a whole number of domains that we don't have time to address adequately. The point that I want to make here, though, is that there are consequences, in terms of incentives and character building, for many of the institutional features of our economy. Many of these features have a far bigger impact on behavior that the welfare state seems to. I am open to the argument that redistribution has a morally significant impact on people's character. I think a careful reader should demand more evidence for this harm, however, before deciding to eliminate programs that have demonstrated benefits in people's lives.

2.4 Waste in Government and Charities

The last pragmatic concern about redistribution that Otteson offers has to do with the wastefulness of government programs. He is concerned that any attempt at redistribution, particularly through social insurance programs, is likely to be inefficient for two broad reasons. First, government agencies lack the immediate accountability that market competition offers, and second, government-provided goods and services lack the price signals necessary to know how much of a good to provide. The result, he argues, is that government programs will inevitably grow and over-provide goods, while also not being held accountable to provide services in a low-cost manner. The exemplar for these problems, in his argument, is the growth over time of the Medicare and Medicaid programs in the United States. Concern with the inefficiency of government provision of goods and services is reasonable, but in this case, the argument does not get us too far, for three reasons. First, in many cases, it is possible to design programs that require relatively little information and are somewhat easy to administer. Second, even if we take the problem of not having prices seriously, I believe that Otteson draws the wrong conclusion. Finally, it is instructive to compare the problems of government programs with Otteson's preferred alternative: charity. It turns out that charitable organizations suffer from exactly the same problems that government programs do.

First, we should take seriously the limitations of government provision when we lack market information. It is true that a government office cannot enter into the life of a poor family in any meaningful way. From the offices in Washington D.C., there is no opportunity to learn precisely what kind of intervention will best help a person get back on their feet. Sometimes people will get benefits that are too small to do much good, or are so poorly targeted that they would be much better off with cash. In practice, however, we can get around some of these problems by having limited goals for the government programs. The government might not be able to help you find a good job, but they can provide unemployment benefits pretty efficiently, and there are multiple reasons why a private-market unemployment insurance system could never work. Programs like food stamps (SNAP) are a great example of a program with modest aims that is relatively easy to administer. The government just needs to process applications based on income (a much easier task than the job of the IRS), and put funds into the

SNAP accounts. For similar reasons, it makes more sense to have the government serve as an insurance provider than as a health care provider.

Second, Otteson argues that the government is never able to know how much of each good a person demands, and will end up over-providing. In the health care domain, the government might end up providing more health insurance to a person on Medicaid than they would want to purchase if they had the means. The problem is that there are no customers weighing the benefits against the price. The solution, though, in Otteson's preferred world, is likely to leave this same person with no health insurance at all. Which is further off the mark? We do have a fair bit of information about the level of insurance that most people demand when they have a moderate income. Providing a similar level of care to those in poverty is a fine approach. Moreover, in practice, we don't see government insurance being too generous. A large number of seniors actually buy additional insurance on top of Medicare because it does not cover all of the care they demand. The growth in Medicare costs is almost entirely attributable not to overly generous benefits, but instead due to the new prescription drug benefit, increasing health care prices, and longer lifespans.

Finally, I think it is worth comparing government programs to Otteson's preferred way of aiding the poor: private charity. Charities don't have any more accountability on the consumer side than governments do. Even more, the incentive that governments have to exaggerate need and expand their reach plagues charities as well. Charities do not access market price information; they don't compete for beneficiaries, and outside the top performers, fraud and waste are rampant. Some charities do great work, but replacing government programs with a dramatic increase in private charitable giving will not result in a revolution of efficient social service provision. To the contrary, all our experience indicates that charitable coverage of basic needs has been, and would be, inconsistent and fairly wasteful on average, with some high performers that do exceptional work.

There is a real pragmatic case for a substantial welfare state. There are some essential needs that are not well-served by the market, and not well-served by private charity. I have highlighted food, education, and health care as key examples. In each of these areas, we have currently operating public programs that have proven to be highly effective. We have good reason to believe, therefore, that we can serve those needs through modest and careful government programs. The outcome is not likely to be a utopia, but it could be far better than the alternatives.

> This section defends the idea that government redistribution can be effective in reducing poverty and improving economic opportunity, without substantial negative side effects. There are four main arguments. First, poverty in the United States remains a problem. Second, government redistribution has been broadly effective in achieving program goals with only small adverse changes in behavior. Third, there should be no concern about the state sheltering people from the consequences of poor choices. Most programs do not reward poor choices, and leave people open to most adverse consequences. Fourth, government programs are not likely to be more wasteful than private charity and private insurance.

3   The Just Society and the Failure of Markets

I will turn now to the real heart of Otteson's argument, in which he argues that a just society will be one in which we respect each person's equal moral agency. A fair system, in his argument, is one that respects people's abilities to make choices for themselves without being second-guessed or limited by government redistribution. The concerns I have raised about economic hardship, in this view, should be resolved through private charity, or beneficence, rather than coercive state action. Government action should be focused on protecting property and enforcing contracts, with some provision for pareto-improving public goods.

In order to illustrate the importance of Otteson's argument, let me offer a description of those cases in which redistribution, because of arbitrariness or favoritism, would clearly not be justified. Imagine a legislature targeted a specific religious or ethnic group with a special tax, or crafted a welfare program that gave payouts only to those who supported the political party in power. These would be unjust, as they violate the basic principle of equality before the law, which, among other things, ensures that government power will not be used in an arbitrary manner against political enemies or against minority groups. In many cases, governments do give subsidies to firms or industries that are politically favored, or issue taxes that will fall on constituents that are not favored. These should always be subject to critical scrutiny. Tax breaks and benefits should be defined as broadly and consistently as possible, and the tax burden spread in a predictable manner. However, it is perfectly consistent for the government to tax or reward people differently based on their circumstances, or based on the choices they make, if the circumstances or choices are subject to an important society-wide interest. So it makes sense to tax carbon emissions if those emissions are imposing costs on the rest of society, or to subsidize research and development, which offers wide benefits.

The difficulty, of course, is that we do not agree on those society-wide interests that justify disparate treatment. At the heart of the debate about redistribution is whether it is fair for the government to tax someone disproportionately (or offer a transfer) based solely on their economic resources. I will dig further into this in the arguments to come. Briefly, I think there are three difficulties with the way Otteson thinks about respecting equal moral agency, which I will discuss here. Over the course of this section, I argue that respect for moral agency should entail a moral obligation to meet the essential needs of other people, and that it should require an economic system that is easy to enter, because participation in economic life is subject to economic constraint.

3.1   Choices, Preferences, and Needs

The first difficulty with Otteson's account is that it depends on a kind of neutrality toward ethically important differences. Consider the role of choices in his argument. He argues that each person's choices should be given equal respect. Redistribution violates this respect by treating people who work hard and save money differently from those who do not. This is a reasonable critique of progressive taxation, but it does not seem to work as a critique of targeted safety-net programs that are open to anyone. Unemployment insurance, for example, is available to those regardless of whether or not they save money, whether or not they pursue an education. The same is true for public education, and a single-payer health insurance system. For all of these kinds of programs, the law treats each person equally by offering all the same benefits, no matter who they are or what choices they have made.

Most importantly, there is one sense in which universal safety net programs, funded by progressive taxes, do treat people differently, and this, I believe, points to a weakness in his minimalist liberal framework. In order to justify redistributing resources, we must believe that some concerns or preferences are more important than others. A social safety net, for example, treats the essential needs of the population (health care, unemployment insurance, food, schooling) as more important than the opportunity of taxpayers to do something else with those same resources. In this sense, the government really is privileging the preference for health care by a relatively poor person above the preference of a relatively rich person for anything else. I think this is justified. While it is elegant to try to craft a system that is neutral with respect to any human differences and any human choices, that way of thinking has some limits. Some essential needs really are more important than a marginal dollar for a wealthy person. It makes sense to do our best to craft a system where people at least have the opportunity to meet those basic needs before fulfilling other preferences. This logic can provide a justification for progressive taxation then, at least for funding for programs that meet those essential needs.

3.2   How Do We Respect People?

The second difficulty with Otteson's argument is the one-dimensional kind of respect that he extols. It is striking that Otteson argues that his proposal is the one that respects the moral agency of individuals, given that egalitarian theorists also base their ideas on respect for individuals. Let me try to parse the difference. Otteson argues that respect requires that we let people make free choices, and that we let people bear the consequences, for good or ill, of those choices. We respect people by assuming that they know what they are doing. Egalitarians like Cohen (2009), Anderson (1999), or Rawls (1999) also make arguments based on respect for individuals, but they are more concerned with political relationships, inclusion, and economic opportunity. For each of these thinkers, respect requires some redistribution so that we not allow poverty to shut people out of economic life, and so that, in most circumstances at least, we don't let people go hungry.

Both ways of showing respect have an internal logic. However, at the margin, when we are deciding how much to redistribute wealth, they are in conflict. We cannot give people the widest margin for individual economic choices and rewards while also designing an effective welfare state. And yet, we can design a system that avoids extremes. We don't have to choose to respect people in only one way. By analogy, think about the way respect is shown among equal co-workers. It makes sense that we give our colleagues a wide latitude to make their own creative decisions. When things work well, we congratulate each other, when they don't go well, we empathize. It makes sense for that kind of collegiality to occur in a structure where each person has some autonomy. It would be perfectly consistent, however, to also have an agreement that when something bad happens, people would pitch in to cover for a sick colleague, or even to aid them on a project that is behind schedule. It would, in fact, be odd to not have both kinds of respect among a community of equals. That is, respect should include both autonomy and a system of mutual obligations to share risk. In a large community, or nation numbering in the millions, taxation and redistribution are the most plausible of ways to organize such a system of mutual obligations. Otteson would encode the first kind of respect into law, and leave the other kind of respect for people or communities to take or leave as they see fit.

These different kinds of respect also show up in the way we think about property. Otteson argues that respect for property entails very limited redistribution. If we think of property rights as reflecting a natural pre-government set of moral obligations to respect others' autonomy, this makes sense. In this view, redistribution is a violation of respect for rights: people create, earn, contract, and accumulate, and then the government comes along after the fact to rearrange everyone's stuff. On the other hand, if we think respect entails basic mutual obligations to other people's material well-being, then the justified claims to property are based not just on individual choices and agreements, but also needs and collective claims. A minimal liberal order that focuses only on maximal individual property protection seems like an arbitrary imposition of walls in the middle of what was held in common.

Both of these views of property are simplistic. In fact, property rights are always determined by social arrangements, sometimes in arbitrary ways. What you consider to be arbitrary, though, depends on some basic account of justice. As Scanlon (2018, chap. 7) helpfully notes, in this debate, we have to consider not only what just action within a system looks like, but also what a just system itself entails. We can put aside, therefore, a concern for second-guessing people's decisions. After a brief transition, all contracts, agreements, plans for the future, and choices about vocation would be made assuming the system of taxation and redistribution that we enact. There is no reason why two individuals cannot take a progressive tax system into account when deciding how to split the gains from a joint enterprise. Absent a really invasive state, therefore, a system of redistribution can respect autonomy free choices while also reflecting people's obligations to other citizens.

3.3   Beneficence and the Poor

The last difficulty with Otteson's proposal is that he does not answer a particularly important and difficult question. He argues that liberal order with a minimal state will ultimately be the best for the poor. In one sense, Otteson is right. Overall prosperity, over the long run, has accompanied liberalization. But there is no such empirical or historic justification for the belief that the poor will not, at times, be left behind. Market economies do not guarantee universal increasing opulence. In the 50 years after Smith wrote the wealth of nations, literacy and social mobility actually declined for people in England (Sanderson 1972). I have already argued that we see something analogous today. Social mobility has declined, standards of living are stagnant for the poor, and the prices of some essential goods have increased. This is the hard question for Otteson: what if the market economy does not provide adequate opportunities for the poor? It is perfectly plausible that for the next 100 years, the real opportunities for the poor in rich countries will continue to decline. In such a world, if we did not have Medicaid, what is the poor person with cancer supposed to do?

Even more seriously, Otteson's account does not deal with the problem of economic opportunity. There is no allowance for the possibility of poverty traps of any kind. There is no reason why governments would want to invest in economic mobility or safety nets. There is no allowance for the fact that a child born into some poor households would need a heroic amount of talent and virtue to become even moderately well off. What of the child whose opportunities are permanently hampered without public education?

There are, it seems to me, two options for Otteson within his framework. First, fall back on charity. As I have noted already, though, charitable organizations are not likely to cover the need. Only extraordinary optimism about human generosity would lead one to believe that health coverage would be offered to even half the population that could not afford it. For every person admitted to St. Jude's Children's Hospital (which does not bill patients), there would be a number of other people without a community willing or able to support their health care or their education.

The second option is simply to argue that such situations are tragic but not unjust. More people will go without food and medicine, but that outcome is just because the process through which health care and food are distributed is procedurally fair. In this view, it doesn't really matter if people actually do end up giving to charity, or if people get adequate food and medicine, from the point of view of the state. What matters is that people are free to choose, individually, how much they want to help those who are poor. The tragedy of deprivation is the fault of a lack of generosity by the wealthy, the fault of the poor themselves, or no person's fault, like bad weather.

I don't think either of these are good responses, so let me finish by offering a kind of technocratic compromise. If we place a high value on people being free to voluntarily give to aid those in need, and if we also believe that there is a strong moral duty for people to do so, could we still support a government-funded welfare state? I think that we could. Consider the fact that, in the United States, money donated to any nonprofit is tax exempt. There are restrictions on these exemptions, but we could make them more generous. If all charitable donations were fully tax-deductible for all taxes, and we impose a progressive income tax, what we are effectively doing is levying extra taxes only on those who earn large amounts of money and do not support those in need. This system allows a person to choose a charity that they could verify was highly effective in addressing the harm that matters most. It would also, of course, allow people to give money to vanity projects, but that seems a small price to pay for a vibrant charitable sector. If the duty to help those with great need is real, then failing to do so should at least weaken one's moral claim to your wealth, and make the progressive taxation, to fund welfare state programs, less objectionable.

This section defends the justice of redistribution in more abstract terms. How we respect individuals and their choices depends on the account of justice that we start with. Similarly, the account of justice also determines what property claims are justified. When we begin with a reasonable account of distributive justice, redistribution can be perfectly consistent with equal respect for people's choices. The section ends with skepticism about the voluntary charity alternative to redistribution offered by Otteson.

4 Conclusion

Otteson's argument is both pragmatic and theoretical. He argues that there is no need to redistribute, that redistribution does not work well as policy, and that doing so often imposes a different kind of injustice. In contrast, I have argued that there are important basic needs that the market is not meeting, that there is no good evidence that the market or charity will meet these needs in the event of an absent government, that at least some social welfare programs have done a good job meeting these needs and expanding opportunity, and that this is all consistent with a theory of justice that prioritizes investing in each person's opportunity to fully participate in economic life. Each of Otteson's arguments is important, and while on balance I disagree with each conclusion, there is a way in which we fundamentally agree. We are both aiming for a free and prosperous society, and we are both working in the liberal tradition, embracing democratic government and market exchange. Hopefully we have illustrated the wide and productive disagreement that can happen within that tradition.

By adopting a classic formulation of liberal thought, Otteson echoes Rawls, arguing that what we need is a system that protects and respects "each individual's maximal scope of individual liberty that is compatible with the same scope of liberty that everyone else enjoys" (p. 10). Clearly, though, Otteson and Rawls do not agree. Their disagreement lies in the definition of liberty. Otteson places freedom from government intervention at the heart of his account of liberty, Rawls, and I, in contrast, place some weight on people's ability to participate in political and economic life, particularly where economic need poses a constraint. My argument is more modest than that of Rawls, and more modest than that of most egalitarians. We don't need to aim for full economic equality in order to justify redistribution. We only need to recognize that there are essential needs that the market will not meet, and basic opportunities that the market will not create. So, instead, I argue that we should respect each individual's maximal scope of liberty that is compatible with the opportunity for everyone to fully participate in economic and political life. It just doesn't make sense to try to build a system that is procedurally free, but that locks some people out, and to then call that system just.

Chapter 4

Difficulties with the Wealth Redistribution Argument
Reply to Steven McMullen

James R. Otteson

Contents

1 Introduction

Steven McMullen is to be commended for his careful and thorough examination of issues at stake in a moral reevaluation of the cases for and against wealth redistribution. It turns out that his argument and mine overlap at several places. In my opening essay, I gave reasons to question both the feasibility and morality of government-directed involuntary wealth redistribution, so I will not recapitulate my argument or revisit the general issue of whether wealth redistribution is a good idea or not.

In this response, I will instead focus on weaknesses in McMullen's argument, particularly places where it suffers from inconclusiveness. McMullen focuses on the obstacles facing poorer parts of the American populace, and he and I agree about many of the instances he

DOI: 10.4324/9780367854263-6

enumerates. Poverty negatively affects people's prospects for a flourishing life in many ways, and thus it is rightly a matter of concern for any just and humane society.[1] McMullen provides an important service by articulating many of the difficulties, challenges, and obstacles poverty creates on the path to human betterment. The main problem with McMullen's argument, then, is not in his concern for the poor, which he and I share; it is instead that the evidence he marshals does not suffice to support his conclusion that government wealth redistribution is required or should be expected to solve the problems poverty creates. Poverty is an ongoing concern, but it is not yet clear that government wealth redistribution is its answer.

This response will take the following steps. First, I will argue that McMullen's basic argument suffers from a logical problem. Second, I will argue that, while many of the problems McMullen articulates with poverty today are indeed real problems, he has not demonstrated that they are problems that government wealth distribution will predictably solve; indeed, some such problems are ones that government redistribution might exacerbate. Third, I will argue that McMullen's neglect to consider several economic concerns weakens his case. Fourth and finally, I will suggest that he overlooks a central moral worry about government wealth redistribution.

2   The Logic of McMullen's Basic Argument

McMullen states his basic argument in the form of three premises and a conclusion (p. 4), and we should thank him for this clear and forthright presentation of his argument in the form of a syllogism. Unfortunately, however, the argument is logically invalid. In logic, the term *valid* applies to the structure of an argument: an argument is valid if and only if the truth of its premises entails or guarantees the truth of its conclusion. That is, if it is the case that *if* the premises are true, then the conclusion *must* also be true, then the argument is logically valid. By contrast, if it could be the case that each of the premises is true while the conclusion is still false, then the argument is *invalid* (even if the conclusion itself is true).[2]

---

1. As I argue in Otteson 2019a.
2. By contrast, a *sound* argument is one that both is valid and has true premises. An evaluation of an argument hence proceeds according to the following steps. First,

This appears to be the case with McMullen's argument: even if we grant each of his premises, the conclusion does not logically follow. Let me elaborate.

McMullen's Premise 1 is: "To meet the demands of distributive justice, we must work to build a legal and economic structure that grants each person the opportunity to participate in and contribute to economic life" (p. 4). Note that this premise begins with assuming the truth of a specific kind of justice—namely, "**distributive**"—which is itself one of the central elements at issue in the debate about wealth redistribution. Assuming it in his first premise therefore begs a very large question. Because, however, McMullen offers reasons to accept his conception of distributive justice—reasons we review below—for the moment, let us grant this premise.

McMullen's Premise 2 states: "In the contemporary United States, basic opportunity is limited by poverty, inequality, and a history of racial oppression" (p. 4). As I argue in the next section, it turns out that McMullen's argument for this premise depends not on the distributive conception of justice he asserts but instead on the **compensatory** conception I defended in my opening essay. That notwithstanding, however, the claim that "basic opportunity is limited by poverty" seems right, so let us also grant Premise 2 for the sake of argument.

Premise 3 is: "There are at least some redistributive government programs that, if expanded, would increase the opportunity to participate and contribute to economic life" (p. 4). Reviewing McMullen's defense of this premise, I do not think he has provided sufficient reason to believe it is true. It might be true, but he has not shown it to be so, and there is reason to doubt it (which I address below). The larger problem with this premise, however, can be seen more clearly by looking at the conclusion he draws from all three

---

we determine whether the truth of the premises entails or guarantees the truth of the conclusion (regardless of whether the premises are in fact true). If not, the argument is *invalid*, and our evaluation of it is complete; we need not consider it further. If so, however, then the argument is *valid*, and we proceed to the second step of determining whether the premises are in fact true. If any of the premises is not true, then our evaluation is again complete and we need not consider it further: the argument is *valid* but *unsound*. If, however, the argument is valid and all its premises are true, then we have a *sound* argument. In that case, the argument commands assent.

premises. So, let us again grant this premise for the time being, and turn to his conclusion.

McMullen's conclusion from these three premises is: "The U.S. government should expand the redistribution in those ways that will expand opportunity." Unfortunately, even if this conclusion is true, it does not follow from the premises (even if we stipulate the three premises). For consider: might there be ways of promoting people's "opportunity to participate in and contribute to economic life" *other than* through government? Other than through the U.S. *federal* government? Even if some programs in the U.S. federal government can contribute toward this goal (as Premise 3 holds), might there be other ways of doing it even better (more efficiently, more morally, more humanely, with greater likelihood of success, and so on)? Absent from McMullen's argument is examination of alternative potential ways to achieve his goals (even granting those goals), including private charity or philanthropy, personal or private group initiative, civic social groups, local or state governments, business activity or entrepreneurship, and so on. Without examining such alternatives, we cannot conclude that we should endorse only action by the U.S. federal government.

Moreover, it is not clear what reason we have to think that resources redirected to government agencies in the ways McMullen recommends would (a) actually be allocated in the ways he wants and (b) actually have the beneficial consequences he anticipates. Given that the U.S. federal government already has numerous programs, offices, agencies, departments, and bureaus dedicated explicitly to exactly the aims McMullen champions; given that the U.S. federal government already spends trillions of dollars annually on such programs (as of 2014, the U.S. federal government had spent a total of approximately $22 trillion on anti-poverty programs[3]); and given what McMullen himself acknowledges is its nonetheless depressingly checkered success: what reason do we have to believe that the next round of programs or the next increase in expenditures will fare any better or will this time achieve what the previous attempts have not?

---

3. See Sheffield and Rector 2014.

2.1   Public Choice and the "Knave Principle"

Because McMullen has not reviewed alternative potential means of achieving the goals articulated in his basic argument, his conclusion is unsupported. Yet let us not rest with a claim of logical invalidity. There is reason to question whether McMullen's advocacy of federal government spending as a means to achieve his goal will actually succeed.

> David Hume (1711–1776), author of *A Treatise of Human Nature* (1739–1740), was one of the great 'skeptical' empirical philosophers. He was a key figure in the Scottish Enlightenment and a close friend of Adam Smith.

When reviewing any government policy proposal, I suggest that we should bear in mind what I call the **Knave Principle**, drawn from philosopher David Hume (1711–1776). Hume writes: "It is, therefore, a just *political* maxim, *that every man must be supposed a knave*" (Hume 1985 [1741], p. 42; italics in the original). As Hume explains, we do not assume this maxim because we believe that everyone is in fact a "knave"—a word that for Hume had a far more negative connotation than it does today, something like a wickedly dishonest scoundrel—but rather for a different, and subtler, reason. Hume argues that all of us have some element of knavery in us, but in our private dealings, our tendency toward knavery is checked. If we indulge it too much, others will dissociate from us; we will lose friends, partners, and associates; we may be unhappy in friendship and love as much as in business or our professional lives. For that reason, we are incentivized to constrain our knavish tendencies and to summon our more generous and humane tendencies.

In politics, however, things are very different, because there we have fewer checks on our knavery. In political life, most of the people who would be subjected to our knavery—the other citizens of our country—are unknown to us, and they individually have little or no recourse if we harm, impose unwelcome costs on, or disappoint them. Hume writes that in private life, "Honour is a great check upon mankind"; in public life, however, where a considerable body of men act together, this check is, in a great measure removed; since a man is sure to be approved of by his own party, for what promotes [his party's] common interest; and he soon learns to despise the clamours of adversaries.

(ibid., 43)

In the past several decades, there has been considerable empirical study and corroboration of the phenomenon Hume articulated some 270 years ago. The subdiscipline of economics now known as "**public choice**" began by asking whether the people who serve in government are similar to those who do not. Discussions of public service (note the term) had long assumed that people in government were more moral—less self-interested, less averse to self-sacrifice for the common good, and more benevolent—than the common run of humankind, and often that they were in addition less biased, possessed of greater knowledge, and so on. If that were true, however, how could we explain the corruption, exploitation, waste, malfeasance, and worse that we so routinely see in government?[4] What if, by contrast (the public choice economists asked), we instead began with the assumption that government officials were not more moral and more rational than others, but rather that they were approximately the same as everyone else, with the same motivations, biases, and so on that characterize humans in other walks of life?[5]

On this latter assumption, we can explain a great deal more of what we in fact observe in government than we can by the alternative assumption that people in public service are unusually moral and rational. If we assume that people in government are, like everyone else, just people, then we should expect that their actions, decisions, and choices would reflect the same motivations and biases that everyone else's actions, decisions, and choices would. If they are not saints and possess no superhuman wisdom, then perhaps that explains why they often seek to benefit themselves or their friends, instead of the society in general; why they often abuse

---

4. See, for example, Schuck 2014. See also Tullock et al. 2002; Simmons 2011; and Acemoglu and Robinson 2012 and 2019.
5. Nobel laureate Richard Thaler catalogues and discusses many of the cognitive biases to which humans are prone in Thaler 2015. See also Ariely 2008 and 2010; and Kahneman 2011.

the power of their offices; why they make so many mistakes, even in apparently good faith; and so on.

The economic school of public choice has been so successful in its application of this assumption that it has led to Nobel prize winners (James Buchanan in 1986) and a now decades-long dedicated peer-reviewed academic journal (called, appropriately enough, *Public Choice*). The upshot of its work that is most relevant here is this: when recommending new or expanded government agencies to address a problem facing society, we should assume not that it will be staffed and administrated by abnormally moral and wise beings, but instead by normal, imperfect human beings. Would we still make our recommendation based on that assumption?

In fact, things could be even worse. Another Nobel laureate, Friedrich Hayek (1899–1992), argued that the people who come to power in politics tend in fact to be even worse than the average run of humanity.[6] The reason, he argued, is that in order to climb the political ladder, people frequently have to be willing to do things they would not do in private associations, including lying, advocating extreme positions, and acting aggressively and sometimes ruthlessly toward adversaries.[7] And they must also be willing to superintend the private activities of their fellow citizens. These are things that most people recoil at. But not everyone recoils at such things—some positively embrace them—and those who do not recoil at them are often the ones who tend to be attracted to and succeed in politics. As Lord Acton (1834–1902) wrote, however, "power tends to corrupt and absolute power corrupts absolutely."[8] The more power such people get, the more they tend to abuse it—and their success in politics may depend in large part on their willingness to use, and even abuse, power. Of course, there have been political leaders who served selflessly and beneficially and who did not abuse their powers, but they are rare. Cincinnatus (ca. 519–430 BC) and Washington (1732–1799), for example, are venerated in part because they were exceptions who seem to prove the rule.

---

6. See Hayek 2007 (1944), chap. 10. Plato made a similar argument in his *Republic*, where he catalogued successive corrupted forms of government as increasingly worse people got in charge; see Plato 1992, bk. 8. I thank an anonymous reviewer for helpful discussion of this point.
7. For more recent discussion of and evidence for this claim, see Sunstein 2011.
8. See Acton 1986 (1887), p. 383.

So, Hayek asks: who is likelier to staff and administrate government agencies? Is it the more moral and generous souls humanity
has to offer, or the less? There seems reason to suppose the latter, not
the former, and a review of the actual character types who occupy
higher offices in politics would seem to provide corroborating evidence. But that means that if we were to recommend government
programs and authorities that could succeed only if the former type
administrated them, then we are constructing an argument that is
premised on an unrealizable ideal: the goals we champion could be
achieved only if the people administrating the required government
agencies possessed attributes they are unlikely to possess.

That is the upshot of Hume's Knave Principle. As mentioned,
Hume does not advocate it because he believes that all people in
politics are in fact knaves. Rather, he advocates the Knave Principle
because by assuming it, we can discipline ourselves to consider the
not unlikely possibility that they *might* be knaves—and thereby
protect ourselves against becoming the victims of political opera-
tors who abuse the power we granted them. If we accept the claim
that there are at least some knaves in all walks of life, as surely
there are, then perhaps we can find ways to corral their potentially
destructive effects by limiting and directing their scope. Because we
know that at least some knaves will find their way into politics
and government—and even, if knaves are positively attracted to the
alluring mechanisms and possibilities that politics and government
offer, a disproportionate proportion of people in politics and government may turn out to be knaves—then we should expect that the
powers and authorities governments possess will often not be put to
the good ends we might ideally wish they would be.

One might object that if there are knaves in every walk of life,
then that would include, for example, in business. CEOs have considerable power, and they can, and sometimes do, wield it detrimen-
tally.[9] So, why, one might ask, should we trust businesspeople or
markets more than government or its agents? In fact, we should be
skeptical and wary of both. The difference, however, is that badly
behaving business leaders do not have coercive power: they can-

---

9. See Anderson 2017. See also Babiak et al. 2010, which claims to find evidence that
   the incidence of psychopathy among corporate executives is over three times as high
   as in the general population.

not make anyone work for them, they cannot prevent anyone from leaving their firms, and they cannot make anyone buy from them or employ their services.[10] Government agents, by contrast, do have coercive powers. So, knaves are always bad, but in politics, they are bad *with power over others*. If only for self-defense, then, and to limit the damage that knaves can wreak in our lives, we should scrutinize the powers and authorities we cede to government agencies. The practical way to do that is to discipline ourselves to grant only those powers and authorities that we believe would yield positive benefit, not if they were wielded by wise saints, but even if they were wielded by knaves.

This discussion suggests that we should temper our confidence that the government agencies McMullen wishes to empower and fund to achieve his goal of enhanced "opportunity to fully participate in economic life" would in fact achieve that end, even granting the attractiveness of the goal. It might also provide some explanation for why the numerous governmental programs already in existence, and the trillions of dollars the government has provided them in funding, has not already solved, or arguably even ameliorated, the problems of poverty McMullen describes.

That it is *possible* that they *might* achieve that end is thus not sufficient. One would instead have to demonstrate that it is *probable* that they *would* achieve that end.[11] McMullen's argument takes a form approximating what economist Harold Demsetz (1969) calls the "nirvana approach" to public policy: subjecting actually existing political or economic situations to searching scrutiny, but then leaving one's own ideal vision of politics or economics as an unexamined nirvana. Just as in engineering almost every goal is easier to

10. G. K. Chesterton wrote: "Very little is left free in the modern world; but private buying and selling are still supposed to be free; and indeed still are free; if anyone has a will enough to use his freedom. Children may be driven by force to a particular school. Men may be driven by force away from a public-house. All sorts of people for all sorts of new and nonsensical reasons, may be driven by force to a prison. But nobody is yet driven by force to a particular shop" (1926, pp. 89–90).

11. Even showing that it is probable that beneficial effects would ensue is not yet sufficient. Because we have limited resources, one would have to show that the proposed policy would lead to better effects than other available alternatives. I return to this issue below, in the section "Good Is Not Good Enough."

achieve if we assume away friction, however, and just as in economics almost every case is easier to make if we assume away transaction costs, so also in political economy almost every case is easier to make if we assume a nirvana government.[12] In all three cases, the assumed conditions do not actually obtain, so a nirvana approach renders their recommendations otiose.

McMullen's argument thus faces two obstacles. First, because there plausibly are means of achieving its stated goals other than what McMullen suggests—alternatives he does not investigate—his conclusion does not logically follow. Second, we have little reason to believe his policy prescriptions would actually achieve the goals he imputes to them.

2.2 What Remains

If McMullen's basic argument is invalid, and if its conclusion is based on dubious assumptions, then why, one might wonder, should one continue reviewing it? Yet perhaps there are other parts of McMullen's larger argument that are worthy of consideration. Perhaps the reasons he offers to support his conception of distributive justice render it more plausible than alternative conceptions of justice; perhaps the evidence he adduces that poverty, inequality, and racial oppression unfairly limit people's opportunity are plausible and thus require consideration; and, more generally, perhaps finding ways to expand economic opportunity is an important and laudable political goal that we should pursue. Perhaps a proposed system of political economy worthy of moral support should include these aims and, hence, merit examination. The arguments and evidence McMullen offers are in fact plausible and his goals are in fact laudable. They therefore do merit examination.

In the remainder of this response, then, let us examine McMullen's argument for each of these claims. We will discover that McMullen vacillates between two different, and incompatible, conceptions of justice as he develops his argument, and that the strongest parts of his argument implicitly rely not on his suggested "distributive" conception of justice but, rather, on the "compensatory" conception

---

12. See also Munger 2014, which discusses the notion of what he calls "unicorn governance."

of justice for which I argued in my opening essay. We will also see that the policies McMullen recommends that are aimed at increasing economic opportunity for the poor are unlikely to achieve that worthy goal. Finally, we will find that McMullen's argument is inconsistent with a foundational moral principle that any morally acceptable political-economic regime should recognize and protect.

> McMullen's basic argument in favor of government wealth redistribution is logically invalid because its premises, even if true, do not entail its conclusion. But there are reasons to be skeptical of his premises as well. The economic field of public choice, and David Hume's "knave principle," give reasons to doubt that government agents would be motivated in the ways required for McMullen's recommended government programs to succeed.

3   Economics and Justice

In my opening essay, I argued for a compensatory conception of justice that required refraining from injuring the persons, the property and possessions, or the voluntary promises of others; punishing transgressions against person, property, and promise; and requiring transgressors to rectify or compensate (hence its name) for their injustice. Because compensatory justice primarily involves restraint, I called it "negative." I argued for this conception for a number of reasons, including: (1) it squares with our intuitions about what injustice is and what should be done when a person commits an injustice; (2) it would not itself occasion further injustice by, for example, punishing innocents, requiring people to compensate for injustices they did not commit, or providing benefit to people against whom no injustice had been committed; and (3) it turns out empirically that this conception of justice is a core pillar of the public institutions required to enable widespread, growing prosperity.

McMullen, by contrast, begins his argument by assuming a different conception of justice, which he calls "distributive," and which he defines as "the domain of justice that pertains to the right distribution of material wealth across a population" (p. 7). A distributive conception of justice takes a broad look at society, identifies the many areas and ways in which society fails to achieve one's imagined ideal, and thence undertakes to articulate the tasks and authorities required to reorganize society so that it will achieve, or make sufficient progress toward, the ideal. This is a time-honored approach favored by many theorists and philosophers.[13]

Adam Smith characterized a political type he called a "man of system," who "is apt to be very wise in his own conceit; and is often so enamoured with the supposed beauty of his ideal plan of government, that he cannot suffer the smallest deviation of any part of it" (Smith 1982 [1759], pp. 233–4). According to Smith, this "man of system":

> seems to imagine that he can arrange the different members of a great society with as much ease as the hand arranges the different pieces upon a chess-board. He does not consider that the pieces upon the chess-board have no other principle of motion besides that which the hand impresses upon them; but that, in the great chess-board of human society, every single piece has a principle of motion of its own, altogether different from that which the legislature might chuse to impress upon it.
>
> (ibid., 234)

Smith goes on to argue that the impulse of the "man of system" to impose his vision of society

> is to erect his own judgment into the supreme standard of right and wrong. It is to fancy himself the only wise and worthy man in the commonwealth, and that his fellow-citizens should accommodate themselves to him and not he to them.
>
> (ibid.)

Although we can all likely call to mind theorists and political leaders who fit this description—people, that is, who overestimate their own wisdom and knowledge, and underestimate the wisdom, knowledge, and capacities of their fellow citizens—nonetheless, the gravamen of Smith's argument lies in the man of system's disrespect

---

13. This approach to politics goes back at least as far as Plato, who argues that philosopher-kings are required to superintend the ideally good society; see book 7 of his *Republic*. See also Gaus 2016.

of his fellow citizens. They are not, in fact, mere chess pieces that we are entitled to move around in society; they are moral agents who are capable of making decisions, evaluating and responding to incentives, and constructing rational plans for their lives. For the theorist or political leader, therefore, to recommend governmental action in the service of his or her "ideal plan of government" that would entail mandated rearranging of the people of society, along with their property and possessions, is not only to disrespect their inherent dignity as full and equal moral agents, but it is also to falsely imagine that they are mere pawns fit to be reconfigured to suit one's own vision and aims.

How does this relate to McMullen's argument for government wealth redistribution and to his conception of distributive justice? If we begin with an assumption of **equal moral agency** for all people, then we are led to a default principle of respecting people and their choices, even when we do not agree with them and even if we think alternative choices might lead to benefit either for them or for others. Because all people are moral agents equal in dignity to us, our first principle of association should be to respect them and their choices, and to trust that they have reasons for what they do, even when we do not know what those reasons are. Proposals to depart from this default principle—what I would call, following Buchanan (1989), a "relatively absolute absolute"—would then have to meet a high justificatory burden. It would require demonstrating not only that some beneficial end could thereby ensue but also (1) that the proposed benefit would *likely* ensue and (2) that the proposed departure is required by concerns of sufficient weight to warrant violating what is otherwise a foundational premise of human morality—namely, the default prohibition against overriding people's voluntary choices or forcing them to behave in ways they do not wish to.

McMullen enumerates several cases in which he believes such overriding is justified, including cases in which one person or party has injured or harmed another person or party: enslavement, for example; the stealing of others' land; and the legal denial of some people's, or some groups', freedom to trade, work, partner, or transact. On the compensatory conception of justice, all of these are straightforward cases of unjust action, and all are therefore cases in which public policy should punish the transgressors, prevent such transgressions from recurring, and require transgressors to indemnify their victims. To make these claims, however, one must rely not on a distributive conception of justice but, instead, on a compensatory conception. Wrongful acts like slavery, theft, appropriation, colonization, and so on could be unequivocally condemned only on a strict compensatory "negative" conception of justice. On a distributional conception, one must instead withhold condemnation of slavery, theft, appropriation, colonization, and so on until one has determined whether their resulting reallocations of land, property, and wealth comport with one's preferred overall signature of wealth distribution.

We can therefore infer from McMullen's condemnation of slavery, appropriation, and so on that, in these cases at least, he relies not on his distributive conception of justice but instead on the compensatory conception of justice. But then McMullen returns to the distributive conception when it suits his other aims. And these aims too are noble. He shows that poverty limits opportunity, for example, because of its deleterious effects in education, in nutrition, and in health care, and he argues that alleviation of poverty could mitigate each of these deficiencies. I join him in believing that poverty has these deleterious effects, and in believing that focusing on the disease of poverty rather than on its unfortunate symptoms stands the best chance of yielding real, long-term improvement in the lives of the poor. In later sections, I will examine whether McMullen's specific proposals are likely to have the desired effects he believes they will. Here, however, let us focus on McMullen's use of justice in his overall argument.

3.1 The Distributive Referee

As I have indicated, McMullen vacillates between the compensatory and distributive conceptions of justice. Deploying different conceptions of justice in different cases is not necessarily a problem, if there is reason in different kinds of cases to treat them differently. And there is a longstanding tradition in philosophy of distinguishing different conceptions of justice, including the compensatory (or "commutative") conception for which I have argued and the distributive conception for which McMullen has argued.

Yet the two conceptions seem to be mutually incompatible. The "negative" compensatory conception calls for action only when someone has already committed an injustice (or, perhaps, when someone is imminently about to commit an injustice). In the absence of unjust action, the compensatory conception is inactive.

Compensatory justice thus serves as something like a referee in a basketball game: when someone commits a foul, the referee must take action to punish the foul; when no fouls are committed, the referee acts merely as an interested bystander and observer of the game. In no case, however, should the referee proactively interfere in the game in order to steer the contest's result in some specific direction that the referee prefers. Indeed, if the referee even *has* a preferred outcome, then that typically counts as a disqualification even to serve as a referee.

By contrast, the distributive conception of justice asks the referee not to call and punish fouls but instead to develop antecedently a preferred outcome of the game and then to enforce play so that it achieves that outcome. The distributive referee wants one team to win and the other to lose, perhaps because the referee believes that one team has won too many times and so the other team should, out of fairness, get a chance to win; or perhaps the referee believes that all players on the team should get playing time, not just the players the coach designates as starters and inserts as back-ups. Whatever the reason—whether good or bad, reasonable or unreasonable—the referee cannot both be a compensatory referee and a distributive referee. To whatever extent the referee engages in distributive activity, to that same extent the referee is negating the compensatory activity.

This is important for the following reason: if one subscribes to the distributive conception of justice, then one can no longer rely on the compensatory conception of justice in those cases in which it seems most apt. If, for example, one were to argue that reparations are owed to Native Americans because their land was stolen by European settlers, or to black Americans because of America's sordid legacy of slavery, one would then rightly invoke a compensatory conception of justice to support one's argument: injustice was committed, and the committers of injustice must therefore be punished or prevailed upon to compensate their victims. If, however, one subscribes instead to a distributive conception of justice, then one could not simply condemn the wrong acts against Native Americans and black Americans outright. Instead, one would have to consider the possibility that the "distribution of material wealth across a population" in light of those wrong acts was actually somehow improved. McMullen's argument thus puts him in the unenviable position of not being able to condemn those wrongful acts simply as unjust, but, rather, to consider whether the resulting reconfiguration of wealth comports with his ideal distribution. Presumably it would not, but why should we wait in the hopes that the preferred signature of wealth distribution will turn out to condemn what we already know should be condemned?

If the advocate of distributive justice were to assure us that his preferred signature of wealth distribution will in fact comport with our antecedent expectations, then that would nevertheless leave us with two remaining concerns, one philosophical and one practical. The philosophical: if one's preferred signature of wealth distribution is calibrated to eventuate in results that comport with what compensatory justice would have indicated, then that means that it is in fact compensatory, not distributive, justice that is operative. In that case, why not simply accept and employ the compensatory conception?

If the answer to that question is that the compensatory conception is not sufficiently capacious to allow the positive government intervention (even in the absence of specific injustice) otherwise desired, then that leads to the second, practical, question: How can we be sure, or even reasonably confident, that whoever administrates the relevant agencies of the government will have visions of wealth distribution that comport with that of the advocate of distributive justice—and will be properly motivated to pursue them? Why should we expect that, were the government to create new or empower existing agencies to expand its positive anti-poverty activities, they would actually effectuate a signature of wealth distribution anything like our imagined ideal? Perhaps McMullen might respond that he is merely attempting to show what justice would require ideally, whether or not it could be implemented in practice or should be attempted in practice. Fair enough, but when he goes on to suggest specific policy proposals that issue from his ideal conception of distributive justice, he owes us an account of why we should reasonably expect that its implementation by policy would match the requirements of his ideal conception.

By articulating the benefits that could accrue if his recommendations were perfectly adopted and if everything else stayed the same, the advocate of distributive justice thus has unfortunately done us little good—because, of course, there is little chance either that his recommendations would be perfectly adopted or that everything else would stay the same. As Smith said, citizens have principles of motion all their own, and hence they will respond to the new programs and policies in ways that are unpredictable and unintended by the theorist. Moreover, the people running the agencies are also certain to have goals, ambitions, and visions of their own—and some of those agents might even be, as Hume warned, knaves. Is it then possible that, once the redistributive agencies and authorities are created, the redistributive activities in which they engage might actually lead, not just to signatures of wealth distribution different from and even perhaps inconsistent with the preferred outcomes, but indeed to new injustices? It does not require a long look at humanity's history, or at the cast of characters who typically line up to exercise political power, to justify a concern that their exercise of the power and discretion McMullen wants to give them might easily be put to different ends from those that he desires—and, indeed, to counterproductive or even unjust ends.[14]

Perhaps a way to reconcile the two conceptions of justice might be revealed with an analogy to golf.[15] Golfers are routinely given "handicaps," or a number of strokes subtracted from a golfer's actual strokes based on that golfer's relative ability. The better the golfer, the lower the handicap, and vice-versa. Golfers are given handicaps to equalize the relative abilities of differently skilled golfers and allow them to compete against one another. Perhaps wealth redistribution might be seen as a "handicap" given to the less advantaged in society to help them "compete" with the more advantaged in society?

A key difference between golf and wealth redistribution, however, is that the strokes awarded as handicaps in golf are not taken away from the other golfers. They are merely awarded from an unlimited supply. Wealth, by contrast, is a scarce resource, and can be awarded, or redistributed, to some only by taking it from others. So, the equalizing effect that handicaps provide in golf comes at no one else's expense, whereas the equalizing effect of wealth redistribution does come at others' expense. That means that a justification of wealth redistribution must meet a higher burden, one that would justify proactive diminishment of some people's prospects in order to bolster others' prospects. It is only because of wealth's scarcity

---

14. McMullen's discussions of European colonization and American slavery are themselves examples. See also Rummel 1996 and 2007; Bourke 1999; Courtois et al. 1999; and Pinker 2011.

15. I thank an anonymous reviewer for helpful discussion on this point.

that a question of its distribution, or redistribution, even arises: if it were unlimited, we could simply give everyone all the wealth they wanted. Because, however, the awarding of handicap strokes in golf issues from an unlimited resource, it is not applicable to wealth redistribution.

> McMullen bases his argument for wealth redistribution on a distributive conception of justice, though at crucial points in his argument he relies instead on a compensatory conception. But the two conceptions seem to be at odds. If he has in mind a third, meta-principle of justice that would enable alternately deploying the distributive and the compensatory conceptions, then he would need (1) to explain what that third conception is, (2) to provide a plausible defense of it, and (3) to explain how it reconciles the seemingly incompatible distributive and compensatory accounts. Moreover, it seems that only a compensatory account is able to condemn cases like the wrongs to Native Americans and to African Americans unequivocally.

4   Limitations on Economic Opportunity

Let us now turn to the limitations on economic opportunity that poverty imposes. McMullen writes: "Distributive justice is not just a debate about the way wealth is accumulated. It is also a debate about the availability of goods that people need" (p. 12). He writes this to support his claim that the "well-being of people matters" (ibid.). Of course, there is likely no one who believes that the well-being of people does *not* matter, but focus for a moment on the end of the second sentence quoted above, that this is "a debate about the availability of goods that people need." This way of framing the "debate" neglects to consider important economic questions about not just wealth redistribution but about wealth *production.*

Before we can redistribute wealth, or make "available" to people the goods they need, there must already exist wealth and goods to redistribute. The way to end poverty, after all, is by generating wealth—by enabling the poor to become wealthy, not by making the poor more comfortable amidst their continuing poverty. But that fact necessitates that we inquire into the nature of wealth production. What are the causes of wealth? What institutions are required to enable its creation? Some places in the world are much wealthier than others. Why? Are there lessons we can learn?

There has been substantial empirical investigation into the institutional and other conditions that have enabled wealth production, and this investigation, especially over the past 40 years or so, has become quite sophisticated—and compelling. I argued in my opening essay that this evidence has converged on a set of institutional requirements that approximate Adam Smith's recommendations of a system protecting principally three things: everyone's bodily persons, everyone's property and possessions, and everyone's voluntary promises, associations, contracts, and agreements (the "3 Ps" of justice: person, property, and promise).

Economic historian Deirdre McCloskey refers to what she calls the "Great Enrichment," and Nobel laureate economist Angus Deaton refers to what he calls the "Great Escape."[16] These terms refer to the unprecedented real increase of wealth and reduction of poverty that began approximately 200 years ago and has now generated more wealth for more people than at any other time in human history. It has now reduced the proportion of the world's population living at the level of absolute poverty to its lowest rate ever, under nine percent, and substantial empirical evidence suggests that it has both arisen and spread in close correlation with the adoption of Smith's "3 Ps" and of the connected Enlightenment ideals of individual liberty, equality before the law, and private property rights.[17] But this large and growing body of evidence has another implication: to whatever extent a country departs from or impinges on those pillars of justice, to that extent it either forgoes the greater prosperity it might otherwise have enjoyed, slows the growth of its prosperity, stagnates, or even—if the departure or impingement is sufficiently widespread or long-lasting—reverses and declines.[18]

I contend that this empirical evidence is now robust enough to justify a presumption in favor of the Smithian "3 Ps" and of those Enlightenment ideals, and thus a presumption against recommendations that propose to limit or depart from them. But perhaps

---

16. See McCloskey 2006, 2010, 2016, and 2019; and Deaton 2013.
17. See Beinhocker 2006; Rose 2011 and 2019; Phelps 2013; Pinker 2018; Rosling et al. 2018; Gwartney et al. 2019; Miller et al. 2019; and Ridley 2020.
18. See North 1981; Rosenberg and Birdzell 1986; Landes 1999; Acemoglu and Robinson 2012 and 2019; Lal 2013; and McCloskey 2021.

one is not persuaded by this evidence about the political, economic, and moral institutions that seem to be required to enable widespread, growing prosperity (including especially among the poor); or, perhaps one does not believe that wealth redistributive policies would have the negative effects this evidence suggests it would. Fair enough. But then one would owe us an explanation why. That is, one owes us a review of this evidence; an analysis of why it is not dispositive; and an argument for why one does not believe that its implication of the precariousness and historically recent appearance of wealth production is worth worrying about as one proposes to change, even marginally, the institutions that this evidence suggests are required to enable wealth production. Wealth does not simply appear; it does not spontaneously generate; it is not created in a vacuum; it has historically been both recent and rare; and its production both historically and logically precedes its redistribution. All this suggests that attention should be paid to the causes and institutional prerequisites of wealth production.

McMullen offers estimates of the direct costs of his recommended expenditures, totaling, he suggests, $276 billion for his four main initiatives (p. 59). Given that the U.S. federal government has spent, since it began its "War on Poverty" as announced by President Johnson in 1964, a total of some $28 trillion on anti-poverty measures; given that the federal government's 2020 budget was approximately $4.8 trillion, including approximately $2.975 trillion already dedicated to anti-poverty measures;[19] and given McMullen's call for government wealth redistribution on top of that, his recommendation of another $276 billion seems a rather deflating culmination of his discussion. $276 billion is a lot of money, of course, but in the days of multi-trillion-dollar federal budgets, not to mention our over $28 trillion current national debt, another $276 billion seems like small potatoes—it would represent only 5.5 percent of the 2020 budget, and less than one-tenth of what the federal government already spent just this year on anti-poverty measures. One thus cannot help but wonder why, if that is all it took, the beneficial effects McMullen predicts have not already happened.

Perhaps the answer lies in McMullen's claim that he is not aiming for a full achievement of what his conception of distributive

---

19. See Amadeo 2020.

justice would require, but instead something more modest, namely, the construction of an economic floor below which citizens would not be allowed to fall, a threshold above which we want everyone to remain whatever else is the case (p. 16). Yet arguments similar to McMullen's have been offered to justify the previous initiations and expansions of anti-poverty measures: each previous instance, the claim was that *this* program or *this* increase in spending would finally achieve the hoped-for result.[20] And yet the promise has gone unfulfilled, as McMullen himself implicitly concedes by arguing that we need yet further expanded spending. Why, then, should we have confidence that the next iteration represented by McMullen's recommended funding expansion will succeed when by his own admission all the other, and much larger and more ambitious, initiatives have failed?

Alternatively, perhaps McMullen does indeed understand the conditions required to enable wealth production, but he believes that the risk of jeopardizing them is worth the goals he has in mind. That is, perhaps he believes that the risk of becoming less wealthy and prosperous overall is worth running if we can thereby enable the poor, or at least more of the poor, to enjoy the economic opportunity that their poverty currently precludes. Before his account can be considered complete, however, and before we can assess it, he needs to show us what we are giving up to devote resources to the ends he recommends, what the opportunity cost is of doing so, and what possible unintended negative consequences there might be—and then he needs to explain why his proposals are to be recommended nonetheless. To illustrate this lacuna in McMullen's argument, let us consider what I call the "Good Is Good Enough" fallacy.[21]

4.1   Good Is Not Good Enough

McMullen lists several good ends that his proposed redistributive policies might effectuate. They can improve education, health, nutrition, and even the poor's faulty "decision-making" (p. 34), all which, McMullen claims, could enable the poor to engage more fully

20. See Haskins 2013.
21. I elaborate on this fallacy in Otteson 2021.

in the productive economy. His policies would break down institutional barriers to economic opportunity and economic mobility;
they would provide some restitution for colonial and racial injustice; they would provide basic needs of the poor, enabling them to
turn their attention to other matters required for a flourishing life of
meaning and purpose. All these seem obviously praiseworthy goals.
Yet a proposed goal's worthiness—or the benefit it might provide
if pursued—is only a necessary, but not by itself a sufficient, reason
to pursue it. We need also to know what other options to achieve
those goals are available, we need to assess those other options, and
we need to compare them with what McMullen is proposing. It is
not clear that we could evaluate one proposal without reference
and comparison with the full menu, or at least a feasible set, of
available options. A worthy proposal *all other things equal* might
not end up as a worthy proposal *all things considered*.

Because we have limited resources, we cannot simultaneously
pursue all our goals: to pursue some, we necessarily have to forgo
others. For every decision or choice we make, there is a tradeoff;
for every allocation of resources, there is an indefinitely large set of
forsaken opportunities, reflected by "**opportunity cost.**"

Opportunity cost: the cost of the most highly valued alternative that is forgone.

Because we have many goals not all of which can be pursued, we
must make choices about which to pursue based on their importance to us: more important goals should be pursued before less
important goals, more important goals should not be sacrificed for
less important goals, and some goals down our list of priorities we
will, unfortunately, be unable to pursue at all.

A consequence of this state of affairs is that we must show not
only that a prospective goal is *good* but also that it is *better than*
other alternative choices or courses of action. Thus, good, by itself, is
not yet good enough. But in order to show that a prospective goal is
better than other available alternatives, we need to know what those
alternatives are. And not just that: we need to assess their prospective
benefits, compare them with the prospective benefits of the course
of action we are contemplating, and then choose that which is likely

to lead to greater benefit. The "Good Is Good Enough" fallacy is to believe that if one has demonstrated that a prospective proposal would, or could, lead to benefit, then one has completed one's case and the argument is closed—one should therefore pursue that goal. But the case is not yet closed, because we do not yet have an accounting of the tradeoffs we would thereby have to make, of the other potential good we are forgoing, or of the opportunity cost involved. Until we have undertaken this latter crucial element of our investigation, we cannot know whether the potential good from Plan A should be pursued over the potential good from Plans B, C, D, and so on.

Exploring the potential good of alternative plans is, however, difficult and uncertain, not least because it involves hypothetical and perhaps conjectural investigation into what might be or what might have been. Partly for that reason, we often forgo that hypothetical investigation, and, once we have hit upon a course of action that we believe might produce benefit, we call an end to our investigation. That appears to be what McMullen's argument does. He outlines the potential good that might result from deploying federal funds to expand nutritional assistance, to expand health insurance coverage, to underwrite universal preschool, and to fund opportunity accounts. A critic might dispute whether those programs are in fact likely to generate the benefits McMullen alleges—there are large literatures debating such programs[22]—but even if we stipulate that McMullen's predictions are likely to ensue, we must still ask: what are we giving up if we devote some portion of our scarce resources to McMullen's recommended ends, compared to what those resources would otherwise have done or what we might otherwise have done with them?

McMullen acknowledges the problem when he writes that "the real cost of these taxes will likely be the simple opportunity cost" (p. 62), and he further claims that a "consequentialist justification of such taxes, then, would depend primarily on the positive impact of the spending they fund" (ibid.). Quite so. Yet he offers

---

22. To take the example of the federal government's Head Start program, which McMullen recommends expanding (p. 54), studies of the program's effectiveness have been mixed. A Brookings study (Bauer and Schanzenbach 2016) finds mixed but overall positive effects, as did an earlier study (Deming 2009). A more recent study, however, found "no statistically significant impacts" from Head Start (Pages et al. 2019).

no exploration of the former, which means he has not yet given an account that meets his own latter criterion. Until McMullen answers that opportunity–cost question, he has not yet completed his case, he has not yet enabled us to evaluate his recommendations, and hence we are not yet in a position to accept them.

Let me be more specific. McMullen writes: "General taxation to provide support for those who are the victims of economic misfortune, then, is a public service that can improve the ex-ante well-being of almost everyone" (p. 20). General taxation might indeed be a public service, and it is easy to imagine the benefit it could provide to victims of economic misfortune. Yet are there alternative ways to provide benefit to those victims of economic misfortune that we might also consider? Might there be other routes to pursue that could produce even greater benefit? And what might those same resources that are to be collected by general taxation have done if they were not collected by the government? Until those questions are answered, McMullen's argument is incomplete and hence inconclusive.[23]

McMullen might respond by claiming that we face uncertainty about both what unfettered markets would do and what markets constrained or regulated by governments would do; given this uncertainty, and given the urgent demands of poverty, it is better to take at least *some* well-intentioned government action rather than to do nothing. Thus, he might claim that, even if my argument shows that his case is inconclusive, nevertheless, it does not show that a market alternative would fare better. I have claimed that there is in fact empirical evidence, as well as theoretical analysis, that supports my position over McMullen's. But here I am content to rest with the more limited claim that McMullen owes us an examination of other

---

23. I note that there are numerous studies finding evidence that very different methods are more effective at helping the poor than what McMullen suggests. See, as one recent example, Lazear 2020, which analyzes data from 162 countries and concludes: "The main conclusion is that the poor, defined as having income in the lowest ten percent of a country's income distribution, do significantly better in economies with free markets, competition, and low state ownership. More impressive is that moving from a heavy emphasis on government to a free market enhances the income of the poor substantially" (1). This study argues, therefore, in essentially the opposite direction of McMullen's recommendation. See also Hoffman 2008; Deaton 2013, Phelps 2013, Hall and Lawson 2014, Pinker 2018, Rosling et al. 2018, and McCloskey 2019.

possible means of achieving his ends and a demonstration that his proposals are likelier to succeed than the alternatives.

McMullen recommends government-provided "education, training, and access to employment"; "insurance against unemployment, disability, illness, and chronic disease"; and a "strong safety net" to ensure "access to capital and financing" (p. 23). These all seem like good things; but the federal government already has numerous agencies, offices, departments, and bureaus dedicated to precisely these aims: Why are they not sufficient? Why have they not already achieved the good McMullen claims these new agencies (or new funding for existing agencies) will?

McMullen's list continues: "At minimum, then, public health programs, food stamps, shelters, and housing subsidies all fit into a category of redistribution that could be worth investing in even if they were not needed to provide longer-term economic opportunities" (p. 25). Again, the federal government currently has numerous programs dedicated to these ends, which are already funded at high levels through general taxation. Perhaps they are not yet funded at a sufficiently high level for McMullen, and his "at minimum" suggests he might have still further things in mind. But he claims that these programs are required to counteract "socially imposed barriers" that prevent the poor from fully participating in economic opportunity, and that these barriers "can be partially remedied by targeted redistribution" (p. 26). He goes on to argue that these barriers place the poor in a position of "precarity" (p. 27): because the poor have fewer reserve resources on which to call in times of need or emergency, their life prospects are more precarious than are the life prospects of the wealthy, who do have reserve resources. He adds: "This precarity is borne disproportionately, moreover, by the young" (p. 27). He is surely right. Note, however, the qualified language McMullen uses: redistribution "*could be* worth investing in"; the social barriers "*can* be *partially* remedied." Perhaps it could and perhaps it (partially) can. But what reason do we have to believe it *will*—especially without reviewing the required tradeoffs or opportunity cost, and without reviewing other possible alternative means to these ends?

4.2   Economic Burdens on the Young

McMullen rightly worries not just about the poor but the young poor, and he argues that the social barriers preventing the poor from rising out of poverty visit their baleful effects particularly on the young—who, after all, are brought into circumstances without their choosing, who hence bear no responsibility for their unfortunate conditions, and who, because of their youth, have limited means to improve their situations.

I argued in my opening essay that the United States has made significant progress in addressing absolute poverty and, particularly, the young in absolute poverty. There is more good news to report: according to the United States Census Bureau, in the 52 years from 1967 to 2019, average income per household member in the United States increased in real (inflation-adjusted) terms by 86.5 percent. The official poverty rate has now declined for the fifth consecutive year, reaching 10.5 percent in 2019, its lowest level in 60 years; and the official poverty rate for children (under age 18) decreased to 14.4 percent, its lowest level in 45 years.[24] Even that good news overstates the levels of poverty, however, because the Census Bureau's official poverty rates do not take into account government in-kind transfers, welfare benefits, reduced and free lunches for children, and so on. Once we take those into account, Meyer et al. (2019) claim that "our best estimate of the extreme poverty rate 'defined as living on less than $2/person/day' is 0.24 percent among households and 0.11 percent among individuals" (1); astonishingly, they find that "after implementing all adjustments, no Survey of Income and Program Participation-interviewed households with children have incomes below $2/person/day" (38)—meaning that there are effectively *no* children in absolute, or "extreme," poverty in the United States today.[25]

These facts support the claim that we are making and have made substantial and unprecedented progress in eradicating extreme poverty in the United States, which means that it is now, thankfully, less of a problem for redistribution to address than ever before. Although we have not yet completely eradicated poverty in the

---

24. Semega et al. 2020.
25. Even including these government transfers still overstates the level of poverty in the U.S., because it does not account for voluntary charitable contributions. As I noted in my opening essay, Americans are remarkably generous: in 2018 (the latest year for which data is available as of this writing), Americans gave an all-time high of $428 billion to charitable causes (Giving USA 2019)—or some 55 percent *more* than the additional $276 billion McMullen claims is required to meet his "minimum" standard.

United States, we have decreased the proportion of people in states of extreme poverty precarity to almost zero. This is great good news, but it further weakens the case for initiating new or expanded funding for addressing extreme poverty in the United States.[26]

In addition to the claim that the circumstances of poverty are particularly punishing and inhumane to children and can exacerbate the young poor's precariousness, McMullen also implicitly invokes the further claim that it is wrong for innocents to suffer through no fault of their own. Such a claim would be an implication of the equal moral agency principle and of the compensatory conception of justice I argued it entailed. If it is wrong for innocents to suffer through no fault of their own, and wrong for them to suffer as a result of unjust actions undertaken by others, then it is also wrong for them to be burdened or punished by the consequences of others' actions over which they themselves had no control. A striking example of such a wrong that McMullen does not explore, however, is our public debt.

As of this writing, the U.S. federal government has a public national debt of approximately $28.4 trillion. The current gross domestic product of the United States is approximately $22.1 trillion, which means that the federal government's current national debt is approximately 30 percent higher than its entire GDP and constitutes approximately $86,000 for every man, woman, and child in America—including every *poor* man, woman, and child. Our debt is rising quickly—the federal government is currently running a budget deficit of over $3.6 trillion, and it is rising[27]—but those numbers, as large as they are, do not include "off budget" liabilities from mandatory spending programs like Social Security,

---

26. McMullen might claim that because these low poverty rates include government transfers, that provides evidence of the effectiveness, or even necessity, of government redistribution. Because a substantial amount of such government redistribution already takes place in the United States, arriving at an accurate picture of poverty in the U.S. requires considering its effects as well. But such redistribution depends on prior or antecedent production of wealth—wealth must first be created before it can be redistributed—which would not only return us to the issues of production and the institutions that enable and encourage it, but it would also further attenuate the case for *new* or *expanded* government programs.

27. Indeed, it is rising so quickly that these numbers will doubtless be far out of date by the time you read this.

Medicare, and Medicaid. Attempting to calculate a full estimate of the federal government's total indebtedness, which would include those "off budget" programs, is difficult, however, because it requires estimates of population growth, longevity, and other factors that are difficult to predict with precision. Yet, using generally accepted accounting principles, as well as conservative estimates of population growth, longevity expectations, and future payouts, a full estimate of the federal government's current indebtedness rises to a staggering $155 trillion, or approximately $470,000 per American. What this means is that Americans have provided enormous benefits to themselves at the expense of future taxpayers—at the expense of those too young to vote or not yet even alive.

That debt will eventually have to be paid by someone, although we often seem to act as if that were not true. A child born today thus faces, before she takes even her first breath, an obligation to pay nearly half a million dollars in other people's debts, for benefits she herself will not receive, and for which she was neither asked permission nor consulted. And this includes every poor child born in America. Americans fought a revolution partly in opposition to what was considered an unjust principle of "taxation without representation." Our government's indebtedness constitutes a massive—indeed, in real, inflation-adjusted terms, a historically unprecedented—wealth transfer from the young and unborn to the currently alive and voting, a "taxation without representation" on a scale never before seen in the entire history of humanity. If one is concerned about disproportionately burdensome weights placed on the poor, and if these burdens fall particularly upon the young poor, then proposing to add yet more financial burden on them would require demonstration that the benefits to them of the programs and increased spending would not be outweighed by the burdens of debt they already face and now would face in addition. Given the enormous amounts involved, that would seem an extraordinarily difficult case to make.

But McMullen does not attempt to make the case. Like many others, he passes over it in silence. Yet closing our eyes to this massive burden does not make it go away.[28] Indeed, it has been precisely

---

28. I note that enriching ourselves at others' unwilling expense would constitute a straightforward injustice on the compensatory account of justice, in the same way that theft, involuntary appropriation, and so on are.

the act of closing our eyes and pretending it does not exist, and our willingness—even, apparently, our eagerness—to benefit ourselves at the expense of our children and grandchildren, of our young and of our unborn, that has allowed it to grow to such almost incomprehensible levels. Proposing to add yet more to this burden requires, therefore, more than a simple aversion of the eyes.

> Before wealth can be redistributed, it must first be produced. Thus, an account of the institutional and other requirements of wealth production must precede and inform any discussion of wealth redistribution. McMullen's claim that another proportionately small increase in current government expenditures could provide benefit does not explain why previous similar, and much larger, expenditures have failed, and it falls prey to the "Good Is Good Enough" fallacy. McMullen's rightful concern with the precarity of the young poor should also consider the enormous debt existing and expanding government programs have accumulated and will visit on the young, including the poor young.

5 The Seen and the Unseen in Redistribution

The 19th-century French political economist Frédéric Bastiat (1801–1850) published a book in 1850 with the title, *What Is Seen and What Is Not Seen*. In it, he argued that the "bad economist" is the one who looks only at the immediately visible effects of an economic transaction or policy but ignores its long-term effects and its opportunity cost, which often need to be foreseen or imagined and are hence difficult to apprehend because they are "unseen." The "good economist," by contrast, is the one who refrains from endorsing a proposed transaction or policy until a good-faith effort is made to assess both the short- and long-term likely effects, as well as the costs, including opportunity costs.

To illustrate his argument, Bastiat offered the now famous example of a broken window. Bastiat's story is of a shopkeeper whose son throws a rock at the window of the shop, breaking it. The shopkeeper is dismayed, but some observers suggest that the breaking of the window is actually something to welcome, because it will lead to economic productivity. After all, a glazier will now get some business—replacing the shopkeeper's window—that the glazier otherwise would not have gotten, which is good for the glazier and, potentially, for the economy generally. So, Bastiat asks whether destruction, despite what we might initially have thought, can actually be productive.

Frédéric Bastiat (1801–1850), author of *The Law* (1850) and *What Is Seen and What Is Unseen* (1850), was a French parliamentarian and political economist. His "broken window" example is credited with formulating the concept of opportunity cost.

Bastiat's answer is no. The appearance of economic benefit arises from looking only at the glazier, whose benefit is "seen." But the appearance is specious because it disregards what Bastiat calls the "unseen." The "unseen" is what the shopkeeper would otherwise have done with the money he now must spend on the window. Bastiat speculates that the shopkeeper had instead wanted to spend that money on either a new pair of shoes or on some books. What is unseen, then, is the value to the shopkeeper of the shoes or books, which he now has to forgo, because the broken window forces him to spend that money on the window instead. The cost of the broken window, then, is not just the money required to replace it, but also the "unseen" lost value of the forgone shoes or books. Once that lost value is reckoned, however, Bastiat argues that destruction is not productive after all. If the shopkeeper had valued a new window more than the shoes or books, he would have already decided to buy a new window before his son threw the rock breaking his existing window. Because, however, he had instead decided to buy shoes or books, that means he must have valued the shoes or books more than he valued a new window.

So, the shopkeeper experiences a loss from the breaking of his window. But what about the economy generally? Does it matter from the perspective of the economy as a whole whether money goes to a glazier, a cobbler, or a bookseller? Yes, it turns out it does matter, which can be seen by distinguishing between "flow" and "stock." It is true that whether a given amount of money goes to a glazier, a cobbler, or a bookseller, it is still flowing to one of them, and so from the perspective of "flow," it makes no difference. Whether a given amount of water, for example, goes into a bucket, a pothole, or a pool, it is still the same amount of water and it is still flowing. But consider instead the "stock," or the overall assets present in an economy or available to society. If the shopkeeper's window had not been broken, the shopkeeper would have had not only the window but also (say) a pair of shoes. Once it was broken, however, he has only the new window. Thus, the breaking of the window has reduced the overall stock of assets in society by one pair of shoes. Because he never actually bought that pair of shoes, however, it is "unseen," and hence easy to forget or neglect. But the unbought shoes are no less a loss for being unconsidered. It represents a loss, and cost, both to the shopkeeper *and* to society. The "broken window fallacy," then, is to believe that destruction can lead to net gain—when, in fact, it leads to net loss. We should hence not go around breaking windows on the theory that we are helping society, even if it is true that we would be helping the local glazier.

One of the claims Bastiat makes that is particularly relevant for our discussion of wealth redistribution is that in the case of the broken window, we might mistakenly believe that only two parties are involved in the transaction—the shopkeeper and the glazier. In fact, there are three parties involved: the shopkeeper, the glazier, *and the cobbler.* The cobbler represents the person who would have received business, and benefit, from the shopkeeper, but who now loses that business and benefit because of the window's having been broken. Because that cobbler never actually received that business—and may not even have known he stood to receive it—it is unrealized, "unseen," and thus typically left out of the accounting. But the fact that we do not pay attention to that loss, or even that the cobbler was unaware of the potential business he did not receive, does not mean the loss is not real. It represents the value of what the shopkeeper's money would otherwise have done, had his window not been broken, and it is thus a loss to the shopkeeper, to the cobbler, and to society.

Who is the "unseen" third person whose interests are not considered in discussions of wealth redistribution?[29] We know who

---

29. William Graham Sumner 1992 (1883) famously calls this person "the forgotten man."

the "seen" parties are: the citizens (current and future) who are taxed to fund the redistribution, and the citizens who are the beneficiaries of the redistributed wealth. A proper cost–benefit analysis begins with estimating the costs to the former and the benefits to the latter, as McMullen has done in making his case for his recommended programs of redistribution. But that is only the first step. The next step is to estimate the lost value to others who would otherwise have been beneficiaries of the taxed citizen's wealth, had it not been redirected. What benefit would that wealth otherwise have created? In whose lives would it otherwise have had an effect? Some of that wealth might have gone to unproductive, perhaps even counterproductive ends; but some of it would have gone to productive, beneficial ends. In the full analysis, would that wealth on balance have been better spent by the taxpaying citizens themselves, or by the government? Two things are important to keep in mind when contemplating this latter question. First, it is an important question: we simply cannot know whether any proposed redistribution of wealth will ultimately be beneficial until we have answered that question. But second, whichever way we are inclined to answer it—whether we are inclined to think it would be better spent by the taxpayers or by the government—the conclusion cannot be merely assumed: it must be demonstrated.

Thus, when reviewing a list of potentially beneficial ends to which redistributed wealth might be allocated, we cannot rely on an only partial reckoning of the benefits and costs. We instead must consider all three parties to the transactions, namely: (1) the would-be beneficiaries, (2) the would-be benefactors, *and* (3) the would-have-been beneficiaries who will now lose the benefit they otherwise stood to receive. Any proposal for mandated wealth redistribution is not complete, and hence has not yet risen to a level enabling evaluation, until it has provided a good-faith attempt at a complete accounting of all these costs and benefits.

But this is required not only because it is the only way to enable us to assess the proposal, but also because policies regarding wealth distribution affect the lives of real human beings. These are not merely academic exercises. People's lives are affected by the political-economic policies their countries adopt, and a historical survey of different systems of political economy provides plentiful examples and evidence that the wrong kinds of systems and policies can and do have deleterious effects on their citizens' ability to prosper, to construct flourishing lives of meaning and purpose, and, in some cases, even to survive. That raises the stakes when proposing to change policies and institutions, and it means we should proceed only once we have used all the care and completeness that befits such a consequential undertaking.

Human beings have, as Smith said, "principles of motion all their own." If we are proposing to take wealth away from them, or to give wealth to them, or to create programs to attend to, train, educate, nurture, or incentivize them—in other words, if we are proposing to introduce ourselves into and alter the directions of their lives away from what they otherwise would have pursued or to override the choices and preferences they otherwise would have made or had—then we need to have a clear and compelling reason to do so, which must include a full accounting of not just the likely benefits but also all the likely costs. Thus, the burden of proof shifts to the person proposing such intervention to offer a complete and sufficiently weighty justification.

The most obvious cases that would satisfy such stringent conditions include punishments for injustice, understood as the infliction of harm or injury on others, as the compensatory conception of justice holds. But proposing to rearrange the signature of wealth and possessions that people in one's community have, beyond rectification for injustice any of them might have committed, involves interposing oneself, or one's agents or delegates, into the lives of otherwise innocent others—which would seem prima facie to constitute a rights violation. Perhaps sometimes rights should be violated, but only with both a due acknowledgment of the violation and a compelling moral justification for doing so.

I have argued that such proposals must therefore meet a high justificatory burden. But here is a specific minimum threshold I would offer as a standard: putting aside cases of unjust harm or injury, an involuntary redistribution of citizens' wealth and possessions is justifiable only if one has demonstrated, with reasonable and probable certainty, that the resulting redistribution will be of net or general benefit. That is: if the benefit accruing to the intended beneficiaries outweighs the cost or loss to those who are taxed *and* the resulting tradeoffs and opportunity cost *and* the cost to the "unseen" others who otherwise stood to benefit—then, at that point, we have a proposal that is complete, and hence worthy of consideration. But not until then.

Bastiat's broken window fallacy illustrates the necessity of considering the "unseen" opportunity cost attendant on any allocation of resources. Even if government programs of wealth redistribution can lead to benefit, before endorsing them, we must demonstrate that they would lead to greater benefit than the benefit of the "unseen" forgone uses to which those resources might otherwise be put.

6 Conclusion

I have claimed that the conclusions of Professor McMullen's argument are not supported by his premises, and that his argument regarding the benefits of government redistribution is inconclusive because it is incomplete. Quite apart from whether the argument I laid out in my own opening essay is sound, McMullen's argument for his position fails to give us sufficient reason to accept it.

Let me now conclude with a final point, which was intimated by the discussion that closed the previous section. The central foundational moral premise on which I built the argument in my opening essay was what I referred to as the "equal moral agency principle." As I suggested, that principle is based on a belief in the inherent dignity, preciousness, and worth of every human being, a dignity that arises in virtue of their essence as rational and autonomous agents who are therefore also moral agents responsible for their choices and accountable for them both to themselves and to others.[30] I further argued that each of us possesses this dignity equally, which therefore implies that we are *equal moral agents*. From this, I concluded that we are morally obligated to respect each other's dignity and agency, which requires a presumptive recognition of and respect for their choices, even when we disagree with those choices or believe they are mistaken. Unless others are undertaking to cause harm or injury to unwilling others—that is, unless they are undertaking, or have undertaken, to commit injustice—our default

---

30. I believe people's dignity arises because they are made in the image and likeness of God, and thus that their equal moral agency entails that they are also accountable to God, but one need not endorse those claims to accept the argument here.

principle should be to refrain from interfering with or preventing their peaceful, voluntary actions, choices, and decisions. I called that the "equal moral agency principle," and I claimed that it is the foundation of a morally acceptable liberal social order.

At the end of the previous section, I offered a threshold that any proposed involuntary redistribution of wealth should meet before it warranted consideration—namely, that it be demonstrated to lead to net benefit, once all costs and all affected persons' interests were fully appraised. But I offered that as only a "minimum threshold," that is, a standard that must be met before we even consider the proposal. Meeting that threshold means that a proposal has provided a complete account of itself, which we require before we can evaluate it. That threshold is therefore necessary, but it is not yet sufficient to warrant assent. Because any such proposal would entail interfering in the lives of innocent others—that is, others who have not committed, or been demonstrated to have committed, harm or injury or injustice against others—it would entail violating the principle of equal moral agency. I believe, on both practical and principled grounds, that we should be sufficiently wary of violating such a fundamental principle that we should closely scrutinize any proposal to do so, and that in most cases, we should end up rejecting it. What might those few cases be, those exceptions to an otherwise foundational rule, when we should *not* reject it?

Vilfredo Pareto (1848–1923) was an Italian engineer and economist. He is credited with formulating the concept of Pareto efficiency, a key element in microeconomics.

Here, I would suggest a further criterion, adapted from a central principle of economics. Economists routinely adopt and apply a standard attributed to the Italian economist Vilfredo Pareto (1848–1923), a standard often called "Pareto optimality" (or "Pareto efficiency"). Pareto optimality identifies an end-point distribution beyond which it is no longer possible to make any one person better off without thereby making someone else worse off. The implied Paretian standard is: we may make distributions, or redistributions, only when we can make at least one person better off while at the same time not thereby making anyone else worse off. There are technical aspects of this standard that make it a challenge to apply in practice, but these technical details are not necessary for us to explore in order to see the import of Pareto optimality here.[31] My suggested use of the Paretian standard would imply a two-step process of evaluation for any proposed involuntary redistribution of wealth or possessions.

Step One would be the full accounting of likely benefits and likely costs discussed earlier, which would include tradeoffs and opportunity cost. Once that (surprisingly difficult) step is completed, we come to Step Two, where we ask: would the proposed redistribution benefit at least some without thereby making any worse off? We are contemplating only cases in which those who would be made worse off are not suffering by consequence of having committed prior injustice, in which case compensatory justice requires punishment or compensation, as appropriate. In other words, we are contemplating only those cases in which the potentially negatively affected persons have not themselves committed injustice.[32] In such

---

31. Some of these challenges are meant to be addressed by, for example, the Kaldor-Hicks amendment to Pareto optimality, which allows for changes if those who gain can, at least hypothetically or in principle, compensate any losers.

32. This qualification allows us to sidestep various species of what I call Original Sin claims, which would include claims that if anyone among one's forebears committed a sin (or injustice), therefore one is also oneself guilty. (Because likely all people have at least someone among their forebears who committed injustice, by this reasoning we would all be guilty from birth; hence the name "Original Sin.") If I stole from you, then I owe you compensation for my injustice. If I stole from you and gave the stolen loot to my children, then I still owe you compensation, even if that means I must take it back from my children. The number of generations down through which compensation is owed, and the duration of time after the initial act of injustice during which compensation can reasonably be expected, is limited, however, by two main considerations: first, the moral agency of new individuals uninvolved in the commission of the injustice (my children, your children, our respective grandchildren, and so on) enters and alters the situation, and their innocence and lack of involvement diminishes both responsibility and entitlement; and second, because those uninvolved others use their agency to respond to their respective situations in new ways, attempts to wind back the clock and imagine what might have been, had the injustice not occurred, become difficult to estimate and increasingly conjectural (as McMullen acknowledges: he writes that it "may be impossible" and "will inevitably be arbitrary" [p. 48]). These two considerations do not mean that no injustice occurred, and they do not mean that no one who was not

cases, my suggestion is that we should consider endorsing proposals for involuntary redistribution only when we have demonstrated that at least one party benefits while no innocent party suffers.

Now, McMullen argues that, owing to the principle of diminishing marginal utility, the next dollar to a wealthy person means less to her than the next dollar means to a poor person (p. 15). A millionaire might hardly notice the loss of, say, $100, but a poor person's life might be measurably and significantly benefited by that same $100. For that reason, McMullen might argue that we can make such transfers while still adhering to the spirit, if not the letter, of the Paretian standard. But recall that the Paretian standard applies—as, indeed, distributive justice requires—to the overall distribution of wealth and possessions in society, not just to individual spot-transactions. And McMullen is calling for wealth redistribution via general taxation, which would apply to undifferentiated groups of people, not to specifically identified persons. That means he would have to show that, even if we grant the principle of diminishing marginal utility, the overall post-redistribution signature of wealth represents a Pareto improvement over the overall pre-redistribution signature.

McMullen has not shown that, but, to be fair, how could he? To do so, he would have to estimate the value to each of the taxed individuals of the amount taxed, including the value to the "unseen" others who might have been beneficiaries of the taxed citizens' wealth; he would then have to estimate the value to each beneficiary of the wealth transferred to each; and then he would have to compare the two—while somehow overcoming the notorious difficulties involved with making intersubjective comparisons of utility.[33]

---

directly involved did not benefit or suffer; they mean only that the practical difficulties of properly adjudicating injustice and required compensation rapidly become intractable over time and run the not insubstantial risk of perpetrating new injustices by punishing innocents, benefiting unwronged, or both. An old adage has it that "justice delayed is justice denied." There is wisdom in that, but it suggests that we must be vigilant in punishing injustice quickly, or we rapidly lose our chance. Statutes of limitation are commonsense responses to this unfortunate reality, but the punishment for the injustice of even murder, which has no statute of limitation, ends with the death of the murderer and is not visited upon the murderer's progeny. For differing views, see Coates 2014 and 2015; and Baptist 2016.

33. McMullen briefly notes these difficulties on p. 15.

Because utility is not a discrete entity that can be weighed or gauged—it is not like marbles that can be counted or water whose volume can be measured—it is not clear how we could show that a reduction or increase in value to one person is measurable against, or even comparable to, reductions or increases in value to others. (The claim that a millionaire would not value $100 as much as a poor person is merely an assumption; it might be true, but it has not been demonstrated to be true, and it is not even clear exactly how it could be demonstrated.[34]) So, McMullen could not reasonably be expected to demonstrate that his post-redistribution signature of wealth is Pareto-superior to the pre-redistribution signature. But if we grant his argument this indulgence, the unfortunate result for his conclusion is that it no longer has an argument to support it.

The goals McMullen articulates are, as I stated at the outset of this response essay and have reiterated throughout, good ones that I share. Poverty remains one of the tragic afflicters of human life, and material poverty generates deleterious consequences beyond just the material, including in psychological and even spiritual ways—and those deleterious effects can propagate down through generations. It is therefore eminently worthy of attention and of serious and concerted study and effort to eradicate. In just the last couple of centuries or so, we have finally, and fortunately, discovered means of generating wealth and thus reducing poverty to levels and at rates never before seen in human history. Despite the over seven-fold increase in worldwide population since 1800, we have reduced the proportion of human beings living at the levels of

---

34. Relatedly, studies that purport to show the diminishing marginal utility of getting richer are based on individuals' evaluations of their own situations and utility (the so-called Easterlin Paradox; see Easterlin 1974). That is, they attempt to ascertain of specific individuals how much happier more money would make them, and whether there is some point at which their happiness plateaus or even diminishes with further increases in wealth. Some such studies claim that there is a limit to how far happiness correlates with increasing wealth. But those studies do not show whether the effect of an increase or decrease in wealth to *one* person's happiness corresponds to, or even relates to, the effects of similar increases or decreases to *different* people's happiness. In any case, more recent studies contest the claim and find evidence that self-reported happiness does indeed increase with increasing wealth. For review and discussion of these studies, see, for example, Kahneman and Deaton 2010; Graham 2011; and Stevenson and Wolfers 2013.

absolute poverty from over 90 percent to below 9 percent. I have argued that the principal causes of this recent, anomalous, and spectacular achievement were the spread of protections of Smith's "3 Ps" of justice—protections of persons, property, and promises—and of Enlightenment ideals of individual liberty and equality before the law. Wealth redistribution has been tried numerous times, across the millennia and in hundreds of human communities, and has yet to prove significantly beneficial.[35] Yet what *has* worked is protection of Smith's "3 Ps" and what Smith calls "the obvious and simple system of natural liberty" (Smith 1981 [1776], p. 687).

On the basis of this evidence and in light of the foregoing argument, then, I offer the following recommendations: Respect all people's persons, respect all people's property and possessions, and respect and enforce all people's voluntary partnerships, contracts, associations, agreements, and promises—and then stand back and watch them improve their lives all on their own. As history and observation have shown, wealth and prosperity will then increase, creating more resources with which each of us can then apply our own time, talent, and treasure to help those who need it, in ways that our own local knowledge can give us confidence that our help will indeed be beneficial and will reduce the risk of unintended negative consequences, of waste and loss, or of unexpected counterproductive outcomes. In other words, as we develop surplus wealth, we are not only enabled but also called to deploy that surplus in ways that benefit not just ourselves but others as well—what the Catholic Church calls the "universal destination of goods," and what Adam Smith calls the "becoming use" of our resources.[36]

We must remember, however, that poverty is as often the result of bad policies as it is of anything else.[37] We should hence first undertake to remove such policies, and disabuse ourselves of viewing the poor as if they were the moral equivalent of chess pieces fitted for benevolent manipulation or machines subject to engineering experiments. The Hippocratic Oath for physicians applies also to eco-

---

35. See Scheidel 2017 for a comprehensive historical review. See also Chandy et al. 2015; Davies 2019; and McCloskey 2019.
36. See *Catechism of the Catholic Church*, §§2403–2404; and Smith 1982 (1759), p. 270.
37. See Easterly 2006, 2008, and 2013; Birdsall 2008; and Coyne 2013.

nomic policy and poverty relief: first, do no harm. Thus, before we start thinking about all the good things we might do *for* the poor, we should first stop doing all the bad things we already do *to* them. We should then have faith in their ability to improve their own lives and expect that they will immediately begin to do so. They are full moral agents, equal in that respect and hence in human dignity to everyone else. Thus, we should enforce and recognize for them the protections and freedoms we ourselves want and enjoy.

We then have an additional moral obligation: we are called to provide our own help to those who need it, joining in partnership with others in ways that, based on our personal knowledge, we can be reasonably confident would actually constitute help. We will not be perfectly successful, but perfection is not a reasonable expectation or standard for imperfect human beings. The enduring scarcity of our resources, the limits of our knowledge, and our self-interest and limited generosity all combine to entail that perfection will not ever be achieved in this world. What we can hope for, however, is improvement. As our wealth and resources increase, we have greater capacity to improve our own and others' situations, and thus our personal moral obligations to do so increase commensurately. Thus, we can and should help those who need our help, both personally and in partnership with others, and we should trust that the poor can and then will use their freedom and security to improve their conditions, as poor people the world over who, when once given the opportunity, have done.

Second Round of Replies

Chapter 5

Distributive Justice, Economic Growth, and the Welfare State

Reply to Otteson's Reply

Steven McMullen

Contents

I Introduction

I have argued that poverty, inequality, and social exclusion are substantial problems, and that they are systemic problems. That is, poverty is not just an individual phenomenon that results from people making particular choices. It is also a problem that results from the rules and institutions that define our economic system. Even more, I have argued that it would be unjust to ignore this element of our economic system, and even worse to exacerbate it. James Otteson has offered a number of objections to my initial case for further redistribution, many of which are helpful and clarifying. It is my belief, however, that all of the major elements of my argument are still justified. This final response is necessarily shorter than the previous chapters, so I will not be able to respond to all of Otteson's arguments or questions. I can respond to most of his major concerns, though, and offer a somewhat clarified argument here.

As I have noted in other parts of this book, there are at least two dimensions in which Otteson and I disagree. First, we disagree on the nature of justice. In the first chapter, I summarize a number of different accounts of justice, not as a blanket endorsement, but only

DOI: 10.4324/9780367854263-8

to note that there are a lot of different ways to think about distributive justice. While these different accounts are incompatible in many ways, many of these accounts of justice can, in practice, justify the kind of proposal I am making. The point here is only that we can disagree somewhat about distributive justice, but may still agree about the kinds of changes we should make to economic policy. In fact, the goals of distributive justice that I support are really somewhat minimal: I argue that each person in society should have the opportunity to participate in economic life in a few essential ways. Otteson does not disagree with this goal, but he does disagree with this as a standard for justice. I will try to clarify our disagreement here and defend my account of distributive justice in Section 5.3.

The more substantial disagreement, in my view, is the more pragmatic question: can redistribution work? This is more substantial in part because, in Otteson's moral framework, one needs a really good reason to redistribute wealth. If the welfare state is highly effective, it might constitute a really good reason. Otteson, however, has argued that redistribution only undermines the one real path out of poverty, which is to embrace a minimal liberal economic order. The evidence on this point, though, is quite clear, as I have already argued at some length. It is quite possible to enjoy the benefits of economic freedom while also having some targeted and generous redistribution. This redistribution can have quite a big impact on the lives of those who are poor. Otteson raises a number of questions about my proposal, though, and in responding to these, in Section 5.4, I will demonstrate that the pragmatic case for expanded redistribution in the contemporary United States is quite strong.

In short, I think we are arguing about two big questions. *What does justice require?* and *Will redistribution help?* Before I delve into these larger issues, though, in the next section, I will take some time to briefly address the places where Otteson questions the structure of my argument and the kind of burden of proof he sets out for a proposal. I will try not to spend too much time on these procedural arguments though, as it seems to me that our end-goal is to allow the reader to engage with the framework and evidence we offer, and then hopefully think more clearly about these hard questions themselves.

2 Argument and Justification

This debate format is excellent in many ways, but given the magnitude of the topic we have decided to consider, it is impossible to do justice to the many lines of argument that might come up. As such,

I left some gaps in my original argument, deciding to pursue only those areas that seemed most consequential for people who wrestle with questions of redistribution. Otteson rightly points out that the overall structure of my argument, then, is not ultimately conclusive. That is, even if you accept all of my premises, there are multiple logically valid conclusions. Put into normal language, there are actually a number of different ways we could pursue justice as I have outlined it. My proposal is but one. Given this, I should have probably offered a simple outline of my argument instead of framing it as a syllogism. I think it should have been clear to all readers, however, that the argument was not intended as a logical proof.

Otteson's response brings to light an important part of my argument, however. I am actually not firmly committed to this specific policy proposal. I cannot hold any specific policy too dear, because I am firmly committed to crafting policy that will do the most to achieve the goals of justice. As a result, I must always be open to new evidence that there might be a better way to do things. How then, should we think about my proposal to expand food assistance, public health insurance, preschool, and to create savings accounts for children? Only that these are the best examples, in my view, of policy changes that would make our system more just, in the contemporary United States, based on the best evidence I can find right now. Since each one clearly involves redistribution, if you agree that policy changes of this kind are justified, you too are embracing redistribution.

Since these policies are not the only possible way to pursue justice, though, Otteson need only offer a different proposal, one that better pursues this account of justice, perhaps without redistribution, and I would be forced to agree with him. That would not be enough to defend his case, though. For him to argue against redistribution, from the premises I have defended, we must have a reason to believe that redistribution will actually limit economic opportunity, and that current programs should be reduced, if not eliminated.

This brings me to the second procedural note in response to Otteson. A number of his arguments seem to depend on there being a really high burden of proof for my proposal. That is, he argues in a couple of places that I have not shown that there is not another way for the government to achieve the same ends. That, of course, would be difficult to demonstrate, given my insistence that we rely on good empirical evidence. I cannot rule out all possible alternatives, because we don't have really good evidence about all alternatives. However, I have argued in some depth that Otteson's alternative, at least, would make these problems worse. The competitive market system that we are operating in is, in many cases, part of the reason for the economic exclusion that is unjust. Given the inability of the private sector, or charitable sector, to make progress on these problems in the United States over the past 40 years, and the relative success of redistributive programs, the path forward seems clear.

Otteson also notes that because people's lives depend on these policies, and that this "raises the stakes when proposing to change policies and institutions, and it means we should proceed only once we have used all the care and completeness that befits such a consequential undertaking" (p. 178). I gladly accept this standard, which is why I have offered multiple peer-reviewed evaluations of each of the programs I aim to alter, and have considered the effects of the associated taxation, and the unintended impacts on the labor market. In the section below, I will further clarify some of the open questions Otteson raises. Compare this with what we have in Otteson's proposal. His principles would eliminate a wide swath of health and education programs, and dramatically change people's income. He does not even detail these changes, however, much less consider the effects on specific populations. I would like to humbly suggest that we must use similar "care and completeness" before walking down the path Otteson seems to prefer.

> In this section, I contend that any major policy change should be subject to careful scrutiny with the best empirical evidence we have. This policy evaluation evidence should then dictate what form redistribution takes, since distributive justice can be achieved in multiple ways.

3   What Are We Aiming for?

While debates about distribution often hinge on economic and policy questions, it is important to start with a clear sense of what we are aiming for. Redistribution should not be arbitrary. It should be focused and purposeful. I have offered this ethical goal: that we should work toward a system in which everyone has an opportunity to participate in the economy in some fundamental ways. As I have noted, this is a pretty minimal ethical standard, and it is consistent with a number of different ways of thinking about distributive justice. This space is too short to work out the numerous interesting details or hard cases, but I believe this account stands up to the scrutiny that Otteson offers. Let me expand on this argument in two parts. First, I will try to make anew the case for this as a good standard for distributive justice. Second, I will respond to Otteson's argument for a narrower compensatory account of justice.

Otteson, along with many other critics of egalitarian ethics, is concerned that redistribution requires an arbitrary punishment of those who make wise choices or who possess a real skill for making others better off. The government, by force, takes more money from the successful and grants it to the unsuccessful. It is important to understand the real power of this argument. Some inequalities *are* morally justifiable. The person who saves scrupulously for a decade may be justifiably richer than the person who spends profligately on trivial things. Not all inequalities are justified though. I offer a long account of how poverty, inequality, and history have put some U.S. citizens in situations where they lack basic opportunities to succeed in today's economy. I will not recount all of this here, but some inequalities are the result of misfortune or good luck, and the most pernicious inequalities develop because we have a social structure that offers an easy path to success for some, while throwing numerous barriers in the path of another. It is that last reality that we must rectify. Real life is complicated, and we cannot tell an easy story about why a person or community is in poverty while their neighbors are not. As such, we must work to eliminate those sources of inequality and poverty that we know are unjust, and give some benefit of the doubt to those in the worst position. Once we have done this, then we can rightly allow differences in effort, skill, luck, and virtue to cause some to prosper more than others.

It is also important to note that this kind of "sufficientarian" or minimal "opportunity to participate" account can be justified using a number of different larger ethical theories. Those who base their egalitarian ethics on a common respect for human dignity might call for more aggressive egalitarianism, but they could still support this minimal standard. So too with utilitarian or prioritarian accounts that offer more explicit ways to adjudicate between ethical claims to wealth. To the extent that past injustices perpetrated by the state have resulted in limited opportunity for racial minorities in the United States, this account would go partway toward addressing those demands for compensatory justice. All this is to say, I don't think we necessarily need to agree about a particular ethical system in order to agree that redistribution is warranted in these kinds of cases. For this reason, when Otteson accuses me of jumping between incompatible theories of justice, it seems somewhat beside the point.

Moreover, the conflict between different kinds of justice claims can easily be overstated. If income or wealth is taxed, according to laws that apply to everyone, in order to pursue justice, then that taxation is just. Similarly, in such a situation, the opposing claim by the taxpayer who would otherwise have that wealth is not just. Property claims are generated by law, if those laws fit this description, then it simply is not the case that we are rearranging people's things by force. On the contrary, the government uses the threat of force only to enforce a rightful claim to that wealth. That is, this theory of justice comes prior to most property claims. We talk about distributive justice as something that happens after the fact, but in legal and ethical terms, it must come first.

Once you recognize that property claims are downstream from just laws, the contradiction that Otteson tries to force between distributive justice and compensatory justice seems somewhat artificial. There are certainly cases in which the goals of distributive justice and compensatory justice might be in tension, but only if the distributive claim is arbitrary or invalid. Moreover, there will always be inconsistencies that result from changes in law. Wealth accumulated in a prior legal framework might be taxed in a later framework. Conflicts and tensions between different ethical goals and legitimate rights claims are common, though. Often they can be resolved, but it would be odd if such conflicts never showed up in our theory of justice.

Otteson's insistence that we can pursue justice merely with an emphasis on compensatory justice, and that distributive justice should be rejected wholesale, has some difficulties. First, distributive justice cannot be escaped. Even his minimal theory of respect for persons is, the way he argues it, a theory of distributive justice. He just argues for a different distributive standard: that of pareto-improving actions, or the funding of pure public goods. This would entail a far smaller government footprint, to be sure, but even the funding of national defense, where well-justified, is a kind of coercive government action. Even this involves the use of force to involuntarily move resources from one group of citizens to another. So his argument that the government should avoid coercive appropriation of wealth is not absolute. He holds only that we need a really good reason. The only difference between this theory and the one I propose is that he does not believe generations of poverty and people dying for lack of health care are good reasons for the government to act. I do.

In short, the more minimal theory of justice that Otteson depends on is just not complete. Consider this: A world in which a few people accumulate vast fortunes, offer low wages to workers who accept because they have no better offer, and in which people live surrounded by great wealth, but without enough resources to fund even a minimal education or health care could be, in Otteson's terms, perfectly just. As long as all trades are voluntary and all wealth was legally gained, his theory would see no injustice here. Otteson is clear that he would find such a world tragic, wrong even, and that individuals would have a moral duty to respond by giving generously to those in need. But those moral claims are pretty weak, apparently, because a wealthy person who chose not to be generous would, apparently, in no way have a weaker moral claim on his/her wealth. The United States is not as bad off, clearly, as this hypothetical thought experiment, but it is an odd theory of justice that finds nothing to condemn in this picture.

> In this section, I argue that distributive justice is inescapable, and that we have to think about justice in distribution before we can really understand property rights. Because of this, thinking only in terms of compensatory justice is not an alternative to reflection about distributive justice.

4   Does Redistribution Work?

In our exchange so far, Otteson and I have both made arguments about the effectiveness of redistribution, but we are not using the same kind of evidence, or making the same kind of argument. I will try to bridge that gap here. First, I will offer a summary of the evidence that redistribution works to accomplish the goals of justice that I have laid out. Second, I will engage the alternative evidence that Otteson offers about the effectiveness of the liberal market order. The odd thing about this argument is that I agree with most of what Otteson contends, though the reverse does not seem to be true. Finally, I will consider the objections that Otteson raises regarding government debt, the production of wealth, and unseen harm.

There are two broad ways in which a redistribution program can "work." The first way is the one that is easy to observe: a program can materially improve the lives of targeted recipients in the intended ways. For the food stamps program, this would mean improving stable access to food for those with a low income. For Medicaid, the goal is to provide medical insurance for those who need it, and for those people to get better care and then have better health outcomes. For a preschool program, the goal would be to provide children pre-K education. These kinds of program outcomes are generally easy to measure using pretty standard before/after comparisons relative to a good control population. Evaluations of this kind have documented that all of these programs achieve these kinds of first-order goals, as I documented in my opening essay.[1]

The other short-term measure of success would be to alter the overall standard of living of those in need in important ways. Using the language that Otteson and I have both offered in previous chapters, I would argue that, for a welfare state to be successful, it must lower the rate of poverty using an absolute measure of some kind. I have offered the clearest evidence about this that I can, in other parts of this debate. In the United States, the welfare state and tax benefits have certainly reduced absolute poverty, at least since the 1960s. The declines in absolute poverty that Otteson and I both celebrate are largely due to a more generous welfare state, not to an increase in market incomes for the poor (Wimer et al. 2016).

The more ambitious metric for success is that a program should have a longer-lasting positive impact on the productive lives of the recipient. It is difficult for statisticians to do a good job estimating these longer-term effects, but as I have noted before, in recent years,

---

1. For those looking to dig deeper into this evidence, the most recent accessible summary of the evidence on these things is *Unbound: How Inequality Constricts Our Economy and What We Can Do about It*, by Heather Boushey (2019).

we have accumulated a considerable amount of evidence documenting substantial long-term positive effects from food stamps, Medicaid, and preschool programs. It is becoming clear that these kinds of programs, which create a stable safety net for basic goods, like food, health care, and education, are part of the recipe for an economy that gives real opportunities to those born into poverty. As I have noted, this should not constitute a blanket endorsement for any redistributive action someone might dream up, nor an endorsement of everything that the U.S. government has tried. I argue only that we have landed on some programs that really do work, and that there are obvious ways in which they should be expanded.

The only program that I advocate that does not have this track record of documented positive results is the "Baby Bonds" program that would give young people a savings account, which slowly grows, and can be used for college, housing, a retirement fund, or starting a small business. This program is a bit more speculative, but the idea grows out of a wealth of evidence and theory. Entrepreneurship is an important vehicle for economic opportunity, as are savings, asset-building, and higher education. For those families who are unable to help their children afford higher education, or get a small business started, these paths to success can be far riskier. These savings accounts could start to bridge that gap.

The evidence that I offer to support an expansion of these programs is not airtight. As with any complicated empirical claim, we need to be on the lookout for better evidence and the chance that we have been wrong. Otteson offers one study that counters one of the above claims. The Pages et al. study (2020) reported that they could not replicate the results from Deming (2009) when using some more recent data. This is certainly a point against the case for the long-run positive impacts of preschool programs. The best way to evaluate empirical evidence, however, is to look for a balance of results across different data sets, using different evaluation methods. The conclusion that Head Start has positive long-run effects is based on a number of different studies, and a rich body of theory, some of which I have cited here (Currie and Thomas, 1993; Carneiro and Ginja, 2014; Baur & Schanzenbach, 2016). While the Pages study makes me somewhat less confident in the result, readers should look at the larger literature.

It is a bit confusing, overall, to have Otteson claim that I have adopted a "Nirvana Approach" by not subjecting such proposals to scrutiny. Or that I have merely claimed it is possible that such programs might achieve my desired ends, without giving reason why it is probable that they would do so (p. 11). On the contrary, I have offered, in the course of my initial argument, at least 30 empirical studies or collections of studies that build this case of the well-documented effects of these specific policies. Despite this evidence, Otteson maintains, boldly, that "Wealth redistribution has been tried again and again, across the millennia and in hundreds, even thousands, of human communities, and has yet to prove significantly beneficial." To buttress this claim, Otteson does not cite any studies of U.S. welfare programs, except for the one study about Head Start. He does cite an interesting study by Ed Lazear (2020) that compares outcomes across countries.[2] But when you examine Lazear's analysis of wealthy countries like the United States, his findings are somewhat tepid. He finds that redistribution can increase income growth among the poor in the short run, but has no effect on the incomes of the poor in the long run. Much of the rest of Otteson's evidence is drawn from the literature on growth in the developing world, the industrial revolution, the failures of global socialism, or the more general phenomenon of government failure. All of this is interesting, but much of it is only tangentially relevant to the proposal that I make. It appears that Otteson's main point is not that these policies are bad, but that they must be bad, because they would be implemented by a government.

What is somewhat odd, in fact, is that I agree with and appreciate the vast majority of the literature that Otteson cites. History is littered with graves that testify to the evils of global communism, and foreign aid has a really mixed track record of success. However, the latest work of Acemoglu and Robinson (2020) (whom Otteson references multiple times for their seminal work on extractive government institutions) concludes that for us to preserve freedom in the midst of global markets and social power, rich countries should invest in universal safety net programs that protect citizens. Whether you agree with that argument or not, it is worth noting that it is perfectly consistent to push for economic freedom

---

2. I favor policy evaluation studies that make comparisons within countries, generally, rather than between countries. The differences between countries are so numerous, that it is really difficult to draw firm conclusions about whether specific government programs are the reason for slower or faster growth in incomes.

and market institutions, on the one hand, and also advocate for a stronger safety net. Even Hayek, no egalitarian himself, thought that a liberal order was consistent with a social insurance function for the state (1944). Moreover, most of the countries with the freest economies have more generous safety nets than the United States. It is also perfectly consistent to think that the impact of a generous welfare state would be different at different points in history, in different countries, and in different government contexts. Despite Otteson's efforts to tell a big, unified story, one cannot responsibly point to failures of government around the world, ignore the record of government successes, and then draw a conclusion about changes on the margin for welfare state policies in the United States.

Even more importantly, even a cursory look at recent U.S. history undermines Otteson's trust that a simple liberal order will provide the best results for the poor. The United States has experienced extraordinary growth over the past 50 years. On average, we are almost twice as wealthy as when my parents were young. And yet, in that time, once you take out the impact of government transfers and tax benefits, the poor have gotten somewhat poorer (Wimer et al. 2016). Perhaps the universal benefits of a liberal economy just stalled for the past 50 years? The more credible story is that while the liberal order is indeed essential for creating wealth, it does not automatically create inclusive growth in the short or medium run. Liberal market orders create opportunities, but they are also perfectly adept at working around exploitation and exclusion for a minority. We have to be intentional about creating and sustaining institutions that do not leave people behind.

In short, there is a sense in which we have talked past each other because we favor different records of evidence. I have favored peer-reviewed journal articles that evaluate the impacts of specific policies; Otteson has generally favored the writing of scholars that are trying to make sense of the big story of wealth creation and growth around the world. If we are going to hold these two bodies of evidence together, as I would like to, I submit that we must accept all four of the following conclusions:

1. Economic growth is essential for long-run gains in standards of living for everyone, including those in poverty.
2. Economic freedom is essential for long-run economic growth.

3. A well-designed welfare state can be an effective way of making sure that some of the gains from wealth creation and growth are shared with those at the margins of the economy.
4. A welfare state may slow the rate of economic growth in the long run.

I believe there is good evidence for all four of these conclusions. Notice that these four conclusions pose a trade-off and invite us to ask questions about moral priorities. I believe that a basic goal of economic justice should be to make sure that everyone has basic economic opportunities, and so I believe it is important that we accept slower growth implied by (4) in order to provide the benefits of (3). Part of this judgment, though, rests on the belief that the growth cost implied by (4) is small. I will turn to Otteson's arguments about that contention shortly. However, once economies are highly developed, they come to face the challenges related to education and technology that currently plague the United States and other rich countries. It seems likely, at this point, that the human capital gains that result from an effective welfare state can largely counteract the costs from labor supply reductions and the impact of taxes. These are things that we have evidence about, though, as I have noted. Given the long debates that we have had about the welfare state in the United States, it is notable that so little of Otteson's favored literature focuses on empirical investigations of this trade-off.

This section compares the bodies of evidence that Otteson and I bring to the debate. I argue that we can hold this evidence together by thinking of our debate as being about a trade-off between long-run growth and short-run equality, and contend that the long-run costs of a well-functioning welfare state are small.

5 Production, Debt, and Unseen Costs

There are three areas where Otteson's critique is quite specific, and each of these warrants a detailed response. First, Otteson argues that my proposal does not consider the effects of redistribution on the overall production of wealth in society. Second, Otteson notes that there is a concerning cost to the ballooning government debt in the United States. Finally, Otteson contends that we need to consider the unseen downstream economic impacts that could be cut short by redistribution. These kinds of arguments are important for justifying a policy in economic terms, and I will respond to each in turn before turning back to the broader argument.

First, we need to consider the impact that redistribution has on wealth production overall. That is, we have good reason to be concerned that both the taxes and the benefits might result in less work, risk-taking, entrepreneurship, investment in education, family formation, and all the other things that make us richer. Most of these effects are small, but economists have particularly focused on two important ways this can happen. The first is that a progressive tax code can discourage work (income tax), and investment (corporate taxes and capital gains taxes). On the benefit side, we worry that those receiving benefits will be less likely to work, or that they might work fewer hours. Readers will remember that I discussed each of these extensively in my opening argument. We have good evidence from a very wide array of studies that these concerns are real and that the effect is small. We should take even these small effects seriously, though, which is why I was careful in considering which welfare state programs to expand, and which taxes to increase. I proposed policies that take these concerns seriously and mitigate the growth-slowing effects. In particular, the preschool policy, the changes to the Supplemental Nutrition Assistance Program (SNAP), and the health care policy that I propose would all effectively reduce the penalty that those in poverty would face if they chose to work. On the tax side, I argue for a very broad, shared income tax increase, and then taxes on capital gains and estates. I will not reiterate the evidence about these specific policy choices, since Otteson does not engage them. In short, however, Otteson claims that I have not given adequate consideration to the concern that these redistributive polices might alter the conditions of wealth creation (pp. 163–66). To the contrary, I have given exactly that question considerable attention, by focusing on the specific ways in which such policies could have that effect.

The second economic concern that Otteson raises pertains to the ever-increasing federal government debt. On this, we don't have much disagreement. Economists, as a guild, have become less wary of debt in recent years, particularly when interest rates are quite low. This is not my area of expertise, but I am a bit more traditionally minded, as is Otteson. I believe that government programs should be funded by current taxation, at least over the business cycle. Our current levels of government spending are too high, and our taxes are too low. The result is a tax burden on future citizens. It is for exactly this reason that I was careful to describe the full funding mechanism for the program changes that I proposed. My proposal would not add to the government debt. As for the current deficit and accumulated debt, we could have a conversation about which areas in the government require reduction and which taxes should be raised, but I judged that a proposal for a full fiscal overhaul of the U.S. federal government was a bit ambitious even for this book.

Perhaps more importantly, it is worth remembering that a good safety net can be an investment. Medicaid is often derided by conservatives as a wasteful entitlement, but the bulk of the scholarly literature shows otherwise. The recent Medicaid expansion, because it rolled out unevenly across the country, has provided a trove of new quasi-experimental evidence in the form of hundreds of research studies. These studies show almost uniformly positive results, including expanded employment for beneficiaries (Guth et al. 2020). The longer-term effects are harder to measure, but two recent high-quality studies that measure this kind of effect are quite positive. Brown et al. (2020) found that Medicaid availability improves economic performance enough that the federal government actually gets back 58 cents for each dollar spent on the program, in the form of increased future taxes and decreased expenditures. Goodman-Bacon (2016) finds that over the long run, Medicaid actually pays for itself, and yields the government a return between two and seven percent. Otteson might not believe these studies, but even if the magnitude of these results is off, there is really good evidence that, in the United States, government provided health care, particularly for the young, can have a strong positive economic effect.

The last economic concern that Otteson raises is that this redistribution will have a large unseen opportunity cost. The heart of his argument seems to be the following: when we levy taxes to fund redistribution, there is an obvious cost to the taxpayer. There is also, however, an unseen cost to the people that would have traded with those taxpayers, and the whole sectors of the economy that they represent. Those tax dollars, if left in the private sector, would have had an impact well beyond the consumption of the taxpayer. This is economically straightforward, but not as consequential as it might seem. In terms of the overall economy, this "unseen opportunity cost" is almost perfectly balanced by a similarly unseen benefit somewhere else. The relatively rich person will spend less money, but the relatively poor person who receives the benefits—or in the case of my proposal, the grocery store, medical system, or preschool teacher—will also spend that money, but on something else. The redistribution shifts spending away from sectors supported by the relatively wealthy toward the sectors providing the goods and services given to those in need, but the overall spending is not lost.

There are two complications with this response. First, there might actually be some loss if the government acts inefficiently in the redistribution. With programs like SNAP, it is fairly easy to show that the program is run fairly efficiently. With the health care benefits, this analysis gets far more difficult and contentious. Suffice it to say, it is possible that there is some loss in the redistribution from poor administration. We should be wary of this. The second complication is ethical, and not just one of accounting. Do we have to justify a move that hurts all of the people economically downstream from the taxpayer, while helping those downstream from the recipient? Isn't this just more redistribution that is even harder to justify? Here I think we can safely put aside the concern. If I normally shop at a local bookstore, but then, one day choose to purchase new book from Amazon instead, I have just hurt the local bookstore, and helped Amazon, in some sense. The local bookstore cannot claim any real harm, though, because they had no real claim to that money. I am sure Otteson would agree. Similarly, if the government's initial redistribution is justified, we don't have to further justify the downstream effects of that redistribution, because those recipients don't have a legitimate claim to that commerce. If the redistribution were illegitimate, or if the government simply took the money and buried it in a pit, then the total harm done to the economy would include those downstream effects. Even then, the claim of harm from the taxpayer would be qualitatively different, and stronger, than the claim from their trading partners.

This section returns to the broader economic impacts of redistribution, arguing that the impact on overall productivity is small, the debt consequences are serious but manageable, and that we should think about redistribution as an investment. Other downstream effects that Otteson is concerned with are, I argue, not important.

6   Conclusion

To conclude, let us review the larger arc of this debate. I have argued that a just economy will be one in which each participant has a real opportunity to participate in some essential ways. People should have the opportunity to get enough schooling to pursue the kinds of careers that are in demand at the time. People should have access to food and medicine even in hard times. Importantly, though perhaps less obviously, people should have access to the funding and institutions that will allow them to be entrepreneurs if they have a good idea and the talent to bring it to fruition. These opportunities are sometimes lacking in contemporary United States. Poverty, inequality, and a dark history of racism have shut some people out of economic life. Children raised in poverty might not have real access to food, medicine, school, and investment. These missing opportunities have real consequences for a whole lifetime. Some will enter poverty or stay in poverty because they make really poor decisions, but everyone, even if they are not the most talented, should at least have a decent shot at leading a productive economic life. I have shown strong evidence that our social safety net has mitigated these problems over the past 50 years, but that there is more to do. A welfare state is not the entire solution, but it has to be part of it. By strategically expanding some redistributive programs that have a proven track record, we can do better.

Otteson, in contrast, has argued that justice requires that we respect individuals as moral agents by giving them wide latitude to make their own decisions and let them enjoy the resulting rewards and consequences. This, he thinks, rules out the taxation and redistribution that I favor. Moreover, he argues that the creation of a wealthy society, and the alleviation of poverty, depends on a liberal order and minimal government intervention. He argues that redistribution runs counter to this recipe for success, and thus that any welfare state actions will be counterproductive. Otteson's contributions here have forced me to reexamine my own thinking on these things, and to work to reconcile two very different accounts of justice and two different kinds of evidence about state action. For the time and effort that Otteson has given to this work, I am thankful. When judged against the status quo, his proposal really is far more ambitious than mine, and so he deserves some credit for that. In the end, though, I am convinced that the weight of evidence and reason lies on my side of the question. That judgment, however, I happily leave to our readers.

Chapter 6

How to Care for the Poor and How Not to

Reply to McMullen's Reply

James R. Otteson

Contents

1 Introduction

Despite the impression our discussion may give, Professor McMullen and I share significant agreement—perhaps even more than we disagree. Here, at the close of our debate, perhaps it is worth reflecting on, and appreciating, some points of commonality.

We both agree that alleviation of misery and suffering are, or should be, primary goals both of public institutions and of people with the means to help. We also agree that poverty is a principal source of misery and suffering, and hence that both public institutions and we as individuals should do what we can to continue the reduction of poverty.

We also agree that all human beings should be treated with dignity and respect, that we are all unique and precious, and that none

DOI: 10.4324/9780367854263-9

of us should ever be disregarded or discarded. I suspect we further agree that, because each person is an equal moral agent, it is wrong for one person or for one group to benefit at the involuntary expense of another person or group, and that a system of political economy that enabled that to happen—or, worse, encouraged it to happen—would be wrong and unjust.

We further agree that prosperity is a key to a flourishing life (it is difficult to lead a full, and fulfilling, life, if one is poor), and that, ultimately, it is prosperity that will be the antidote to poverty. I also hold, and I believe McMullen would agree, that increasing prosperity has not only material benefits, especially for the poor, but also nonmaterial benefits like liberty, independence, and security, and that prosperity can give ever more of us a chance at leading flourishing, even genuinely happy, lives.

So, where do we disagree? We disagree primarily on the proper or best means to achieve those goals. The question of proper or best means actually has two components: one, as it were, a principled consideration, the other a consequentialist consideration. The first we might call the "justice question": is it just for the government to take from some to give to others? The second we might call the "welfare question": would some benefit more from government wealth redistribution than those from whom it is taken would suffer? I argue for a lexical priority of these questions. Because human beings are equal moral agents who therefore should be treated as ends in themselves and not as mere means to others' ends, before we consider to what extent recipients of government wealth redistribution might benefit from it we first need to ask whether we have the right to take it from the (prior) possessors. If we determine that it is right to take wealth from some to give to others, or that there are at least some cases in which it can be justified, then we can ask whether doing so creates benefit for the recipients that outweighs the loss to those from whom it is taken. My argument has been that there are indeed cases in which the "justice question" can be answered in the affirmative—primarily cases in which the (prior) possessor of wealth committed some injustice or other wrongdoing and thus rightly owes compensation to the person(s) who were wronged. But the lexical priority of the "justice question" entails that we sometimes do not get to the "welfare question."

By contrast, McMullen revises his conception of justice to include, or incorporate, the "welfare question." In his response essay, he offers a new definition of justice that "prioritizes investing in each person's opportunity to fully participate in economic life" (p. 144). This definition bypasses concerns about identifying specific acts of injustice (understood as causing harm or injury to others), and it also bypasses his own conception of "distributive" justice (understood as effectuating the proper overall distribution of wealth and resources in society). Instead, it points to the fact that some people are limited, or even prevented, by economic constraints from constructing lives of meaning and purpose, and it appeals to our humanity to convince us that something should be done for people in such circumstances. In a society in which some are wealthy, even extremely wealthy, the resources to do something are available. So, McMullen argues, we should.

And indeed, we should. Here again, then, is another point of agreement. Yet several questions remain: What, exactly, should we do? Who, exactly, should do it? And how, exactly, should we do it? On these questions, McMullen's position differs from mine.

In this final response, I address these questions. I first indicate some remaining weaknesses in McMullen's argument for government wealth redistribution, including its neglect to consider alternative means of achieving the goals we agree are worthy. I also suggest what I think is the appropriate standard for evaluating potential means to these goals, and I offer some evidence that meets the standard I believe is appropriate and explain why it supports my position. I then address McMullen's new definition of justice and explain why I think it is nevertheless insufficient. I also discuss what I believe is the strongest argument for wealth redistribution. In the final section, I explain what I believe our personal moral duties are in light of the important aim of alleviating poverty.

I note that although the following discussion primarily addresses McMullen's argument, much of it applies to arguments supporting government wealth redistribution generally.

2   Debating Controversial Issues

There is always a risk in debating a controversial issue, particularly for the person defending a position that differs from the prevailing view.[1] In his 1850 *What Is Seen and What Is Not Seen,* Frédéric

---

1. For a discussion of some of the risks involved, see Otteson 2019b. See also Rothschild 2021.

Bastiat voices a sharp criticism of his intellectual opponents. He had pointed out that people who advocate for government subsidy of things like the arts often do so not only on the grounds that "the arts expand and elevate the soul of a nation and make it more poetic" (2016 [1850], p. 413), but also on the grounds that they lead to overall *economic* gain—the subsidies give employment and resources to actors and singers, painters and sculptors, theaters and opera houses, museums, and so on.

Bastiat has no argument against the former claim: if people judge that elevating the soul of a nation warrants public expenditures on the arts, he has no objection. On the other hand, he does demur from the latter argument: yes, resources would flow to these people and places and would thus benefit them, but that is the "seen" benefit. There is also, however, an "unseen" *cost*, namely, what those resources would otherwise have done had they not been redirected to these ends by the state. When these "unseen" but nevertheless real costs are reckoned, it turns out that such subsidies often do not, in fact, lead to overall economic gain. If we believe the moral, cultural, or aesthetic value of the arts is worth the cost, then Bastiat raises no opposition to subsidizing them. In that case, however, he insists that we acknowledge that we *are* paying a cost for them, not pretend that they are costless or even lead to economic gain. Reallocations, as Bastiat reminds us, are not increases.

The "unseen" cost Bastiat discusses is what economists have come to call "**opportunity cost**," and it is reflected by the most highly valued forgone alternative. When resources are expended in one direction, those same resources cannot be expended anywhere else; thus, any particular allocation entails forsaking indefinitely many alternative allocations. The first problem Bastiat points out with such arguments, then, is that they often fail to account for opportunity cost. But the second problem is that advocates for government-directed shifting of resources in directions that the (prior) possessors of those resources had not wanted them to go often fail to consider the possibility that the prior possessors might actually have *preferred* their resources to go elsewhere. If taxpayers did prefer those resources to go elsewhere—and the fact that they were not already dedicating them to, for example, the arts, suggests that they did believe their resources were otherwise better spent—then this new, and "artificial," redirection represents a loss to them. That loss is the "unseen" cost, the unseen lost value, and it is what underpins Bastiat's claim that the subsidies funded by taxation represent a net economic loss.

But to Bastiat's criticism. He asks his reader, "do you know what economists [who make arguments like Bastiat's] are accused of? It is that when we reject subsidies, we are rejecting the very thing that is to be subsidized and are the enemies of all these types of activities" (2016 [1850], p. 415). Bastiat continues: "Thus, if we demand that the State not intervene in religious matters through taxation, we are atheists [...]. If we think the State ought not to subsidize artists, we are barbarians who think that art is of no use" (ibid.). Because McMullen similarly mischaracterizes my argument, Bastiat's reply is worth quoting:

> I protest here as forcefully as I can against these deductions. Far from entertaining the absurd notion of abolishing religion, education, property, production, and the arts, when we demand that the State protect the free development of all these kinds of human activity without having them in its pay at the citizens' mutual expense, we believe on the contrary that all these life-giving forces in society would develop harmoniously under the influence of freedom, that none of them would become, as we see today, a source of unrest, abuse, tyranny, and disorder. Our adversaries believe that an activity that is neither in the pay of the State nor regulated is an activity that has been destroyed. We believe the contrary. Their faith lies in the legislator, not humanity; ours lies in humanity, not in the legislator.
>
> (2016 [1850], 415)

Similarly to Bastiat's "adversaries," McMullen claims that if one raises challenges to state-directed redistribution of wealth, one must therefore oppose "public education, or health care" (p. 124). So: "Millions of people would," on my watch, "end up going without health insurance and health care" (p. 123), and I therefore must want people not to have health insurance or health care. I must want the "homeless person [who] is brought to an emergency room for acute care" to be turned away and left to the wolves (ibid.). I must want "real standards of living [to] substantially drop," and I must desire "worse education and healthcare" (p. 124). In my "preferred world," people would be left "with no health insurance at all" (p. 137). And for the poor, I must want their "real economic opportunities [to] diminish as well" (p. 124). Against all which McMullen intones: "I am unwilling to call that world just" (ibid.).

As Bastiat explains, however, these are false deductions. Of course we all want prosperity; of course we all want people to have the health care and education they need; of course we all want people to have economic opportunity. Our question for this volume was whether government wealth redistribution could be morally justified or could serve properly moral ends. As I have reiterated, the goals of such redistribution—whether benefiting the poor, punishing injustice, or instantiating fairness, equality, or equity in society—are worthy goals that all sides endorse. The question was whether government wealth redistribution could predictably make progress toward these goals, and whether it could do so consistently with morality. I argued that there were reasons to be skeptical of both. But I also offered alternative means of making progress toward those goals that I argued could do so more predictably and more consistently with morality—which implies that I endorse the goals. McMullin's response reveals, however, that questioning either the efficacy or morality of government wealth redistribution entails for him that one must oppose its putative goals as well. Yet just as opposition to state subsidy of religion does not imply opposition to religion, pointing out difficulties with government wealth redistribution does not imply opposition to prosperity.

2.1 Reality Proves Possibility

McMullen claims that private initiative cannot provide the goods and services required to enable people, especially the poor, to lead fulfilling lives. But he underestimates what private initiative is capable of. The strongest evidence for private, as opposed to governmental, provision of goods, services, and benefits such as education, health care, job training, and so on is that *private initiative already does it*. There are private hospitals, doctors, nurses, and medical clinics; there are private primary, secondary, undergraduate, and graduate educational institutions; there are private charities giving hundreds of billions of dollars annually toward health care, education, job training, and moral, social, and spiritual development. There are millions of charities, NGOs, civic groups, religious groups, and so on, privately funded and dedicated explicitly to these worthy aims.[2] And there is much more: there are privately sponsored and regulated mutual-aid clubs and associations, funeral service providers, stock markets and exchanges, risk management assessors, security and police, contract dispute resolution and arbitration agencies, goods and services inspectors, pollution abatement programs, and so on, not to mention many other privately maintained goods and services that might surprise one, such as roads, bridges, waterways, parks, libraries, museums, theaters, opera houses, and on and on.[3] And the wealthier people become, the more they give to these and many other private initiatives that safeguard, enrich, and uplift human life.[4]

The nonprofit RIP Medical Debt, for example, buys people's medical debts and forgives them. To date, it has forgiven some $3 billion in people's medical debts.[5] In 2020, the Capitol Hill Lutheran Church in Iowa bought *all* of Iowans' medical debt—and forgave it. It now plans to do the same for Missouri.[6] Medi-Share is a voluntary Christian health care cost-sharing nonprofit. It currently has some 500,000 members who pay a monthly fee to share in and pay each other's medical bills.[7] There are many other private organizations that also help people pay their medical bills.[8] Similarly, numerous charities and for-profit companies help pay educational expenses and student debt.[9] Hundreds of nonprofits and for-profits provide college scholarships for the poor.[10] Many other examples could be adduced.

Now, they do so imperfectly, but humans are imperfect creatures and so no system or program they develop will ever be perfect.

---

2. In 2018, there were 1.54 million registered nonprofits in the United States, an increase of 4.5 percent since 2016, with some $3.8 trillion in assets; and in 2017, 25.1 percent of all American adults volunteered, contributing 8.8 billion hours of volunteer work (Urban Institute 2020). Additionally, Americans gave some $428 billion to charitable causes in 2018, over and above the time and skills they donated and after paying their taxes (Giving USA 2019).
3. See, for example, Beito 2000; Beito et al. 2002; and Stringham 2015.
4. See, for example, Brooks 2006 and 2015; and Yunus 2017.
5. See RIP Medical Debt n.d.
6. See Martin 2020.
7. See Medi-Share n.d.
8. See, for example, Amplify Credit Union 2020.
9. See, for example, Glassdoor 2020.
10. See, for example, CollegeScholarships.org n.d.

But McMullen holds private initiative to a standard of "universal" perfection, and when he finds it imperfect, as it inevitably is, he declares against it. His own recommendations, however, he holds to a much lower standard of *might be possible that it could lead to benefit*.[11] If perfection is the standard, however, then both our sets of recommendations come up short, as do all others. On the other hand, if incremental but real improvement is the goal, then the evidence suggests that private initiative has substantially more to recommend it than McMullen allows.

2.2   A New Great Society

McMullen endorses a world of welfare and benefits, a world without suffering, misery, or deprivation. His description is reminiscent of what President Lyndon Johnson stated in 1964 announcing his "Great Society" initiative: "The Great Society rests on abundance and liberty for all. It demands an end to poverty and racial injustice, to which we are totally committed in our time. [...] The Great Society is a place where every child can find knowledge to enrich his mind and to enlarge his talents."[12] In my opening and response essays, I showed that, both in the United States and in the rest of the world, absolute poverty has been on a precipitate and unprecedented decline, especially over the past 40 years. McMullen concedes that point, but he objects that the condition of the poor (if not the absolute poor, then perhaps the poor in, say, the bottom quarter of wealth in the United States) has stagnated over the past few decades. Though the situation is complicated—for example, the prices of many goods and services, including previously unavailable goods and services (smartphones, flat-screen televisions, internet access, and so on), have declined faster than inflation has risen, implying greater purchasing power even for the poor—nevertheless, the poor have not increased their welfare as much as either McMullen or I would have liked.

Yet this relative stagnation has occurred precisely during the time of massively increased wealth redistribution. The rates of poverty

---

11. The "government might end up providing" benefit (p. 137), government wealth redistribution "could be far better than the alternatives" (p. 138), and so on.
12. Johnson 1964.

in the United States were declining faster *before* the Great Society programs were initiated, and they have plateaued since.[13] And yet, Great Society programs have spent some $28 *trillion* since their inception. In other words, exactly the kinds of government wealth-redistribution programs McMullen recommends have already been in place, and have grown enormously, over the past five decades. That raises the question of whether it should give us pause in advocating more of the same.

McMullen's own Great Society can be achieved, he suggests, with slightly more wealth redistribution. Yet, why should we believe that (slightly) more of the same—just $276 billion more in federal government spending[14]—will this time achieve its promise? After surveying decades of government attempts to increase economic opportunity and spur economic growth, Pritchett and Woolcock (2008) conclude: "The old king—that agencies of the nation-state organized through a bureaucratic (in the good sense) civil service were *the* development solution, or at least, the instrument for the development solution—is dead, wounded by disappointing experience and stabbed fatally from both the political left (Scott 1998) and the political right (de Soto 2000)" (170; italics in the original).[15]

McMullen alleges that I endorse a world "without a welfare state, public education, or health care" (p. 124). Rather, I argued that because government wealth redistribution involves uninvited

---

13. "In 1950, roughly 25 percent of Americans were officially poor. By 1966, just two short years after the War on Poverty formally began, the number was down to 14.7 percent. That 10 percent drop translates into a 41 percent cut in the poverty rate—a truly amazing accomplishment. Surely, you must be thinking, Johnson's government-centered agenda was a stunning success! There's just one problem with that narrative. Almost all of the decrease in poverty took place *before* Johnson's policies went into effect. It was a vibrant economy that did the trick" (Brooks 2015, p. 60; italics in the original). Other countries have followed similar trajectories. Economic historians Ian Gazeley and Andrew Newell studied "the almost complete elimination of absolute poverty among working households in Britain between 1904 and 1937," concluding that "the elimination of destitution among working families was almost complete by the late thirties, earlier than previously thought and well before the Welfare State reforms of the post-WW2 government" (2010, p. 33).

14. I note that this would constitute less than a one percent increase over what the federal government has already spent on similar programs.

15. See the bibliography for Pritchett and Woolcock's references to Scott 1998 and de Soto 2000.

interference in the lives of human beings who are our moral equals, it therefore needs to meet a high burden of justification—a burden McMullen's argument does not meet. But just as opposing state subsidy of religion does not mean one therefore wants people to go to hell, pointing out that McMullen's argument for government wealth redistribution fails to make its case does not entail wanting people to be poor, wanting them to go without education or health care, wanting "a system [...] that locks some people out, and to then call that system just" (p. 145), and so on.

> Opposing government subsidy of religion or the arts does not equate to opposing religion or the arts. Similarly, raising moral or economic concerns about government wealth redistribution to alleviate poverty or to provide benefits to the poor does not equate to opposing poverty alleviation or benefit to the poor. The best means of achieving those important goals is what is at issue, not the goals themselves.

3   Perfection and Appropriate Standards

McMullen writes: "there is no such empirical or historical justification for the belief that the poor will not, at times, be left behind. Market economies do not guarantee universal increasing opulence" (p. 142). I argued in both of my previous essays that perfection is not possible on *any* system of political economy; it follows that perfection is not possible in a market-based system. It is also not possible on McMullen's preferred welfare-state system. Of course market economies do not "guarantee universal increasing opulence." What economy does?

When McMullen asserts that there is no empirical evidence supporting a belief that in a market economy "the poor will not, at times, be left behind," he is thus correct—but only trivially so because there is no empirical evidence supporting a belief in any economic system that in it "the poor will not, at times, be left behind." There are today scores of countries that employ varieties of welfare states, yet in none of them do we observe universally increasing opulence or no person ever being left behind. There is also no empirical evidence supporting a belief that if people get vaccinated "the sick will not, at times, be left behind." Does that therefore count against the medical consensus that people should get vaccinated? No. Holding medicine to such a standard—unless you can *guarantee universal increasing health*, your advice may be dismissed, and you must therefore wish for people to be sick—would not only unjustly impugn the motives of medical professionals but would also mean that real if imperfect improvement in health is irrelevant. Should we prohibit anyone who has cancer from receiving treatment until we can first "guarantee" that all cancer patients can and will be cured? Of course not.

What the empirical evidence I adduced does claim to show is that in market economies all economic classes of society, *and especially the poorest*, improve *to a greater extent than they do in other kinds of economies*. It does not propose, let alone guarantee, perfection; it suggests improvement, and more improvement than should be expected from other systems. After reviewing data from 162 countries, Lazear (2020) finds: "The main conclusion is that the poor, defined as having income in the lowest 10 percent of a country's income distribution, *do significantly better in economies with free markets, competition, and low state ownership*. More impressive is that *moving from a heavy emphasis on government to a free market enhances the income of the poor substantially*" (1; italics supplied). This study does not claim a "guarantee" of "universal increasing opulence"; it claims instead that the poor "do significantly better"—as both I and the other studies I cited claimed. Moreover, it shows that the relative degree to which an economy depends on an "emphasis on government" as opposed to an emphasis on "free markets" correlates strongly with benefit to the poor. In other words, moving away from a market economy is attended by decreasing benefit to the poor, while moving toward a market economy is attended by increasing benefit to the poor.

McMullen offers what he considers "the hard question for Otteson: what if the market economy does not provide adequate opportunities for the poor?" (p. 142). He predicts that the prospects of the poor will stagnate or even decline in a market economy, so perhaps we might reinterpret his "hard question" as: "What if the market economy leads to a decline in the poor's condition?" If that is the question, then it is not hard: if empirical evidence showed that a market economy would predictably lead to a decline in the prospects of the poor, then that would constitute significant reason to oppose a market economy. There might yet be other reasons to support a market economy, but a final judgment in its favor would, in that case, have to overcome this substantial objection—and it might well be unable to overcome it.

The empirical evidence, however, does not show that market economies lead to a decline in the prosperity or prospects of the poor. It shows the reverse. Indeed, it shows more than that: it shows that market economies are the only systems of economics that have ever led to widespread increases in prosperity and opportunity, including especially for the poor. It also shows that countries like the United States, as well as those many other countries that, to varying extents, base their economies on markets but also have public policies of wealth redistribution are able to sustain those redistributive programs only when, and to the extent that, they also have market economies.[16] And it shows that the conditions of the poor vary directly with their countries' emphasis on markets: the more market-oriented a country's economy is, the better its poor fare; the less market-oriented a country's economy is, the worse its poor fare.

McMullen claims that my argument provides "no allowance for the possibility of poverty traps of any kind" (p. 142). One poverty trap that McMullen does not consider is government welfare itself. Harvey and Conyers (2016) undertook to survey recipients of federal welfare. Their conclusion: "Although we found that many people abuse today's welfare programs, it is important to remember that the great majority of welfare recipients need the help, and that most do not abuse the rules. Rather, *they feel trapped*. Most want to work, but the system can be stultifying. It deadens the spirit, undermines morale, and takes participants down a path that leads away from work and *away from the chance for a satisfying life*" (xix; italics supplied).[17] These findings challenge McMullen's argument for more government wealth redistribution because he bases it in part on the claim that such aid can help people lead fulfilling lives. If it

---

16. See Otteson 2014, esp. chap. 5.
17. In his study of 20th-century experiments in centralized social and economic planning, James Scott concluded: "high-modernist designs for life and production tend to diminish the skills, agility, initiative, and morale of their intended beneficiaries. They bring about a mild form of institutional neurosis" (1998, p. 349). See also the tragic story of the Austrian village of Marienthal in Brooks 2008, chap. 7.

often has the effect of demoralizing people and increasing a sense of defeated purposelessness, then that seems worthy of consideration.

McMullen continues: "There is [on Otteson's account] no allowance for the fact that a child born into some [poor] households would need a heroic amount of talent and virtue to become even moderately well-off. What of the child whose opportunities are permanently hampered without public education?" (p. 142). Well, in fact, I am one of those children—or, at least, I was. I was raised by an uneducated single teenage mother, in an environment marked by petty criminality and illicit drug use; I spent much of my childhood below the poverty line and many of my younger days hungry. Through both hard work and good fortune, I have thankfully managed to rise above the poverty level and to "become even moderately well-off." It was not easy, but it did not require "a heroic amount of talent and virtue"—because I am not heroically talented or virtuous. Now, my case is my own, and not necessarily like or applicable to anyone else's; and, of course, this is not to depreciate or deny the real difficulties of poverty. But it does suggest that McMullen's assumption that the poor are incapable of improving their own conditions might be overstated. Referring to positions like McMullen's, political scientist James Scott argues that what "is perhaps most striking about" them, "despite their quite genuine egalitarian and often socialist impulses, is how little confidence they repose in the skills, intelligence, and experience of ordinary people" (1998, p. 346).

McMullen asks: "What of the child whose opportunities are permanently hampered without public education?" (p. 142). Indeed. But what of the child whose opportunities are "permanently hampered" by being forced to attend subpar public education? Is there any evidence that some public schools do not, in fact, help children, but might even hamper their proper development? Is there any evidence that the worst-performing public schools are often precisely those to which poor children are sent? Is there any evidence that it is poor children in particular who would benefit most from educational opportunities other than government-mandated and supported public schools? There is.[18] Indeed, what often requires "a heroic amount of talent and

---

18. For two recent studies that survey a great deal of empirical evidence, see Caplan 2018 and Sowell 2020.

virtue" is precisely to succeed in some of the public schools to which poor children are frequently consigned.

3.1 A Third Option

McMullen aims, finally, to put me on the horns of a dilemma: either I have to rely (naively) on charity to help the poor, when he predicts that charity will not be up to the task; or I must harden my heart, conclude that their situations are "tragic but not unjust" (p. 143), and expect (I suppose) that God will sort it all out in the end. I am pleased to report that there exists a third alternative, which is neither naively optimistic nor cruelly hard-hearted. In addition to charity, there is a substantial other route for providing the poor the goods and services they want and need: private enterprise.

Consider Walmart, for example. It is one of the largest companies in the world—it has a market capitalization of some $400 billion, some $540 billion in revenues, and employs some 2.2 million people worldwide—and it has achieved this spectacular success by catering not to the rich but to the poor. A majority of its shoppers have household incomes under $75,000, and approximately 40 percent of its shoppers have household incomes under $50,000.[19] Indeed, the shoppers at Walmart and Walmart Superstores, at Target and Target Superstores, at Costco, Kroger, and Amazon have similar demographics, and these are among the largest and most successful companies in the world. Perhaps you have also heard of companies like Dollar Tree, Variety Store, Family Dollar, Dollar General, Five Below, and many others, which also cater to those of more modest means.

Walmart also strives to provide health care to the poor, including routine checkups, vaccinations, wellness checks, and care for other non-life-threatening health concerns; it would do more if the government allowed it to do so.[20] Many other companies strive to do the same.[21] There is hence significant interest in the private

---

19. See Hanbury 2020.
20. See Walmart n.d.
21. One other example, from hundreds that might be chosen (this example was brought to my attention by a student), is AgroAmerica, a family-owned business with some 13,000 employees in over a dozen countries, which, among its initiatives, offers its employees educational training, nutritional advice, family

sector to address the concerns of, and provide goods and services to, the poor. Many pharmaceutical companies provide their drugs at reduced or no cost to those who need them but cannot afford them;[22] many stores and restaurants provide discounts to students, veterans, and the elderly; at every emergency room in America, a person in need of immediate health care can get it without paying; there are numerous companies that provide health, life, and auto insurance specifically to the poor; there are numerous companies that provide job and skills training for the poor and unskilled; there are numerous companies that provide banking and financial services to the poor; and so on.

Now, if you disdain these realities, perhaps because you yourself would not like to go to Walmart for your health care, fair enough—and good for you: it means you are wealthy enough to enjoy other options. But there is tremendous interest among private enterprise, and among millions of people of goodwill, for providing goods and services to the poor. They are doing so to the tune of billions of dollars annually—and that is in addition to direct charity. Perhaps you do not avail yourselves of these opportunities; perhaps you do not even know of them. If so, once again, good for you: it means you have other options. But they exist, and thus a claim that the only possibility the poor have to obtain these goods and services is through the government is false.

Do these private, for-profit, and not-for-profit, enterprises do so perfectly? Do they guarantee that everyone who wants or needs something will always get it? Again, no. We still live in an imperfect world of fallen creatures and scarce resources, which means, unfortunately, that not everyone will get everything he or she wants or needs. But McMullen ignores private provision of benefit to the poor, which means that his claim that direct charity is all the poor have to rely on, or hope for, in a market economy is false. His further claim that the poor can be served only by government wealth redistribution is therefore also false. Assuming that McMullen is not prepared

---

counseling, and medical services, and builds and repairs local roads, purifies local water sources, and so on. See AgroAmerica n.d.

22. The pharmaceutical company Merck's free provision of its proprietary drug Mectizan to countries whose residents suffered from onchocerciasis, or "river blindness," is a famous example. See *New York Times* 1987.

to argue that we should expect perfection from the government programs he recommends, we are thus led to compare the actually existing alternatives and see which are likelier to lead to improvement. In that case, the wealth, opportunity, and prosperity created in market economies enables far more benefit for their citizens, including especially the poor, than the alternatives McMullen recommends.[23]

Because humans are imperfect, perfection is not an appropriate standard against which to judge any human plan or construction. We live in a world of second-bests, which means that the standard to evaluate alternative proposals for addressing any large-scale issue, including poverty, should be what is relatively better. The economic argument for market economies is based not on the claim that they are or can be perfect, but instead on the claim that they enable increasing prosperity, including especially for the poor, better than other actually available alternatives. They also enable private enterprise to provide goods and services to poorer communities, in addition to charity.

4 Some Further Evidence

McMullen claims that the conditions of the poor stagnate or even decline under market-based systems of economics. That is a testable empirical proposition. Is it true? It would not appear so. Here are some further empirical findings to consider:

- Van Zanden et al. (2014) survey changes in material well-being since 1820 for 25 major countries in 8 regions of the world, covering more than 80 percent of the world's population. Their finding: "The rich have gotten richer *and* the poor have also gotten much richer because of capitalism."[24]
- Market economies enable and encourage innovation (Ridley 2020). But to whom do the gains from innovations primarily

---

23. One might argue that government wealth redistribution should add to, or couple with, private initiative, instead of replace it. Such an argument might risk the "Good Is Good Enough" fallacy, to which I return below.
24. Quoted in Whaples 2017, p. 20; italics in the original.

go? Nobel laureate William Nordhaus (2004) estimates that from 1948 to 2001, only 2.2 percent of the gains from technological innovations were captured by producers themselves; the other 97.8 percent went to consumers.

- McMullen claims that charity is not up to the task of meeting the needs of the poor (pp. 142–3). Yet, the increasing wealth that is generated in market-based economies results in greater philanthropy and charity. McQuillan and Park (2017) review the empirical evidence and conclude: "Economic freedom and private property help drive unbridled individual giving and effective private charity. Freer economies supply greater abundance, leaving individuals with more money to give to the charities of their choice. Freer economies also foster a sense of individual moral responsibility toward the less fortunate, resulting in true giving that comes from compassion as opposed to forced redistribution by governments" (111). Moreover, there is evidence that government-funded welfare succeeds rather in "displacing local initiatives," whereas "privatizing welfare enhances them" (Harvey and Conyers 2016, 159; see also Slavov 2013).

- McMullen is correct that the cost of education, health care, and housing has increased. But those are sectors of the economy that are especially subject to government restriction, regulation, and subsidy, more than are "manufactured goods and most food items," as well as most other consumer goods, whose real prices have decreased. Thus, as Perry (2018) shows, "almost all of the items above the line [i.e., those whose real costs have increased since 1997, including education, health care, and housing] are protected industries while those below the line [i.e., those whose real costs have decreased since 1997, including cars, household furnishings, clothing, cellphone services, software, toys, and televisions] are subject to generally robust competition"; Perry thus concludes, "prices are cheaper with more competition and less government involvement." As McCloskey and Carden (2020) state: "US medicine is expensive because it is a great assemblage of monopolies enforced by the government" (34).

- Government policies of wealth redistribution have shown little long-term benefit for the poor. After surveying four decades of data from 92 countries, Dollar and Kraay (2002) conclude: "the view that a basic policy package of private property rights, fiscal discipline, macroeconomic stability, and openness to trade on average increases the income of the poor to the same extent that it increases the income of the other households in society." Moreover, "It is worth emphasizing that our evidence does not suggest a 'trickle-down' process or sequencing in which the rich get richer first and eventually benefits trickle down to the poor. The evidence, to the contrary, is that private property rights, stability, and openness contemporaneously create a good environment for poor households—and everyone else—to increase their production and income"; and, finally, "we find little evidence that formal democratic institutions *or a large degree of government spending on social services systematically affect incomes of the poor*" (218–19; italics supplied). In other words, McMullenesque recommendations have been tried many times over long periods of time in many countries, and yet they have not been found to be beneficial to the poor.[25]

I emphasize once again, however, that market economies are not perfect. There continue to be problems, including various problems connected particularly to poverty, in market economies. The claim instead is that market-based economies do relatively better than other economies, and that they are more effective in combating many of the problems humanity faces—including poverty—than other systems of economics. The poor are benefited much more across a large number of measures of well-being by living in a more market-based country than they are by government wealth redistribution.

One final, but telling, indicator: the poorest 10 percent of the populace in the 40 countries that have the most market-oriented economies in the world today are nearly *eight times wealthier* than are the poorest 10 percent of the populace in the 40 countries with the least market-oriented economies.[26] McMullen claims that most of that differential is due to government wealth transfer (p. 196), but the preponderance of evidence disputes that.[27] The more market-based

---

25. For a wide review of extant literature supporting this conclusion, see Lawson et al. 2020.

26. See Gwartney at al. 2020, chap. 1.

27. I note that the study McMullen cites to substantiate his claim, Wimer et al. (2016)—which, according to McMullen, "show[s] that the declines in poverty are due to the increasing effect of government redistributive programs" (p. 126)—relies on a dubious assumption and makes a dubious argument. The

a country's economy is, the better the well-being of its poor, and the less market-based a country's economy is, the worse the well-being of its poor; and government wealth redistribution has not been found to provide long-term or systematic benefit to the poor.

4.1 Improvement Is Improvement

By focusing on what the poor in America and in the world still do not have, we often neglect to consider not only what they *do* have but how much their lives have been improved in recent history. Consider: "In 2011, the average poor American possessed more living space than the U.S. average for all citizens in 1980," which is "even more living space than the average person today across all economic classes in France, Sweden, Germany, and the United Kingdom." Moreover, "Three-quarters of poor Americans today have one or more cars. Most have refrigerators, dishwashers, televisions, and microwave ovens. Enjoyable items like personal computers, video game consoles, and Internet access have become commonplace."[28] Perhaps on other issues, this might be dismissed as a glass-is-half-full vs. glass-is-half-empty dispute with little real import. But when actual human lives are at stake, and when we consider the well-being of the poor in particular, improvements are crucially important and not to be dismissed.

Consider an analogy to medicine. Suppose a medical unit during wartime is inundated with a flood of injured. Some are gravely injured; others are moderately injured; some have only light injuries. The medical unit staff unfortunately does not have the resources to give all of them all the care they need, so they adopt a policy of giving approximately equal time and resources for all the injured. What is the result? Most of the gravely injured

---

dubious assumption is that if government anti-poverty programs were cut, then the wealth that funded them would simply vanish, instead of being returned to the private sector where it would have other effects against which the effect of the government transfers would have to be measured. The dubious argument is that because a substantial proportion of the transfers to the poor that the study measures were financed by public debt, claiming that that has reduced their poverty is like claiming that I can make myself wealthier by taking out more credit cards and spending them up.

28. Brooks 2015, pp. 60–1. See also Sheffield and Rector 2014.

are brought from critical condition to serious; the moderately injured are brought from serious to fair; and the lightly injured are brought from fair to good. Some of the gravely injured are, alas, lost. Nonetheless, the medical unit staff celebrate having improved the conditions of almost everyone.

McMullen, however, would call them a failure: they lost some of the gravely injured. If the medical staff responded that there was likely nothing more they could have done for them, or that if they had devoted substantially more of their scarce resources to just those few, it would have led to declining conditions of most of the others, McMullen would be unmoved. They must *guarantee universal increasing health*, or the gains to others are irrelevant. But that is an unreasonable standard. Improvements are improvements, even when not everyone improves. As economists McCloskey and Carden put it: "That people still sometimes die in hospitals does not mean that medicine should be replaced by witch doctors, so long as death rates are falling" (2020, 20).

4.2   Ends and Moral Means

It is true, as McMullen claims, that market economies and the wealth they produce do not lead to equal benefit for everyone. It is also true that in market economies, some people will inevitably not be helped in the way that any of us would ideally like. And it may be true in addition that at least some of the federal programs McMullen champions "decrease real poverty, and increase access to essential food, healthcare, and education" (p. 132). In all these cases, however, we must ask: compared to what? And: at what cost, either economic or moral?

> Alfonse Capone (1899–1947) was a Chicago mobster who also gave to charitable causes. He was convicted on charges of tax evasion in 1931.

Consider another analogy. Suppose the notorious Chicago gangster Al Capone (1899–1947) pointed out that he gave generously to local parochial schools, to food banks, to local hospitals, and to various other charitable causes—as he apparently did.[29] Suppose he was even so bold as to claim that he had thereby "decreased real poverty [in Chicago], and increased access to essential food, health-care, and education." Would we respond with "thank you very much," and look no further into the matter? Or might we instead be inclined to inquire, perhaps delicately, into the method by which Capone attained the wealth he is so generously donating, asking whether it was justly acquired or not, and perhaps also investigate whether there might be other ways of working toward decreasing poverty and increasing access to food, health care, and education that might be preferable or better, all things considered?

This exposes a lacuna in McMullen's argument. He claims to have evidence that government wealth redistribution can lead to good ends. Suppose he is right. Still, that no more ends the argument or closes the case than do Capone's assurances about the ben-eficial effects of his largesse—even if Capone's assurances are true. Of course, McMullen's ends are well-intentioned, whereas Capone's were not. The analogy pertains not to the intentions, however, but to the means employed to achieve their results. Before endorsing any redistribution of wealth, we need to know whether the redistri-bution is effectuated through moral means consistent with justice, and we also need to know whether there are other ways of making progress toward those goals that might be morally or economically better.

> There is substantial evidence that the poor fare better in market economies than in other economies, and that their prosperity varies directly with the degree to which their countries' economies approxi-mate market economies. Market economies are not perfect, but they enable real improvements. Alternative proposals to benefit the poor should be judged, however, not only on whether they provide gains to their intended beneficiaries, but also on whether the benefits they provide were created or acquired through moral means.

---

29. See Klein 2019.

5   Good Is (Still) Not Good Enough

•In my opening essay, I argued that because people are equal moral agents, any proposal to intervene uninvited into their lives to rearrange or reorder their property or possessions, or to override their preferences and choices, would have to meet a high justificatory burden. I did not argue that no circumstances could ever justify such intervention or overriding; indeed, I enumerated specific cases in which I believed it could be justified. Instead, I argued that the burden of proof is on the person advocating to do so to explain why the proposed intervention or overriding met this high justificatory burden. I proposed respecting others' peaceful and voluntary choices, exchanges, transactions, and associations as a robust default—a "relatively absolute absolute"—that could be overridden only in cases specifically demonstrated to warrant departure from this otherwise foundational moral principle. I specified a "minimum threshold" for any such proposal: before the proposal warranted consideration, it should provide a complete account of both its likely benefits and its likely costs, including opportunity costs; it should be demonstrated to predictably lead to greater benefit and lower cost than other plausible alternatives; and it should confer real benefit at least to some without thereby making any innocents worse off.

Those are high bars to cross, but, because we are dealing with equal moral agents and their lives, it should be a high bar to cross. Not impossible, but challenging—as it should be. Many proposals for wealth redistribution do not meet that standard. Indeed, many proposals for wealth redistribution make no real attempt to meet that standard—such as McMullen's.

In the end, McMullen's position can be summarized in the following two claims: first, it is possible that government wealth redistribution, perhaps at slightly higher levels of funding, could have beneficial effects; and second, the only way to show proper concern for the poor is through government-mandated wealth redistribution. In the remainder of this response, let me address these by turn.

McMullen's first claim—that it is possible that government wealth redistribution could lead to benefit—commits the "Good Is Good Enough" fallacy. Many things we might do could possibly lead to benefit. Because our resources are scarce, however, and because some of the things we might do that could lead to benefit would entail violating moral principles that we should not violate, pointing out the potential benefit from some proposed course of action does not yet make a convincing case that we should therefore do it.

To see why this undermines this part of McMullen's argument, consider substituting other potential proposals for McMullen's recommended government wealth redistribution. Suppose, for example, someone were to claim that empirical evidence suggests that religious belief correlates with positive benefits in people's lives—a not implausible claim.[30] Suppose this person then makes the following *religious-welfare* argument:

1. To meet the demands of religious justice, we must work to build a legal and economic structure that grants each person the opportunity to participate in and contribute to religious life.
2. In the contemporary United States, basic religious opportunity is limited by poverty, inequality, and a history of religious oppression.
3. There are at least some redistributive government programs that, if expanded, would increase the opportunity to participate in and contribute to religious life.
4. Therefore, the U.S. government should expand the redistribution in those ways that will expand opportunity.

Suppose this person then claims, on the basis of this argument, that we should implement a fine of, say, $100 for every person who does not attend a weekly religious service; and a modest, say just 1 percent, income tax on all citizens that would generate funds from which the government would provide grants to—that is, 'invest' in—religious institutions.

Or consider another substitute proposal—say, marriage. Suppose someone claims that marriage is a key to a flourishing life (for which there is some evidence).[31] This *marital-welfare* argument could run:

1. To meet the demands of marital justice, we must work to build a legal and economic structure that grants each person the opportunity to participate in and contribute to marital life.

---

30. See, for example, Pew Research Center 2019. See also Carroll et al. 2020, which finds "a strong correlation between home-centered religious worship patterns and positive relationship outcomes" (3), including overall levels of happiness and even "sexual satisfaction" (25).
31. See, for example, Stutzer and Frey 2006; Regnerus 2015; and Girgis et al. 2020.

2. In the contemporary United States, basic marital opportunity is limited by poverty, inequality, and a history of marital oppression.
3. There are at least some redistributive government programs that, if expanded, would increase the opportunity to participate in and contribute to marital life.
4. Therefore, the U.S. government should expand the redistribution in those ways that will expand opportunity.

As you may have noticed, these religious- and marital-welfare arguments follow McMullen's argument for wealth redistribution exactly, substituting "religious opportunity" and "marital opportunity," respectively, as their goals instead of McMullen's "economic opportunity." How should we respond to our hypothetical religious- or marital-welfare arguments? Several responses suggest themselves.

First, the use of the phrase "religious justice" (or "marital justice") begs the question by assuming into its definition the very question at issue. Why should we accept a conception of "religious justice" (or "marital justice"), as opposed to longstanding alternative conceptions of justice, especially when "religious justice" (or "marital justice") conflicts with these other conceptions of justice? Second, the claim that "at least some" redistributive government programs could potentially increase the opportunity to participate in and contribute to religious life or married life does not mean that they actually would—especially once opportunity cost is considered, not to mention the public-choice concerns and the Knave Principle I discussed in my response essay.[32]

Third, and most important, the conclusions are unsupported by the premises[33]—because of this signal fact: as equal moral agents, people have the right to religious and marital freedom. That means you may not intrude into their religious or marital affairs, or rearrange their wealth or resources in the service of religious or marital affairs, *even if it is true that they could thereby potentially be benefited.* As equal moral agents, they have the right to decide which religious beliefs to subscribe to (if any), whether to attend or support religious institutions, and whether to give their time, money, or other resources to any religious institution, as well as to decide

---

32. See also Heath 2020.
33. In other words, the arguments are logically invalid.

whom to marry, whether to get married, and whether to contribute to others' marital arrangements.

This rejection of religious and marital interference seems absolute. The argumentative threshold that I offered was less stringent, however, proposing a relatively looser standard of Pareto efficiency, which allows exceptions in cases in which one could demonstrate that at least some would benefit while no innocent party would be harmed (or in which any harmed innocents could be compensated in a way that they would themselves reasonably accept). Ultimately, however, a rejection of the religious- and marital-welfare arguments is based not on a cost–benefit analysis (even a full one, including opportunity cost), but, instead, on a moral constraint that I suspect most, including me, hold sacrosanct.

But what would distinguish the religious-welfare argument and the marital-welfare argument from a redistributionist argument? The redistributionist claims that empirical evidence indicates an important lack in some people's lives, including especially in the lives of the poor; so do the religious- and marital-welfare arguments. The redistributionist claims that government wealth redistribution could prove beneficial with regard to this lack; so do the religious- and marital-welfare arguments. The redistributionist concludes that the government should therefore engage in wealth redistribution to serve that end; so do the religious- and marital-welfare arguments. While McMullen advocates his wealth-redistribution version of this argument, I suspect that he would oppose the religious- and marital-welfare versions of the same argument. But on what grounds could he do so? This therefore appears to put McMullen on the horns of his own dilemma: if he supports government wealth redistribution, then it seems he must also be open to the religious- and marital-welfare arguments (and perhaps a range of other similarly constructed arguments); if, however, he wishes to oppose the religious- and marital-welfare arguments, then it seems he must also oppose his own government wealth redistribution argument.

5.1   The Redistributionist's Strongest Argument

Perhaps the strongest argument McMullen makes to justify government wealth redistribution relates to the "poverty traps" he describes. I discussed above one potential poverty trap McMullen does not consider, namely welfare itself. But the argument that poverty can make it difficult to take even a first step toward prosperity suggests that merely removing formal (legal) obstacles to improvement is insufficient. The evidence that market economies lead to overall improvement leaves open the possibility that, for some at least, whatever indirect benefit they might enjoy by living in a society in which overall living standards are rising, various obstacles might nevertheless remain that inhibit their betterment.

What might be only minor setbacks for wealthier people can be devastating to the poor. Losing one's job, or losing one's health care or health care insurance, is difficult for anyone, but it can particularly affect the poor, who do not have the reserve resources the wealthy do to call upon in times of exigency. Instead of claiming that government redistribution in such cases should count as "investment"—which would imply that those paying for the redistribution do so voluntarily and should expect a direct return—a stronger argument would be to acknowledge that such programs are indeed costly, but to claim that this cost is worth bearing out of humane concern for and in fraternal solidarity with the poor. In other words, whether such programs lead to economic productivity or not, providing help to the poor is often the right thing to do, even if it leads to a net economic loss. Sometimes proper concern for others requires genuine sacrifice.

> An argument for wealth redistribution on grounds that it can lead to benefit is too broad, as it would seem to justify redistribution not only to alleviate poverty but also to support religion, marriage, and potentially other practices that might also lead to benefit. A stronger argument for wealth redistribution would rely not on claims that it would lead to net economic gains, but would instead acknowledge that it could be a net cost—but claim that doing the right thing sometimes requires sacrifice.

6 Conclusion: True Charity

True charity makes a demand on us. It often requires an economic sacrifice, and I submit that the increasing wealth generated by a market economy is accompanied by an increasing moral expectation, and even obligation, that we dedicate our wealth—including not only our money, but also our time and talent—to the creation of as much value, or the alleviation of as much misery and suffering, as we are able. Having made my case and offered my criticisms of McMullen's argument, let me now, in response to McMullen's second claim that the only way to show proper concern for the poor is through government wealth redistribution, conclude by reflecting on the nature of the personal moral obligation I believe we have.

We have, as I have indicated, evidence suggesting that societies with market-based economies increase in wealth, that people in wealthier societies tend to give more, and that, thus, the more market-based a society's economy is, the more its citizens will likely give. Nevertheless, it is difficult to make any confident predictions regarding precisely what kinds of charitable activities would be summoned or to which people would contribute if the government approximated what I have recommended. Thus, McMullen is right to point out that there would be no guarantees. But I can describe what I think our personal moral calling would be in such a society, and why I think it would be preferable for a society to rely on such personal moral callings than to transfer our responsibilities of caring for others to the state.

Thirty years ago, Pope St. John Paul II (1920–2005) discussed the welfare state in *Centesimus Annus*. He wrote: "In recent years the range of such intervention has vastly expanded, to the point of creating a new type of state, the so-called 'welfare state'" (1991, §48). The Holy Father was not happy with what he saw. He says we observe in these federal government agencies "excesses and abuses," and he offers this as an explanation:

> Malfunctions and defects in the social assistance state are the result of an inadequate understanding of the tasks proper to the state. Here again the principle of subsidiarity must be respected: a community of a higher order should not interfere in the internal life of a community of a lower order, depriving the latter of its functions, but rather should support it in the case of need and help to coordinate its activity with the activities of the rest of society, always with a view to the common good.
>
> (ibid.)

He continued:

> By intervening directly and depriving society of its responsibility, the social assistance state leads to a loss of human energies

St. John Paul II (1920–2005) was the Pope of the Roman Catholic Church from 1978 to 2005. He was the author of 14 papal encyclicals, addressing issues from sexual reproduction to family life to the dignity of work to canon law to Communism. He escaped Nazi capture during World War II and was canonized in 2014.

and an inordinate increase of public agencies, which are dominated more by bureaucratic ways of thinking than by concern for serving their clients, and which are accompanied by an enormous increase in spending. In fact, it would appear that needs are best understood and satisfied by people who are closest to them and who act as neighbors to those in need. [...] One thinks of the condition of refugees, immigrants, the elderly, the sick, and all those in circumstances which call for assistance, such as drug abusers: all these people can be helped effectively only by those who offer them genuine fraternal support, in addition to the necessary care.

(ibid.)

John Paul II's argument makes several claims, but a few are worth emphasizing. First, he suggests that federal government welfare programs crowd out other kinds of charitable activity, including local government charity and private initiatives. As we have seen, empirical studies corroborate this claim.

But second, he argues that true charity must be "fraternal," that is, arising from genuine community and relationship between the giver and the receiver and motivated by a real concern for the dignity and well-being of the receiver.[34] The way to do that is to take personal initiative, to personally undertake the hard work of getting to know the people who need help, learning their situations and challenges and hardships, and fraternally seeking ways to work in solidarity with them not only for their benefit but for the benefit also of the giver and the larger community. Knowing what kinds of assistance would actually constitute help for others requires

---

34. See also Olasky 2008.

knowing about them and their situations. Sometimes giving money is best; other times, other things are needed; sometimes nothing is needed other than kindness and moral support. Knowing how best to help requires this personalized, localized knowledge, and that is much more difficult, indeed perhaps impossible, to get from afar. Transferring this responsibility of ministering to the poor to the government puts the poor at the mercy of the "bureaucratic" public agencies John Paul II describes, which, because of their distance from and inability to know the personal circumstances of those to whom they would minister, he decries for their inability to give "genuine fraternal support."

What, then, *is* the solution to helping the poor? Alas, there is likely no single solution, no "magic bullet," no single comprehensive plan for alleviating the plight of the poor—because "the poor" are not all the same, are not all in the same circumstances, and thus do not all need the same kinds of assistance. Grand social plans imagine what James Scott calls "standardized citizens," who "have, for the purposes of the planning exercise, no gender, no tastes, no history, no values, no opinions or original ideas, no traditions, and no distinctive personalities to contribute to the enterprise. They have none of the particular, situated, and contextual attributes that one would expect of any population and that we, as a matter of course, always attribute to elites" (1998, p. 346). If the multiple attempts over the past many decades to find the one comprehensive plan, the one solution, to poverty have taught us anything, it is that a 'plan' to solve poverty is likely to fail. As development economist William Easterly notes, "we already have quite a large surplus of action plans": "A recent study by a couple of World Bank authors found that 31 per cent of the World Bank's 'knowledge products' have never been downloaded; and 87 per cent were never cited. 'Never cited' means, basically, nobody ever read them" (Easterly 2016, p. 11).[35] So we have had numerous plans to solve poverty, to which we can add McMullen's, though we have disheartening little to show for them.

---

35. Elsewhere, Easterly notes that the United Nations Millennium Project of 2000 "listed 449 separate interventions to achieve the MDGs [Millennium Development Goals]. For this number, even a probability of success of each intervention of 99 percent would yield an overall success probability for the comprehensive plan of 1 percent" (Easterly 2008, pp. 22–3).

My argument for a government based on protecting Adam Smith's "3 Ps" of justice—person, property, and promise—does not constitute a 'plan' for solving poverty. I have presented some of the evidence indicating that the well-being of the poor in those countries that most closely approximate this Smithian government is much higher than that of the poor in those countries furthest away from such a government, and I have argued that that was one main reason to support such a system of government, along with the market economy it entails. But that does not constitute a 'plan' for solving poverty. Rather, it enables the opportunity to increase prosperity. But it does so by enabling greater generation of resources with which each of us can then more fully accept our own personal moral obligation to help those who need help when and where we can.

This is actually a more demanding moral call than the redistributionist's. Paying for someone else to take responsibility for the poor is an ultimately inadequate route to fulfill our moral obligation to the poor. It can relieve us of the burden of undertaking to learn about them and their circumstances, and of seeking ways to help them communally, fraternally, and in solidarity. But it purchases that by forgoing engaging them as persons, as moral agents of dignity and value, as unique individuals deserving respect and care. It thus gives us no moral credit, and it is thus a false charity. True charity, by contrast, requires solidarity, or "acting out of a sense of identification with the other" and "treating their interests on a par with [one's] own and experiencing their misfortunes as [one] would [one's] own" (Zhao 2019, pp. 8 and 13). But to identify with another in this way requires one to *know* that other. As Pope Benedict XVI argued in *Caritas in Veritate:* "Solidarity is first and foremost a sense of responsibility on the part of everyone with regard to everyone, and it cannot therefore be merely delegated to the State" (2009, §38). And as Pope Francis claimed in *Fratelli Tutti,* what is needed "is not a case of implementing welfare programs from the top down, but rather of undertaking a journey together" (2020, §129).

I therefore call instead for a renewed *personal* moral obligation to minister to the poor. This requires us to actively engage all our gifts—all our time, talent, and treasure—to create the most productive value that we can, seeking to benefit ourselves only while benefiting others. Sometimes this requires charitable giving, but sometimes it requires engaging with others in the market. As Pope

Benedict argues: "In a climate of mutual trust, the *market* is the economic institution that permits encounter between persons, inasmuch as they are economic subjects who make use of contracts to regulate their relations as they exchange goods and services [...] in order to satisfy their needs and desires" (2009, §35; italics in the original). In this way, writes Pope Benedict, "The poor are not to be considered a 'burden,' but a resource, even from the purely economic point of view" (ibid.). Meeting the poor where they are, and, in fraternal solidarity, ministering to them—or working, partnering, exchanging, or transacting with them—are the only ways to develop the "authentically human relations" (ibid., §36) I believe we are morally called to build.[36]

There is no single route to accomplishing this, and none of us can fully accomplish it alone. But each of us can, and should, affirmatively seek ways to create at least some positive benefit in not only our own lives but in the lives of at least some others as well. In this way, in Pope Benedict's words, "charity goes beyond justice" (2009, §6). Embracing and pursuing such charity beyond justice can enable us to get better—together.

---

36. My reference to Catholic social thought should not be taken to imply that all of it would agree with my argument. Catholic social thought typically calls for a range of strategies to address poverty, often including properly oriented and limited governmental welfare.

Further Readings

Suggested Readings (Steven McMullen)

The topic of our debate is a large one, but if the reader wants to dig deeper into the questions we raise, here are a few books that are worth further study. In this list, I avoid some of the classic books that have shaped the field, and instead look to more recent work that will give readers a sense of where scholars are working today.

First, to understand the considerable literature on distributive justice, I recommend T.M. Scanlon's recent book, *Why Does Inequality Matter?* (Oxford University Press, 2018). It is a thorough treatment of one of the central questions in this literature. For a somewhat more libertarian view, read also John Tomasi's book *Free Market Fairness* (Princeton University Press, 2012). Both of these books offer moderate and thoughtful discussions of some of the big questions. Finally, a reader approaching the field would learn much from studying *The Oxford Handbook of Distributive Justice* (2018) edited by Serena Olsaretti.

Second, I have found it enormously helpful to think carefully about how we conceive of poverty and economic progress. Toward this end, I recommend that philosophers and social scientists both think carefully about the capabilities approach developed by Martha Nussbaum and Amartya Sen. The two works that I would start with are Sen's "Equality of What?" published in *The Tanner Lectures on Human Values I* (Cambridge University Press, 2011), and then Nussbaum's more comprehensive *Creating Capabilities: The Human Development Approach* (Harvard University Press, 2013). For an understanding of how to think about economic opportunity in both philosophical and policy terms, I recommend Joseph Fishkin's *Bottlenecks* (Oxford University Press, 2016).

Finally, while the policy evaluation literature is vast and daunting, we cannot do a good job understanding welfare state programs without digging into this empirical evidence. I recommend two recent books that offer reliable tours of this evidence. First, Heather Boushey's *Unbound: How Inequality Constricts Our Economy and What we Can Do about It* (Harvard University Press, 2019) is readable and thorough. For those less excited about state action, Michael Tanner's *The Inclusive Economy: How to Bring Wealth to America's Poor* (Cato Institute, 2018), offers an up to date look at the evidence as well.

Suggested Readings (James R. Otteson)

I have cited many works relevant to our discussion in the bibliography, but here are some works I would particularly recommend for those wishing to investigate further.

G. A. Cohen's brief *Why Not Socialism?* (2009) argues in defense of socialism, but it also develops several moral arguments against relying on markets to provide ethical mechanisms to prosperity. Cohen's earlier *If You're an Egalitarian, How Come You're So Rich?* (2000), especially Chapter 10, makes a related moral case against wealth inequality. See also the collection of Cohen's essays in *On the Currency of Egalitarian Justice* (2011), which raises further arguments against inequality and in favor of wealth redistribution. For a criticism of Cohen's arguments, see James R. Otteson, *The End of Socialism* (2014).

Mariana Mazzucato's *The Entrepreneurial State* (2015) complements Cohen's argument by arguing that the state should engage in wealth redistribution for the purpose of enhancing prosperity, and by arguing that the state can do so more competently than critics allege. For a criticism of Mazzucato's claims and an argument that state wealth investment is actually malinvestment, see Deirdre Nansen McCloskey and Alberto Mingardi's *The Myth of the Entrepreneurial State* (2020).

For a historical review of varied attempts at reducing wealth inequality and their perhaps surprising ineffectiveness, see Walter Scheidel's *The Great Leveler* (2017). David T. Beito's *From Mutual Aid to the Welfare State* (2000) reviews the extensive history of voluntary mutual aid societies in the United States in the period of 1890–1967, and argues that they were more effective at serving the needs of the poor than were federal government programs. Arthur

Brooks's *The Conservative Heart* (2015) makes a similar case for the superiority of voluntary poverty relief programs to government initiatives. And Edward Peter Stringham's *Private Governance* (2015) argues for private solutions to various social problems.

Finally, Michael Munger's *Is Capitalism Sustainable?* (2019) reviews several of the practical problems with wealth distribution as a vehicle to poverty relief and prosperity, as does James R. Otteson's *Seven Deadly Economic Sins* (2021).

Glossary

Absolute Poverty a poverty line, usually marking a minimum standard of living, that does not change over time, and does not depend on the incomes of others in society. One absolute poverty cutoff is the "extreme poverty" or "international poverty" threshold often used by the United Nations, which is just under $2 a day. Contrasts with **Relative Poverty.**

A priori able to be apprehended by pure reason or without empirical investigation; that the interior angles of a triangle are equal to two right angles can be known a priori, whereas what the current population of the United States is can be known only by empirical investigation (or *a posteriori*).

Capabilities Morally important opportunities or "functionings" that are essential to a minimally good human life. Examples include food, shelter, freedom of movement, and education. Capabilities theory was pioneered by Amartya Sen and Martha Nussbaum.

Capital Gains Tax in the United States, this tax is paid on the increase in the value of an asset between the time you purchase it and the time you sell it. This is the primary tax paid on non-income increases in individual wealth.

Capitalism a system of economics that includes strong private property rights, allows individualized or decentralized economic decision-making, and allows free trade and free enterprise; contrasts with **socialism.**

Compensatory Justice a conception of justice relating primarily to a requirement to make an injured or harmed party whole; if A visited injury, harm, or cost on an unwilling or unwitting B, compensatory justice requires A to indemnify B through compensation.

Competitive Consumption   consumption that is motivated by interpersonal comparisons and/or intended to signal status.

Cooperative Transactions   mutually voluntary and typically mutually beneficial transactions; positive sum; contrasts with extractive transactions.

Deontic Egalitarians   find inequality objectionable only when those inequalities are the result of another injustice.

Distributive Justice   a conception of justice pertaining to the right or proper distribution of material wealth across a population.

Earned Income Tax Credit   A refundable tax credit that offers a tax reduction for those who have low incomes and offers a cash rebate for the working poor. It is structured to encourage entry into the labor market and phase out slowly.

Effective Marginal Tax Rate   The percentage of each dollar earned that a person loses to taxes and reduced government benefits due to **means-tested** government programs.

Egalitarian   a person who argues for a more equal distribution of resources. Egalitarians differ greatly in the kinds of arguments they make for greater equality, and in the kinds of equality that they are seeking.

Equal Moral Agency Principle   based on the claim that all people have equal moral dignity, this principle holds that, except under extraordinary circumstances, everyone's agency and choices should be respected equally.

Estate Tax   In the United States, this tax is paid on the value of an inheritance. Under current law, no taxes are paid on inheritances valued at less than $11.5 million.

Extractive Transactions   involuntary or nonconsensual zero sum (or negative-sum) transactions in which one party to the transaction benefits at the other party's expense; contrasts with cooperative transactions.

Formal Opportunity   is ensured when there are no legal barriers preventing a person from achieving any important kind of economic success; compare with **substantive opportunity**.

Head Start   A publically funded U.S. preschool program available to children in low-income families.

Homeostasis (or risk compensation)   the phenomenon by which people adjust their behavior according to their perceptions of risk; a belief that an activity is risky tends to lead people to avoid it, whereas a belief that an activity is less risky tends to lead people to engage in it more.

Invisible Hand an argument from Adam Smith (1723–1790) that holds that under the right institutional environments, individual, self-interested economic activity tends to conduce to the benefit of others, even if unintentionally.

Knave Principle an argument from David Hume (1711–1776) claiming that we should endorse only those governmental policies whose likely benefits would outweigh their likely costs on the assumption that they would be managed and administered not by saints but by knaves.

Labor Supply Disincentive (or work disincentive) a side effect of some tax and redistribution policies, in which the policy reduces the benefit of working, either because the take-home income is reduced through taxes or because additional wages reduce the person's eligibility for government benefits.

Libertarian A person who places a high value on individual liberty and a minimal exercise of state power, particularly in regard to property and economic activity.

Luck Egalitarians are those thinkers that, in a variety of different ways, believe that society should equalize the benefits of good luck, and compensate people who have bad luck; usually these theories concern individual characteristics that cannot be easily changed, like race, intelligence, or physical attractiveness.

***Malum in Se* Crimes** Crimes that are evil or wrong in themselves because they inherently involve harm or injury, such as murder, rape, and theft; in contrast to *malum prohibitum* crimes, which are criminal only because they violate some rule, law, or regulation, such as renovating one's house without a legally required permit.

Market Power refers to the ability of a market actor (buyer or seller) to exert power in a negotiation because there is limited competition on their side of the market. Extreme cases would include monopolies.

Means-Tested Programs Government programs that are only available to those with limited economic means. Usually, the means-test is based on income. Examples include **SNAP** and Medicaid.

Medicaid a means-tested public health insurance program for those with low incomes in the United States.

Moral Hazard a case in which a policy of compensating people for loss, or protecting them against loss, unintentionally leads people to engage in more, not less, of a risky behavior.

Natural Law   a set of principles for moral conduct and behavior that is envisioned to be willed by God or written into the fabric of the universe; it precedes and is independent of human-made governments, law, and so on; it holds that people have natural rights that no human-made institutions should violate.

Naturalistic Fallacy   the fallacy of directly deriving a normative or prescriptive statement or judgment from a factual statement, or deriving an "ought" from an "is"; for example, it would not follow from the fact that people are self-interested (a purported factual or "is" statement) that therefore people *should* act self-interestedly (a normative, prescriptive, or "ought" statement).

Opportunity Cost   the cost of the most highly valued alternative that is forgone.

Opt-Out Option (or exit option)   the right to refuse any offer, proposition, or proposal to exchange, collaborate, or partner; the right to say "no, thank you" and walk away.

Pareto Improvement   a criterion for evaluating a proposed policy or course of action by which the policy or course of action is recommended if it results in a benefit or improvement to at least one member of a group without any other members suffering a loss; named after Vilfredo Pareto (1848–1923), who is credited with its formulation.

Positive Sum   a primary characteristic of an exchange or transaction in which both, or all, parties benefit; an increase in value to all parties entails a positive net or overall benefit; contrasts with zero sum.

Public Choice Economics   the use of economic tools to analyze the behavior of people and institutions in political settings; based on the assumption that people in politics, as in other realms of human behavior, have normal motivations, biases, etc.

Public Goods   are those goods that are non-rival and non-excludable, meaning one person's enjoyment does not preclude someone else from benefiting from the good, and that you cannot prevent people from enjoying the good once it is produced.

Redistribution   when the government engages in public spending, either in cash benefits or the provision of services, to benefit a particular group of people, at the cost of others. Usually, redistribution intends to provide material resources to those who are poor using taxes paid by those who are wealthier.

Relative Poverty the fact or condition of one person or one group being poor in comparison with another person or group; contrasts with **absolute poverty**; it is possible to be *relatively poor* (that is, in comparison with some other person or group), while simultaneously being *absolutely rich* (by historical, objective, or world standards).

Rent-Seeking economic behavior that seeks economic benefit without providing a service to society. Often this term is used to describe firms that seek regulation that will give them an advantage over their competitors.

Risk-Averse (Risk Aversion) refers to the attitude someone has toward uncertainty. If someone is risk-averse, then they will be less likely to take risks, those who are less risk-averse will be more likely to take risks, both good and bad.

Safety Net Redistribution that aims to provide a minimum standard of living, below which no one will fall. Basic food, housing, or medical benefits for the poor might fit this model, as could **social insurance** programs.

Section 8 Housing Voucher Program provides a government-funded discount on housing costs for some people who are in or near poverty.

Social Capital the network of valuable interpersonal connections that grant economic opportunities.

Socialism a system of economics that includes government ownership or control of property, that engages in government-directed or centralized economic decision-making, and that grants government-wide control over trade, industry, and business; contrasts with **capitalism.**

Social Insurance a way of thinking about government redistribution as protection against economic misfortune. In the United States, for example, there is an unemployment insurance program and a disability insurance program, which replaces a portion of workers' wages if they are laid off or become unable to work.

Starting-Gate Theories An egalitarian theory that argues that a just system is one in which each person starts with the same opportunities for success. They sometimes adopt the metaphor of a fair race, in which everyone is starting from the same position.

Substantive Opportunity is ensured when there are no material or social constraints that prevent people from achieving any important kind of economic success; compare with **formal opportunity.**

Supplemental Nutrition Assistance Program (SNAP, formerly food stamps)   a safety-net program in the United States that gives low-income households funds that can only be used to buy food.

Telic Egalitarians   are those who think that the fact of inequality is necessarily objectionable, no matter how the inequality was generated.

Temporary Assistance for Needy Families (TANF)   A federal government program of temporary cash aid to those in or near poverty with children.

Time Preference   the degree to which a person cares more about the present than the future.

Utilitarianism   a moral theory that holds that the right action is the one that leads to the largest increase in overall or net utility (utility is variously conceived of as usefulness, pleasure, preference-satisfaction, or happiness); it typically counts all persons' utility equally, though it typically does not presume or hold that persons have natural rights.

"Veil of Ignorance"   a device offered by philosopher John Rawls that restricts agents' knowledge, when in the "original position" deliberating about the basic rules of justice to be applied to society, of what position the agents will occupy in the society under the rules they endorse.

Welfare State   A term that encompasses all state-administered safety-net programs. In the United States, this would likely include food assistance (**SNAP**), cash benefits (**TANF, Social Security, Unemployment Insurance**), housing assistance (**Section 8 Housing Vouchers**), and health insurance (**Medicaid** and **Medicare**).

Zero Sum   a primary characteristic of an exchange or transaction in which one party benefits but only at the expense of the other party; positive value for one party, when added to the same negative value for the other party, leads to no, or zero, net benefit; such transactions can also be *negative-sum* if assets or benefit are lost in the exchange; contrasts with **positive sum.**

Bibliography

Acemoglu, D., and J. A. Robinson. 2012. *Why Nations Fail: The Origins of Power, Prosperity, and Poverty.* New York: Crown Business.

Acemoglu, D., and J. A. Robinson. 2019. *The Narrow Corridor: States, Societies, and the Fate of Liberty.* New York: Penguin.

Acemoglu, D., and J. A. Robinson. 2020. *The Narrow Corridor: States, Societies, and the Fate of Liberty.* New York: Penguin Books.

Acton, J. E. E. D. (Lord). 1986 (1887). "Acton-Creighton Correspondence." P. 383 in *Selected Writings of Lord Acton,* vol. 2, *Essays in the Study and Writing of History,* edited by J. R. Fears. Indianapolis, IN: Liberty Fund.

Adams, J. 2011. "The Failure of Seat Belts Legislation." Pp. 132–56 in *Clumsy Solutions for a Complex World: Governance, Politics, and Plural Perceptions,* edited by M. Verweij and M. Thompson. New York: Palgrave Macmillan.

AgroAmerica. N.d. "Community Development." Retrieved here: https://agroamerica.com/en/community-development/.

Alaimo, K., C. M. Olson, and E. A. Frongillo. 2001. "Food Insufficiency and American School-Aged Children's Cognitive, Academic, and Psychosocial Development." *Pediatrics* 108(1):44–53.

Alesina, Alberto, and Eliana La Ferrara. 2000. "Participation in Heterogeneous Communities." *The Quarterly Journal of Economics* 115(3):847–904. doi: 10.1162/003355300554935.

Almlund, Mathilde, Angela Lee Duckworth, James Heckman, and Tim Kautz. 2011. "Personality Psychology and Economics." Pp. 1–181 in *Handbook of the Economics of Education,* edited by E. A. Hanushek, S. Machin, and L. Woessmann. Amsterdam: Elsevier.

Almond, Douglas, Hilary W. Hoynes, and Diane Whitmore Schanzenbach. 2010. "Inside the War on Poverty: The Impact of Food Stamps on Birth Outcomes." *The Review of Economics and Statistics* 93(2):387–403. doi: 10.1162/REST_a_00089.

Altig, David, Alan Auerbach, Laurence Kotlikoff, Elias Ilin, and Victor Ye. 2020. *Marginal Net Taxation of Americans' Labor Supply.* NBER Working Paper. 27164. National Bureau of Economic Research, Inc.

Altschuler, Glenn, and Stuart Blumin. 2009. *The GI Bill: The New Deal for Veterans*. Oxford University Press.

Amadeo, K. 2020. "FY 2020 Federal Budget: Trump's Budget Request." *The Balance*. Retrieved here: https://www.thebalance.com/fy-2020-federal-budget-summary-of-revenue-and-spending-4797868.

Amplify Credit Union. 2020. "11 Organizations That Will Help You Pay Your Medical Bills." Retrieved here: https://www.goamplify.com/blog/improvecredit/organizations-that-help-pay-medical-bills/.

Anderson, E. 2017. *Private Government: How Employers Rule Our Lives (and Why We Don't Talk about It)*. Princeton, NJ: Princeton University Press.

Anderson, Elizabeth S. 1999. "What Is the Point of Equality?" *Ethics* 109(2):287–337. doi: 10.1086/233897.

Anderson, Lisa R., Jennifer M. Mellor, and Jeffrey Milyo. 2008. "Inequality and Public Good Provision: An Experimental Analysis." *The Journal of Socio-Economics* 37(3):1010–28. doi: 10.1016/j.socec.2006.12.073.

Andrews, Dan, and Andrew Leigh. 2009. "More Inequality, Less Social Mobility." *Applied Economics Letters* 16(15):1489–92. doi: 10.1080/13504850701720197.

Antel, John J. 1992. "The Intergenerational Transfer of Welfare Dependency: Some Statistical Evidence." *The Review of Economics and Statistics* 74(3):467–73. doi: 10.2307/2109491.

Ariely, D. 2008. *Predictably Irrational: The Hidden Forces that Shape Our Decisions*. New York: Harper.

Ariely, D. 2010. *The Upside of Irrationality: The Unexpected Benefits of Defying Logic*. New York: Harper Perennial.

Arneson, Richard J. 2000. "Luck Egalitarianism and Prioritarianism." *Ethics* 110(2):339–49. doi: 10.1086/233272.

Arrow, Kenneth J. 1963. "Uncertainty and the Welfare Economics of Medical Care." *The American Economic Review* 53(5):941–73.

Ashenfelter, Orley, and Cecilia Rouse. 2000. "Schooling, Intelligence, and Income in America." Pp. 89–117 in *Meritocracy and Economic Inequality*, edited by K. Arrow, S. Bowles, and S. N. Durlauf. Princeton, NJ: Princeton University Press.

Autor, David H. 2014. "Skills, Education, and the Rise of Earnings Inequality among the 'Other 99 Percent.'" *Science* 344(6186):843–51. doi: 10.1126/science.1251868.

Autor, David H., Lawrence F. Katz, and Melissa S. Kearney. 2008. "Trends in U.S. Wage Inequality: Revising the Revisionists." *Review of Economics and Statistics* 90(2):300–23. doi: 10.1162/rest.90.2.300.

Babiak, P., C. S. Neumann, and R. D. Hare. 2010. "Corporate Psychopathy: Talking the Walk." *Behavioral Sciences and the Law* 28:174–93.

Bailey, Martha J., Hilary W. Hoynes, Maya Rossin-Slater, and Reed Walker. 2020. *Is the Social Safety Net a Long-Term Investment? Large-Scale Evidence from the Food Stamps Program*. Working Paper. 26942. National Bureau of Economic Research.

Bailey, R. and M. L. Tupy 2020. *Ten Global Trends Every Smart Person Should Know: And Many Others You Will Find Interesting.* Washington, DC: Cato.

Baptist, E. E. 2016. *The Half Has Never Been Told: Slavery and the Making of American Capitalism.* New York: Basic Books.

Barr, Andrew C., and Chloe Gibbs. 2019. "Breaking the Cycle? Intergenerational Effects of an Anti-Poverty Program in Early Childhood." EdWorkingPapers.Com.

Bastiat, F. 2016 (1850). "What Is Seen and What Is Not Seen, or Political Economy in One Lesson." Pp. 401–52 in *The Collected Works of Frédéric Bastiat: Economic Sophisms and "What Is Seen and What Is Not Seen,"* edited by J. de Guenin. Indianapolis, IN: Liberty Fund.

Bauer, L. and D. W. Schanzenbach. 2016. "The Long-Term Impact of the Head Start Program." The Hamilton Project, Brookings Institution. Retrieved here: https://www.hamiltonproject.org/assets/files/long_term_impact_of_head_start_program.pdf.

Baumol, William J., and William G. Bowen. 1968. *Performing Arts, the Economic Dilemma; a Study of Problems Common to Theater, Opera, Music and Dance.* Cambridge: M.I.T. Pr.

Baur, Lauren, and Diane Schanzenbach. 2016. *The Long-Term Impact of the Head Start Program | The Hamilton Project.* Economic Analysis. Washington, DC: The Brookings Institution.

Becker, Gary S., and Casey B. Mulligan. 1997. "The Endogenous Determination of Time Preference." *The Quarterly Journal of Economics* 112(3):729–58.

Beinhocker, E. D. 2006. *The Origin of Wealth: The Radical Remaking of Economics and What It Means for Business and Society.* Cambridge, MA: Harvard Business School.

Beito, D. T. 2000. *From Mutual Aid to the Welfare State: Fraternal Societies and Social Services, 1890–1967.* Chapel Hill, NC: University of North Carolina.

Beito, D. T., P. Gordon, and A. Tabarrok, eds. 2002. *The Voluntary City: Choice, Community, and Civil Society.* Ann Arbor: University of Michigan.

Benedict XVI, Pope. 2009. *Caritas in Veritate.* Retrieved here: http://www.vatican.va/content/benedict-xvi/en/encyclicals/documents/hf_ben-xvi_enc_20090629_caritas-in-veritate.html.

Berger, R. 2017. "The New 2018 Federal Income Tax Brackets and Rates." *Forbes.* Retrieved here: https://www.forbes.com/sites/robertberger/2017/12/17/the-new-2018-federal-income-tax-brackets-rates/#49638422292a.

Berkowitz, Seth A., Hilary K. Seligman, Joseph Rigdon, James B. Meigs, and Sanjay Basu. 2017. "Supplemental Nutrition Assistance Program (SNAP) Participation and Health Care Expenditures Among Low-Income Adults." *JAMA Internal Medicine* 177(11):1642–49. doi: 10.1001/jamainternmed.2017.4841.

Bertrand, Marianne, and Sendhil Mullainathan. 2004. "Are Emily and Greg More Employable Than Lakisha and Jamal? A Field Experiment on Labor Market Discrimination." *American Economic Review* 94(4):991–1013. doi: 10.1257/0002828042002561.

Bhattacharya, Jayanta, Thomas DeLeire, Steven Haider, and Janet Currie. 2003. "Heat or Eat? Cold-Weather Shocks and Nutrition in Poor American Families." *American Journal of Public Health* 93(7):1149–54.

Birdsall, N. 2008. "Seven Deadly Sins: Reflections on Donor Failings." In *Reinventing Foreign Aid*, edited by W. Easterly. Cambridge: MIT Press.

Blanchflower, David G., Phillip B. Levine, and David J. Zimmerman. 2003. "Discrimination in the Small-Business Credit Market." *The Review of Economics and Statistics* 85(4):930–43. doi: 10.1162/003465303772815835.

Blau, David M. 1999. "The Effect of Income on Child Development." *Review of Economics and Statistics* 81(2):261–76. doi: 10.1162/003465399558067.

Bourke, J. A. 1999. *An Intimate History of Killing: Face-to-Face Killing in 20th Century Warfare.* New York: Basic Books.

Boushey, Heather. 2019. *Unbound: How Inequality Constricts Our Economy and What We Can Do About It.* Cambridge, MA: Harvard University Press.

Breed, Allen G. 2001. "Prosperity Made Blacks a Target for Land Grabs." *Los Angeles Times*, December 9.

Brennan, J. 2016. *Against Democracy.* Princeton, NJ: Princeton University Press.

Brooks, A. C. 2006. *Who Really Cares? The Surprising Truth about Compassionate Conservatism: Who Gives, Who Doesn't, and Why It Matters.* New York: Basic Books.

Brooks, A. C. 2008. *Gross National Happiness: Why Happiness Matters for America—And How We Can Get More of It.* New York: Basic Books.

Brooks, A. C. 2015. *The Conservative Heart: How to Build a Fairer, Happier, and More Prosperous America.* New York: Broadside Books.

Brown, David W., Amanda E. Kowalski, and Ithai Z. Lurie. 2020. "Long-Term Impacts of Childhood Medicaid Expansions on Outcomes in Adulthood." *The Review of Economic Studies* 87(2):792–821. doi: 10.1093/restud/rdz039.

Buchanan, J. M. 1979 (1999). "Politics without Romance: A Sketch of Positive Public Choice Theory and Its Normative Implications." Pp. 45–59 in *The Collected Works of James M. Buchanan, Vol. I: The Logical Foundations of Constitutional Liberty,* edited by G. Brennan, H. Kliemt, and R. D. Tollison. Indianapolis, IN: Liberty Fund.

Buchanan, J. M. 1989. "The Relatively Absolute Absolutes." Pp. 32–46 in *Essays on the Political Economy.* Honolulu: University of Hawai'i.

Buchanan, J. M. 2003. "Public Choice: Politics Without Romance." *Policy* 19(3):13–8.

Burman, Leonard E., Robert McClelland, and Chenxi Lu. 2018. *The Effects of Estate and Inheritance Taxes on Entrepreneurship*. Washington, DC: Tax Policy Center.

Caplan, B. 2018. *The Case Against Education: Why the Education System Is a Waste of Time and Money*. Princeton, NJ: Princeton University Press.

Cappelen, Cornelius, and Jørgen Pedersen. 2018. "Just Wealth Transfer Taxation: Defending John Stuart Mill's Scheme." *Politics, Philosophy, & Economics* 17(3): 317–35.

Card, David, Thomas Lemieux, and W. Craig Riddell. 2004. "Unions and Wage Inequality." *Journal of Labor Research* 25(4):519–59. doi: 10.1007/s12122-004-1011-z.

Carlson, Devon, Robert Haveman, Tom Kaplan, and Barbara Wolfe. 2009. "Long-Term Effects of Public Low-Income Housing Vouchers on Labor Market Outcomes."

Carneiro, Pedro, and Rita Ginja. 2014. "Long-Term Impacts of Compensatory Preschool on Health and Behavior: Evidence from Head Start." *American Economic Journal: Economic Policy* 6(4):135–73. doi: 10.1257/pol.6.4.135.

Carroll, J. S., S. L. James, and H. Boyd. 2020. "Religion in the Home: Do Individuals and Couples Benefit from Home-Based Religious Practices?" The Wheatley Institution, Brigham Young University. Retrieved here: http://wheatley.byu.edu/wp-content/uploads/2020/10/Religion-in-the-Home10.13.20.pdf.

Catechism of the Catholic Church, 2nd. ed. 1997. The Vatican. Retrieved here: http://www.vatican.va/archive/ENG0015/_INDEX.HTM.

Chandy, L. and G. Gertz. 2011. "Poverty in Numbers: The Changing State of Global Poverty from 2005 to 2015." Washington, DC: Brookings Institution. Retrieved here: https://www.brookings.edu/research/poverty-in-numbers-the-changing-state-of-global-poverty-from-2005-to-2015/.

Chandy, L. and C. Smith. 2014. "How Poor Are America's Poorest? U.S. $2 a Day Poverty in a Global Context." Washington, DC: Brookings Institution. Retrieved here: https://www.brookings.edu/research/how-poor-are-americas-poorest-u-s-2-a-day-poverty-in-a-global-context/.

Chandy, L., H. Kato, and H. Kharas. 2015. *The Last Mile: Ending Extreme Poverty*. Washington, DC: Brookings Institution.

Chantrill, C. 2019a. "US Government Spending: Medicare Spending Analysis." Retrieved here: https://www.usgovernmentspending.com/medicare_spending_analysis.

Chantrill, C. 2019b. "US Government Spending: Medicaid Spending Analysis." Retrieved here: https://www.usgovernmentspending.com/medicaid_spending_analysis.

Chesterton, G. K. 1926. *The Outline of Sanity*. San Francisco, CA: Ignatius Press.

Chetty, Raj. 2009. "Is the Taxable Income Elasticity Sufficient to Calculate Deadweight Loss? The Implications of Evasion and Avoidance." *American Economic Journal: Economic Policy* 1(2):31–52. doi: 10.1257/pol.1.2.31.

Chetty, Raj, David Grusky, Maximilian Hell, Nathaniel Hendren, Robert Manduca, and Jimmy Narang. 2017. "The Fading American Dream: Trends in Absolute Income Mobility since 1940." *Science* 356(6336):398–406. doi: 10.1126/science.aal4617.

Chetty, Raj, John N. Friedman, Emmanuel Saez, Nicholas Turner, and Danny Yagan. 2017. *Mobility Report Cards: The Role of Colleges in Intergenerational Mobility*. Working Paper. 23618. National Bureau of Economic Research.

Chetty, Raj, John N. Friedman, and Jonah E. Rockoff. 2014. "Measuring the Impacts of Teachers II: Teacher Value-Added and Student Outcomes in Adulthood." *American Economic Review* 104(9):2633–79. doi: 10.1257/aer.104.9.2633.

Chetty, Raj, and Nathaniel Hendren. 2018. "The Impacts of Neighborhoods on Intergenerational Mobility I: Childhood Exposure Effects." *The Quarterly Journal of Economics* 133(3):1107–62. doi: 10.1093/qje/qjy007.

Chetty, Raj, Nathaniel Hendren, and Lawrence F. Katz. 2016. "The Effects of Exposure to Better Neighborhoods on Children: New Evidence from the Moving to Opportunity Experiment." *American Economic Review* 106(4):855–902. doi: 10.1257/aer.20150572.

Chetty, Raj, Nathaniel Hendren, Maggie R. Jones, and Sonya R. Porter. 2020. "Race and Economic Opportunity in the United States: An Intergenerational Perspective." *The Quarterly Journal of Economics* 135(2):711–83. doi: 10.1093/qje/qjz042.

Chetty, Raj, Nathaniel Hendren, Patrick Kline, Emmanuel Saez, and Nicholas Turner. 2014. "Is the United States Still a Land of Opportunity? Recent Trends in Intergenerational Mobility." *The American Economic Review* 104(5):141–47.

Chin, Mark J., David M. Quinn, Tasminda K. Dhaliwal, and Virginia S. Lovison. 2020. "Bias in the Air: A Nationwide Exploration of Teachers' Implicit Racial Attitudes, Aggregate Bias, and Student Outcomes." EdWorking Papers.Com.

Clark, G. 2009. *A Farewell to Alms: A Brief Economic History of the World*. Princeton, NJ: Princeton University Press.

Clark, Gregory, and Marianne E. Page. 2019. "Welfare Reform, 1834: Did the New Poor Law in England Produce Significant Economic Gains?" *Cliometrica* 13(2):221–44. doi: 10.1007/s11698-018-0174-4.

Coase, R. H. and N. Wang. 2012. *How China Became Capitalist*. New York: Palgrave Macmillan.

Coates, T.-N. 2014. "The Case for Reparations." *The Atlantic*. Retrieved here: https://www.theatlantic.com/magazine/archive/2014/06/the-case-for-reparations/361631/.

Coates, T.-N. 2015. *Between the World and Me*. New York: One World.

Cohen, G. A. 1995. *Self-Ownership, Freedom, and Equality*. Cambridge; New York: Paris, France: Cambridge University Press.

Cohen, G. A. 2000. *If You're an Egalitarian, How Come You're So Rich?* Cambridge, MA: Harvard University Press.

Cohen, G. A. 2009. *Why Not Socialism?* Princeton, NJ: Princeton University Press.

Cohen, G. A. 2011. *On the Currency of Egalitarian Justice, and Other Essays in Political Philosophy*. Princeton, NJ: Princeton University Press.

CollegeScholarships.org. N.d. Retrieved here: http://www.collegescholarships.org/scholarships/low-income.htm.

Committee for a Responsible Federal Budget. 2020. *Primary Care: Estimating Democratic Candidates' Health Plans*. Washington, DC.

Congressional Budget Office. 2004. *The Estate Tax and Charitable Giving*. CBO Paper. Washington, DC: Congressional Budget Office.

Congressional Research Service. 2019. "Federal Workforce Statistics Sources: OPM and OMB." Congressional Research Report R43590. Washington, DC: Congressional Research Service. Retrieved here: https://fas.org/sgp/crs/misc/R43590.pdf.

Cook, A. 2004. "Mind Your Head: The Data and Debate on Bicycle Helmet Effectiveness." *Significance* 1(4):162–3.

Cook, Karen S. 2014. "Social Capital and Inequality: The Significance of Social Connections." Pp. 207–27 in *Handbook of the Social Psychology of Inequality, Handbooks of Sociology and Social Research*, edited by J. D. McLeod, E. J. Lawler, and M. Schwalbe. Dordrecht: Springer Netherlands.

Courtois, S., N. Werth, J.-L. Panné, A. Paczkowski, K. Bartošek, and J.-L. Margolin. 1999. *The Black Book of Communism: Crimes, Terror, Repression*. Cambridge, MA: Harvard University Press.

Coyne, C. J. 2013. *Doing Bad by Doing Good: Why Humanitarian Action Fails*. Stanford, CA: Stanford University Press.

Crisp, Roger. 2003. "Equality, Priority, and Compassion." *Ethics* 113(4):745–63. doi: 10.1086/373954.

Cunha, Flavio, and James Heckman. 2010. "The Economics and Psychology of Inequality and Human Development." *Journal of the European Economic Association* 7(2-3):320–64. doi: 10.1162/JEEA.2009.7.2-3.320.

Currie, Janet M. 2006. *The Invisible Safety Net: Protecting the Nation's Poor Children and Families*. Princeton, NJ: Princeton University Press.

Currie, Janet M., and Duncan Thomas. 1993. *Does Head Start Make a Difference?* Working Paper. 4406. National Bureau of Economic Research.

Currie, Janet M., and Jonathan Gruber. 1996. "Saving Babies: The Efficacy and Cost of Recent Changes in the Medicaid Eligibility of Pregnant Women." *Journal of Political Economy* 104(6):1263–96.

Dague, Laura, Thomas DeLeire, and Lindsey Leininger. 2017. "The Effect of Public Insurance Coverage for Childless Adults on Labor Supply." *American Economic Journal: Economic Policy* 9(2):124–54. doi: 10.1257/pol.20150059.

Darity, William A., and A. Kirsten Mullen. 2020. *From Here to Equality: Reparations for Black Americans in the Twenty-First Century.* Chapel Hill: University of North Carolina Press.

Darling-Hammond, Linda. 2001. "Inequality in Teaching and Schooling: How Opportunity Is Rationed to Students of Color in America." Pp. 208–33 in *The Right Thing to Do, The Smart Thing to Do: Enhancing Diversity in the Health Professions,* edited by B. D. Smedley, A. Y. Stith, L. Colburn, and C. H. Evans. Washington, DC: National Academies Press.

Davies, S. 2019. *The Wealth Explosion: The Nature and Origins of Modernity.* Sussex: Edward Everett Root.

De Soto, H. 2000. *The Mystery of Capital: Why Capitalism Triumphs in the West and Fails Everywhere Else.* New York: Basic Books.

Deaton, A. 2013. *The Great Escape: Health, Wealth, and the Origins of Inequality.* Princeton, NJ: Princeton University Press.

DeLong, J. B. 1998. "Estimating World GDP, One Million B.C.–Present." Retrieved here: http://www.j-bradford-delong.net/TCEH/1998_Draft/World_GDP/Estimating_World_GDP.html.

Deming, David. 2009. "Early Childhood Intervention and Life-Cycle Skill Development: Evidence from Head Start." *American Economic Journal: Applied Economics* 1(3):111–34. doi: 10.1257/app.1.3.111.

Demsetz, H. 1969. "Information and Efficiency: Another Viewpoint." *The Journal of Law and Economics* 12(1): 1–22.

DePolt, Richard A., Robert A. Moffitt, and David C. Ribar. 2009. "Food Stamps, Temporary Assistance for Needy Families and Food Hardships in Three American Cities." *Pacific Economic Review* 14(4):445–73. doi: 10.1111/j.1468-0106.2009.00462.x.

Diette, Timothy M. 2012. "The Whiter the Better? Racial Composition and Access to School Resources for Black Students." *The Review of Black Political Economy* 39(3):321–34. doi: 10.1007/s12114-011-9101-7.

Dobkin, Carlos, Amy Finkelstein, Raymond Kluender, and Matthew J. Notowidigdo. 2018. "Myth and Measurement: The Case of Medical Bankruptcies." *The New England Journal of Medicine* 378(12):1076–78. doi: 10.1056/NEJMp1716604.

Dolan, Ed. 2020a. "It Is Time to Rethink the Capital Gains Tax Preference." Niskanen Center Commentary. Retrieved July 14, 2020 (https://

www.niskanencenter.org/it-is-time-to-rethink-the-capital-gains-tax-preference/).

Dolan, Ed. 2020b. "New Research Revives Debate Over a Poverty Trap." Niskanen Center Commentary. Retrieved July 16, 2020 (https://www.niskanencenter.org/new-research-revives-debate-over-a-poverty-trap/).

Dollar, D. and A. Kraay. 2001. "Trade, Growth, and Poverty." World Bank Policy Research Working Paper No. 2615. Retrieved here: http://documents.worldbank.org/curated/en/278551468743972606/Trade-growth-and-poverty.

Dollar, D. and A. Kraay. 2002. "Growth Is Good for the Poor." *Journal of Economic Growth* 7:195–225.

Donaldson, J. 2017. "Poverty Reduction in China: Stellar, but Misunderstood." *Brink Asia.* June 7. Retrieved here: https://www.brinknews.com/poverty-reduction-in-china-stellar-but-misunderstood/?utm_source=BRINK+Asia.

Downey, Douglas B., Paul T. von Hippel, and Beckett A. Broh. 2004. "Are Schools the Great Equalizer? Cognitive Inequality during the Summer Months and the School Year." *American Sociological Review* 69(5):613–35. doi: 10.1177/000312240406900501.

Duke, G. and R. P. George, eds. 2017. *The Cambridge Companion to Natural Law Jurisprudence.* New York: Cambridge University Press.

Duquette, Nicolas J. 2018. "Inequality and Philanthropy: High-Income Giving in the United States 1917–2012." *Explorations in Economic History* 70:25–41. doi: 10.1016/j.eeh.2018.08.002.

Durlauf, Steven N. 1996. "A Theory of Persistent Income Inequality." *Journal of Economic Growth* 1(1):75–93. doi: 10.1007/BF00163343.

Dynan, Karen, Douglas Elmendorf, and Daniel Sichel. 2012. "The Evolution of Household Income Volatility." *The B.E. Journal of Economic Analysis & Policy* 12(2). doi: 10.1515/1935-1682.3347.

East, Chloe N. 2020. "The Effect of Food Stamps on Children's Health Evidence from Immigrants' Changing Eligibility." *Journal of Human Resources* 55(2):387–427. doi: 10.3368/jhr.55.3.0916–8197R2.

Easterlin, R. A. 1974. "Does Economic Growth Improve the Human Lot? Some Empirical Evidence." Pp. 89–126 in *Nations and Households in Economic Growth*, edited by P. A. David and M. W. Reder. New York: Academic Press.

Easterly, W. 2007. *The White Man's Burden: Why the West's Efforts to Aid the Rest Have Done So Much Ill and So Little Good.* New York: Penguin.

Easterly, W. 2008. "Introduction: Can't Take It Anymore?" Pp. 1–43 in *Reinventing Foreign Aid*, edited by W. Easterly. Cambridge: MIT Press.

Easterly, W. 2013. *The Tyranny of Experts: Economists, Dictators, and the Forgotten Rights of the Poor.* New York: Basic Books.

Easterly, W. 2016. *The Economics of International Development: Foreign Aid versus Freedom for the World's Poor*. London: Institute for Economic Affairs.

Ekins, Emily. 2019. *What Americans Think About Poverty, Wealth, and Work. Survey Reports*. Washington, DC: The Cato Institute.

Epstein, R. A. 2017. *The Classical Liberal Constitution: The Uncertain Quest for Limited Government*. Cambridge, MA: Harvard University Press.

Evans, Gary W. 2004. "The Environment of Childhood Poverty." *American Psychologist* 59(2):77–92. doi: 10.1037/0003–066X.59.2.77.

Feiveson, Laura, and John Sabelhaus. 2019. *Lifecycle Patterns of Saving and Wealth Accumulation. 2019–010*. Board of Governors of the Federal Reserve System (U.S.).

Ferguson, N. 1999. *The House of Rothschild: Money's Prophets 1798–1848*. New York: Penguin.

Fischer, Will. 2015. *Research Shows Housing Vouchers Reduce Hardship and Provide Platform for Long-Term Gains among Children*. Washington, DC: Center on Budget and Policy Priorities.

Fishkin, Joseph. 2016. *Bottlenecks*. Reprint edition. Oxford New York: Oxford University Press.

Fleischacker, S. 1999. *A Third Concept of Liberty: Judgment and Freedom in Kant and Adam Smith*. Princeton, NJ: Princeton University Press.

Follett, C. 2015. "Extreme Poverty's End in Sight." Washington, DC: HumanProgress.org. Retrieved here: https://humanprogress.org/article.php?p=845.

Francis, Pope. 2020. *Fratelli Tutti: On Fraternity and Social Friendship*. Retrieved here: http://www.vatican.va/content/francesco/en/encyclicals/documents/papa-francesco_20201003_enciclica-fratelli-tutti.html.

Frank, Robert H. 2005a. "Positional Externalities Cause Large and Preventable Welfare Losses." *The American Economic Review* 95(2):137–41.

Frank, Robert H. 2005b. "The Mysterious Disappearance of James Duesenberry." *The New York Times*, June 9.

Frank, Robert H. 2010. *Luxury Fever: Weighing the Cost of Excess*. Princeton, NJ: Princeton University Press.

Frank, Robert H. 2017. *Success and Luck: Good Fortune and the Myth of Meritocracy*. Reprint edition. Princeton University Press.

Frankfurt, Harry G. 2015. *On Inequality*. First Edition. Princeton, NJ: Princeton University Press.

Furman, Jason. 2016. "Productivity, Inequality, and Economic Rents." *The Regulatory Review*. Retrieved June 1, 2020 (https://www.theregreview.org/2016/06/13/furman-productivity-inequality-and-economic-rents/).

Furman, Jason, and Peter Orszag. 2018. "A Firm-Level Perspective on the Role of Rents in the Rise of Inequality." Pp. 19–47 in *Toward a Just Society: Joseph Stiglitz and Twenty-First Century Economics*, edited by M. Guzman. New York: Columbia University Press.

Gaddis, S. Michael. 2015. "Discrimination in the Credential Society: An Audit Study of Race and College Selectivity in the Labor Market." *Social Forces* 93(4):1451–79. doi: 10.1093/sf/sou111.

Garces, Eliana, Duncan Thomas, and Janet Currie. 2002. "Longer-Term Effects of Head Start." *American Economic Review* 92(4):999–1012. doi: 10.1257/00028280260344560.

Gaus, G. 2016. *The Tyranny of the Ideal: Justice in a Diverse Society.* Princeton, NJ: Princeton University Press.

Gazeley, I. and A. Newell. 2020. "The End of Destitution." IZA Discussion Paper No. 4295. Retrieved here: https://ssrn.com/abstract=1434629.

Geremek, Bronislaw. 1991. *Poverty: A History.* Oxford: Wiley-Blackwell.

Girgis, S., R. T. Anderson, and R. P. George. 2020. *What Is Marriage? Man and Woman: A Defense.* New York: Encounter.

Giving USA Foundation. 2019. *Giving USA 2018: The Annual Report on Philanthropy for the Year 2018.* Chicago, IL: Giving USA Foundation.

Glassdoor. 2020. "12 Companies That Will Pay Off Student Loans." Retrieved here: https://www.glassdoor.com/blog/12-companies-that-will-pay-off-student-loans/.

Goldin, Claudia Dale, and Lawrence F. Katz. 2008. *The Race Between Education and Technology.* Cambridge, MA: Harvard University Press.

Goodman-Bacon, Andrew. 2016. *The Long-Run Effects of Childhood Insurance Coverage: Medicaid Implementation, Adult Health, and Labor Market Outcomes.* Working Paper. 22899. National Bureau of Economic Research.

Goodman-Bacon, Andrew. 2018. "Public Insurance and Mortality: Evidence from Medicaid Implementation." *Journal of Political Economy* 126(1):216–62. doi: 10.1086/695528.

Gottschalk, Peter. 1992. "The Intergenerational Transmission of Welfare Participation: Facts and Possible Causes." *Journal of Policy Analysis and Management* 11(2):254–72. doi: 10.2307/3325367.

Graham, C. 2011. *The Pursuit of Happiness: An Economy of Well-Being.* Washington, DC: Brookings Institution.

Gregory, Christian A., and Partha Deb. 2015. "Does SNAP Improve Your Health?" *Food Policy* 50:11–19. doi: 10.1016/j.foodpol.2014.09.010.

Gronholt-Pedersen, J. 2019. "Danes Make Welfare a Hot Election Issue as Cracks Show in Nordic Model." *U.S. News and World Report.* Retrieved here: https://www.usnews.com/news/world/articles/2019-05-29/danes-make-welfare-a-hot-election-issue-as-cracks-show-in-nordic-model.

Guth, Madeline, Rachel Garfield, and Robin Rudowitz. 2020. *The Effects of Medicaid Expansion under the ACA: Updated Findings from a Literature Review - Report.* San Francisco, CA: Kaiser Family Foundation.

Gwartney, J., R. Lawson, J. Hall, and R. Murphy. 2020. *Economic Freedom of the World: 2020 Annual Report.* Vancouver, BC: Fraser Institute.

Hall, J. C. and R. A. Lawson. 2013. "Economic Freedom of the World: An Accounting of the Literature." *Contemporary Economic Policy* 32(1) (March): 1–19.

Hamermesh, Daniel S., and Jeff E. Biddle. 1994. "Beauty and the Labor Market." *The American Economic Review* 84(5):1174–94.

Hamersma, Sarah. 2013. "The Effects of Medicaid Earnings Limits on Earnings Growth among Poor Workers." *The B.E. Journal of Economic Analysis & Policy* 13(2):887–919. doi: 10.1515/bejeap-2012-0048.

Hamilton, Darrick, and William Darity. 2010. "Can 'Baby Bonds' Eliminate the Racial Wealth Gap in Putative Post-Racial America?" *The Review of Black Political Economy* 37(3–4):207–16. doi: 10.1007/s12114-010-9063-1.

Hanbury, M. 2020. "This Is What the Average Walmart Shopper Looks Like." *Business Insider.* Retrieved here: https://www.businessinsider.com/walmart-shopper-demographics-average-is-white-woman-2020-1?op=1.

Harari, Y. N. 2015. *Sapiens: A Brief History of Humankind.* New York: Harper.

Hardin, Russell. 1990. *Morality within the Limits of Reason.* Reprint edition. Chicago, IL: University Of Chicago Press.

Harvey, Phil, and Lisa Conyers. 2016. *The Human Cost of Welfare: How the System Hurts the People It's Supposed to Help.* Santa Barbara, CA: Praeger.

Haskins, R. 2013. "The War on Poverty: What Went Wrong?" Washington, DC: Brookings Institute. Retrieved here: https://www.brookings.edu/opinions/the-war-on-poverty-what-went-wrong/.

Haushofer, Johannes, and Ernst Fehr. 2014. "On the Psychology of Poverty." *Science* 344(6186):862–67. doi: 10.1126/science.1232491.

Hayek, F. A. 2007 (1944). *The Road to Serfdom: The Definitive Edition,* edited by B. Caldwell. Chicago, IL: University of Chicago Press.

Heath, J. 2020. *The Machinery of Government: Public Administration and the Liberal State.* New York: Oxford University Press.

Heckman, James. 2007. "The Economics, Technology, and Neuroscience of Human Capability Formation." *Proceedings of the National Academy of Sciences* 104(33):13250–55. doi: 10.1073/pnas.0701362104.

Heckman, James, Jora Stixrud, and Sergio Urzua. 2006. "The Effects of Cognitive and Noncognitive Abilities on Labor Market Outcomes and Social Behavior." *Journal of Labor Economics* 24(3):411–82.

Heckman, James, Rodrigo Pinto, and Peter Savelyev. 2013. "Understanding the Mechanisms through Which an Influential Early Childhood Program Boosted Adult Outcomes." *American Economic Review* 103(6):2052–86. doi: 10.1257/aer.103.6.2052.

Helland, Eric, and Alexander Tabarrok. 2019. *Why Are the Prices So Damn High?* Arlington, VA: Mercaus Center.

Hippel, Paul T. von, and Ana P. Cañedo. 2020. "Is Ability Group Placement Biased? New Data, New Methods, New Answers." EdWorkingPapers.Com.

Hirschfeld, M. L. 2018. *Aquinas and the Market: Toward a Humane Economy.* Cambridge, MA: Harvard University Press.

Hirschman, A. O. 1970. *Exit, Voice, and Loyalty: Responses to Decline in Firms, Organizations, and States*. Cambridge, MA: Harvard University Press.

Hoffman, K. 2008. "Placing Enterprise and Business Thinking at the Heart of the War on Poverty." Pp. 485–502 in *Reinventing Foreign Aid*, edited by William Easterly. Cambridge: MIT Press.

Hoynes, Hilary. 2016. *The Supplemental Nutrition Assistance Program: A Central Component of the Social Safety Net*. Policy Brief. Berkeley, CA: Institute for Research on Labor and Employment.

Hoynes, Hilary W., and Diane Whitmore Schanzenbach. 2009. "Consumption Responses to In-Kind Transfers: Evidence from the Introduction of the Food Stamp Program." *American Economic Journal: Applied Economics* 1(4):109–39. doi: 10.1257/app.1.4.109.

Hoynes, Hilary W., Diane Whitmore Schanzenbach, and Douglas Almond. 2016. "Long-Run Impacts of Childhood Access to the Safety Net." *American Economic Review* 106(4):903–34. doi: 10.1257/aer.20130375.

Huemer, M. 2013. *The Problem of Political Authority: An Examination of the Right to Coerce and the Duty to Obey*. New York: Palgrave Macmillan.

Huemer, Michael. 2017. "Is Wealth Redistribution a Rights Violation?" Pp. 259–71 in The Routledge Handbook of Libertarianism, edited by J. Brennan, B. van der Vossen, and D. Schmidtz. New York: Routledge.

Hume, D. 1985 (1741). "Of the Independency of Parliament." In *David Hume: Essays Moral Political and Literary*, rev. ed. E. F. Miller, ed. Indianapolis, IN: Liberty Fund.

Hume, D. 1985 (1748). "Of the Original Contract." Pp. 465–87 in *David Hume: Essays Moral, Political, and Literary*, edited by E. F. Miller. Indianapolis, IN: Liberty Fund.

Hyman, Joshua. 2017. "Does Money Matter in the Long Run? Effects of School Spending on Educational Attainment." *American Economic Journal: Economic Policy* 9(4):256–80. doi: 10.1257/pol.20150249.

Ingram, G. and J. McArthur. 2018. "From One to Many: Cash Transfer Debates in Ending Extreme Poverty." Washington, DC: Brookings. Retrieved here: https://www.brookings.edu/blog/future-development/2018/12/19/from-one-to-many-cash-transfer-debates-in-ending-extreme-poverty/.

Isaacson, W. 2014. *The Innovators: How a Group of Hackers, Geniuses, and Geeks Created the Digital Revolution*. New York: Simon and Schuster.

Jackson, C. Kirabo, Rucker C. Johnson, and Claudia Persico. 2016. "The Effects of School Spending on Educational and Economic Outcomes: Evidence from School Finance Reforms." *The Quarterly Journal of Economics* 131(1):157–218.

John Paul II, Pope St. 1991. *Centesimus Annus*. Retrieved here: http://www.vatican.va/content/john-paul-ii/en/encyclicals/documents/hf_jp-ii_enc_01051991_centesimus-annus.html.

Johnson, L. B. 1964. "The Great Society" (remarks at the University of Michigan). Retrieved here: https://www.pbs.org/wgbh/americanexperience/features/lbj-michigan/.

Jones, Sonya J., Lisa Jahns, Barbara A. Laraia, and Betsy Haughton. 2003. "Lower Risk of Overweight in School-Aged Food Insecure Girls Who Participate in Food Assistance: Results From the Panel Study of Income Dynamics Child Development Supplement." *Archives of Pediatrics & Adolescent Medicine* 157(8):780–84. doi: 10.1001/archpedi.157.8.780.

Joulfaian, David. 2006. "The Behavioral Response of Wealth Accumulation to Estate Taxation: Time Series Evidence." *National Tax Journal* 59(2):253–68.

Kahneman, D. 2011. *Thinking, Fast and Slow.* New York: Farrar, Straus and Giroux.

Kahneman, D. and A. Deaton. 2010. "High Income Improves Evaluation of Life but Not Emotional Well-Being." Princeton University: Center for Health and Well-Being. Retrieved here: https://www.princeton.edu/~deaton/downloads/deaton_kahneman_high_income_improves_evaluation_August2010.pdf.

Kant, I. 1929 (1781). *Critique of Pure Reason,* N. K. Smith, trans. New York: St. Martin's.

Karelis, Charles H. 2009. *The Persistence of Poverty: Why the Economics of the Well-Off Can't Help the Poor.* London: Yale University Press.

Katz, Lawrence F., and Alan B. Krueger. 2017. "Documenting Decline in U.S. Economic Mobility." *Science.* doi: 10.1126/science.aan3264.

Khullar, Dhruv, and Dave Chokshi. 2018. *Health, Income, & Poverty: Where We Are & What Could Help.* Health Policy Brief. Health Affairs.

Klein, C. 2019. "Mobster Al Capone Ran a Soup Kitchen during the Great Depression." History.com. Retrieved here: https://www.history.com/news/al-capone-great-depression-soup-kitchen.

Kleiner, Morris M., and Alan B. Krueger. 2013. "Analyzing the Extent and Influence of Occupational Licensing on the Labor Market." *Journal of Labor Economics* 31(2):S173–202. doi: 10.1086/669060.

Kliff, Sarah. 2018. "An Exclusive Look at Cory Booker's Plan to Fight Wealth Inequality: Give Poor Kids Money." *Vox.* Retrieved July 11, 2020 (https://www.vox.com/policy-and-politics/2018/10/22/17999558/cory-booker-baby-bonds).

Kopczuk, Wojciech, Emmanuel Saez, and Jae Song. 2010. "Earnings Inequality and Mobility in the United States: Evidence from Social Security Data since 1937." *The Quarterly Journal of Economics* 125(1):91–128. doi: 10.1162/qjec.2010.125.1.91.

Krass, P. 2002. *Carnegie.* New York: Wiley.

Kreider, Brent, John V. Pepper, Craig Gundersen, and Dean Jolliffe. 2012. "Identifying the Effects of SNAP (Food Stamps) on Child Health Outcomes When Participation Is Endogenous and Misreported."

Journal of the American Statistical Association 107(499):958–75. doi: 10.1080/01621459.2012.682828.

Lal, D. 2013. *Poverty and Progress: Realities and Myths about Global Poverty.* Washington, DC: Cato Institute.

Landes, D. S. 1999. *The Wealth and Poverty of Nations: Why Some Are So Rich and Some Are So Poor.* New York: Norton.

Lawson, R., R. Murphy, and B. Powell. 2020. "The Determinants of Economic Freedom: A Survey." *Contemporary Economic Policy* 38(4):622–42.

Lazear, E. P. 2020. "Socialism, Capitalism, and Income." Stanford University: Hoover Institution. Retrieved here: https://www.hoover.org/sites/default/files/research/docs/prosperityproject_lazear_final.pdf.

Lewan, Todd, and Dolores Barclay. 2001. "'When They Steal Your Land, They Steal Your Future.'" *Los Angeles Times*, December 2, Online.

Lindsey, Brink, and Steven M. Teles. 2017. *The Captured Economy: How the Powerful Enrich Themselves, Slow Down Growth, and Increase Inequality.* Oxford: Oxford University Press.

Machin, Stephen. 1997. "The Decline of Labour Market Institutions and the Rise in Wage Inequality in Britain." *European Economic Review* 41(3):647–57. doi: 10.1016/S0014–2921(97)00027-5.

Mack, J. 2016. "Absolute and Overall Poverty." *Poverty and Social Exclusion.* Retrieved here: http://www.poverty.ac.uk/definitions-poverty/absolute-and-overall-poverty.

Maddison, A. 2007. *Contours of the World Economy, 1–2030 AD: Essays in Macro-Economic History.* New York: Oxford University Press.

Mani, Anandi, Sendhil Mullainathan, Eldar Shafir, and Jiaying Zhao. 2013. "Poverty Impedes Cognitive Function." *Science* 341(6149):976–80. doi: 10.1126/science.1238041.

Mankiw, N. Gregory. 2013. "Defending the One Percent." *Journal of Economic Perspectives* 27(3):21–34. doi: 10.1257/jep.27.3.21.

Mankiw, N. Gregory, and Matthew Weinzierl. 2010. "The Optimal Taxation of Height: A Case Study of Utilitarian Income Redistribution." *American Economic Journal: Economic Policy* 2(1):155–76. doi: 10.1257/pol.2.1.155.

Martin, J. 2020. "Iowa Church Clears $5 Million in Medical Debt for Christmas, and Aims for Millions More." *Newsweek*. Retrieved here: https://www.msn.com/en-us/news/politics/iowa-church-clears-5-million-of-medical-debt-for-christmas-and-aims-for-millions-more/ar-BB1bRgh0?fbclid=IwAR1uno7h0h-xzwN6aJN6eS1uTYf74MsToSNU-BKf9BIwViGHnTZhT31fqPk.

Massey, Douglas S., and Nancy A. Denton. 1993. *American Apartheid: Segregation and the Making of the Underclass.* Later Printing edition. Cambridge, MA: Harvard University Press.

McCabe, Helen. 2021. *John Stuart Mill, Socialist.* McGill-Queen's University Press.

McCloskey, D. N. 2006. *The Bourgeois Virtues: Ethics for an Age of Commerce*. Chicago, IL: University of Chicago Press.

McCloskey, D. N. 2010. *Bourgeois Dignity: Why Economics Can't Explain the Modern World*. Chicago, IL: University of Chicago Press.

McCloskey, D. N. 2016. *Bourgeois Equality: How Ideas, Not Capital or Institutions, Enriched the World*. Chicago, IL: University of Chicago Press.

McCloskey, D. N. 2019. *Why Liberalism Works: Why True Liberal Values Produce a Freer, More Equal, Prosperous World for All*. New Haven, CT: Yale University Press.

McCloskey, D. N. 2021. *Bettering Humanomics: A New, and Old, Approach to Economic Science*. Chicago, IL: University of Chicago Press.

McCloskey, D. N. and A. Carden. 2020. *Leave Me Alone and I'll Make You Rich: How the Bourgeois Deal Enriched the World*. Chicago, IL: University of Chicago Press.

McCloskey, D. N. and A. Mingardi. 2020. *The Myth of the Entrepreneurial State*. Great Barrington, MA: American Institute for Economic Research.

McIntosh, Kriston, Emily Moss, Ryan Nunn, and Jay Shambaugh. 2020. *Examining the Black-White Wealth Gap*.

McMullen, Steven. 2021. "Competition, Regulation, and the Race to the Bottom in Animal Agriculture." Pp. 113–30 in *Animals and Business Ethics*, edited by N. Thomas. New York: Springer.

McQuillan, L. J. and H. C. Park. 2017. "Pope Francis, Capitalism, and Private Charitable Giving." Pp. 87–117 in *Pope Francis and the Caring Society*, edited by R. M. Whaples. Oakland, CA: Independent Institute.

Mechling, George, Stephen Miller, and Ron Konecny. 2017. "Do Piketty and Saez Misstate Income Inequality? Critiquing the Critiques." *Review of Political Economy* 29(1):30–46. doi: 10.1080/09538259.2017.1255439.

Medi-Share. N.d. "About Us." Retrieved here: https://www.medishare.com/about.

Mettler, Suzanne. 2002. "Bringing the State Back in to Civic Engagement: Policy Feedback Effects of the G.I. Bill for World War II Veterans." *The American Political Science Review* 96(2):351–65.

Meyer, B. D., D. Wu, V. R. Mooers, and C. Medalia. 2019. "The Use and Misuse of Income Data and Extreme Poverty in the United States." NBER Working Paper Series, Working Paper 25907. Retrieved here: http://www.nber.org/papers/w25907.

Meyer, Bruce D., and James X. Sullivan. 2012. "Winning the War: Poverty from the Great Society to the Great Recession." *Brookings Papers on Economic Activity* 45(2):133–200.

Milanovic, B. 2010. *The Haves and the Have-Nots: A Brief and Idiosyncratic History of Global Inequality*. New York: Basic Books.

Milanovic, B. 2016. *Global Inequality: A New Approach for the Age of Globalization*. Cambridge, MA: Harvard University Press.

Miller, T., A. B. Kim, and J. M. Roberts. 2019. *2019 Index of Economic Freedom: 25th Anniversary Edition.* Washington, DC: The Heritage Foundation.

Moffitt, Robert A. 2002. "Chapter 34 Welfare Programs and Labor Supply." Pp. 2393–2430 in *Handbook of Public Economics*, edited by S. McMullen. Vol. 4. Elsevier.

Moffitt, Robert A. 2014. "Multiple Program Participation and the SNAP Program I RSF." P. 45 in *Five Decades of Food Stamps.* University of Kentucky Center for Poverty Research: Russell Sage Foundation.

Monnery, N. 2019. *A Tale of Two Economies: Hong Kong, Cuba and the Two Men Who Shaped Them.* London: Gulielmus Occamus & Co.

Mullainathan, Sendhil, and Eldar Shafir. 2014. *Scarcity: The New Science of Having Less and How It Defines Our Lives.* Reprint edition. New York: Picador.

Munger, M. 2014. "Unicorn Governance." Foundation for Economic Education. Retrieved here: https://fee.org/articles/unicorn-governance.

Munger, M. 2015. "One and One-Half Cheers for a Basic Income Guarantee: We Could Do Worse, and Already Have." *The Independent Review* 19(4):503–13.

Munger, M. 2019. *Is Capitalism Sustainable?* Great Barrington, MA: American Institute for Economic Research.

Murphy, J. M., C. A. Wehler, M. E. Pagano, M. Little, R. E. Kleinman, and M. S. Jellinek. 1998. "Relationship between Hunger and Psychosocial Functioning in Low-Income American Children." *Journal of the American Academy of Child and Adolescent Psychiatry* 37(2):163–70. doi: 10.1097/00004583–199802000-00008.

New York Times. October 22, 1987. "Merck Offers Free Distribution of New River Blindness Drug." Retrieved here: https://www.nytimes.com/1987/10/22/world/merck-offers-free-distribution-of-new-river-blindness-drug.html.

Newhouse, Joseph P. 1993. *Free for All?: Lessons from the RAND Health Insurance Experiment.* Cambridge, MA: Harvard University Press.

Nielsen, Kai. 1981. "A Rationale for Egalitarianism." *Social Research* 48(2):260–76.

Nielsen, Kai. 1985. *Equality and Liberty: A Defense of Radical Egalitarianism.* Totowa, NJ: Rowman & Littlefield Publishers.

Niemietz, K. 2019. *Socialism: The Failed Idea that Never Dies.* London: Institute for Economic Affairs.

Nordhaus, W. 2004. "Schumpeterian Profits in the American Economy: Theory and Measurement." National Bureau of Economic Research Working Paper no. 10433. Cambridge, Mass.: NBER.

North, D. C. 1981. *Structure and Change in Economic History.* New York: Norton.

Nozick, Robert. 1974. *Anarchy, State, and Utopia.* Oxford: Blackwell.

Olasky, M. 2008. *The Tragedy of American Compassion*. Wheaton, IL: Crossway.

Oman, N. B. 2016. *The Dignity of Commerce: Markets and the Moral Foundations of Contract Law*. Chicago, IL: University of Chicago Press.

Otteson, J. R. 2006. *Actual Ethics*. New York: Cambridge University Press.

Otteson, J. R. 2014. *The End of Socialism*. New York: Cambridge University Press.

Otteson, J. R. 2017. "Opting Out: A Defense of Social Justice." *The Independent Review* 24(1):13–24.

Otteson, J. R. 2019a. *Honorable Business: A Framework for Business in a Just and Humane Society*. New York: Oxford University Press.

Otteson, J. R. 2019b. "Escaping the Social Pull: Nonconformists and Self-Censorship." *Society* (December 2019): 1–10.

Otteson, J. R. 2021. *Seven Deadly Economic Sins: Obstacles to Prosperity and Happiness Every Citizen Should Know*. New York: Cambridge University Press.

Overpeck, Mary D., and Jonathan B. Kotch. 1995. "The Effect of US Children's Access to Care on Medical Attention for Injuries." *American Journal of Public Health* 85(3):402–4.

Pager, Devah. 2007. *Marked: Race, Crime, and Finding Work in an Era of Mass Incarceration*. Chicago, IL: University of Chicago Press.

Pages, R. J.-C., D. L. Lukes, D. H. Bailey, and G. J. Duncan. 2019. "Elusive Longer-Run Impacts of Head Start: Replications Within and Across Cohorts" (EdWorkingPaper No.19–27). Retrieved from Annenberg Institute at Brown University: http://edworkingpapers.com/ai19-27.

Pages, Remy, Dylan J. Lukes, Drew H. Bailey, and Greg J. Duncan. 2020. "Elusive Longer-Run Impacts of Head Start: Replications Within and Across Cohorts." *Educational Evaluation and Policy Analysis* 42(4):471–92. doi: 10.3102/0162373720948884.

Parfit, Derek. 1997. "Equality and Priority." *Ratio* 10(3):202–21. doi: 10.1111/1467–9329.00041.

Payne, Keith. 2017. *The Broken Ladder: How Inequality Affects the Way We Think, Live, and Die*. New York: Viking.

Peltzman, S. 2004. "Regulation and the Natural Progress of Opulence." American Enterprise Institute. Washington, DC. Retrieved here: https://www.aei.org/publication/regulation-and-the-natural-progress-of-opulence/.

Pepper, John V. 1995. "Dynamics of the Intergenerational Transmission of Welfare Receipt in the United States." *Journal of Family and Economic Issues* 16(2):265–79. doi: 10.1007/BF02353711.

Perry, M. J. 2018. "Chart of the Day (Century?): Price Changes 1997 to 2017." Washington, DC: American Enterprise Institute. Retrieved here: https://www.aei.org/carpe-diem/chart-of-the-day-century-price-changes-1997-to-2017/.

Pew Research Center. 2018. "Mobile Fact Sheet." Retrieved here: https://www.pewinternet.org/fact-sheet/mobile/.

Pew Research Center. 2019. "Religion's Relationship to Happiness, Civic Engagement and Health around the World." Washington, DC: Pew Research Center. Retrieved here: https://www.pewforum.org/2019/01/31/religions-relationship-to-happiness-civic-engagement-and-health-around-the-world/.

Phelps, E. 2013. *Mass Flourishing: How Grassroots Innovation Created Jobs, Challenge, and Change.* Princeton, NJ: Princeton University Press.

Phillips, Richard, and Steve Wamhoff. 2018. *The Federal Estate Tax: An Important Progressive Revenue Source.* Washington, DC: Institute on Taxation and Economic Policy.

Piketty, Thomas, and Emmanuel Saez. 2003. "Income Inequality in the United States, 1913–1998." *The Quarterly Journal of Economics* 118(1):1–41.

Pinker, S. 2011. *The Better Angels of Our Nature: Why Violence Has Declined.* New York: Viking.

Pinker, S. 2018. *Enlightenment Now: The Case for Reason, Science, Humanism, and Progress.* New York: Viking.

Plastrik, Peter, Betsy Campbell, Sheri Gasche, Neal Halfon, Jessica Laufer, and Sybil MacDonald. 2002. *Building Assets to Reduce Poverty and Injustice.* New York: Ford Foundation.

Plato. 1992. *Republic.* G. M. A. Grube, trans., rev. by C. D. C. Reeve. Indianapolis, IN: Hackett.

Pritchett, L. and M. Woolcock. 2008. "Solutions When the Solution Is the Problem: Arraying the Disarray in Development." Pp. 147–77 in *Reinventing Foreign Aid*, edited by W. Easterly. Cambridge: MIT Press.

Prucha, Francis Paul. 1986. *The Great Father: The United States Government and the American Indians.* Abridged edition. Lincoln: University of Nebraska Press.

Putnam, Robert D. 2000. *Bowling Alone: The Collapse and Revival of American Community.* New York: Simon & Schuster.

Putnam, Robert D. 2016. *Our Kids: The American Dream in Crisis.* Reprint edition. New York: Simon & Schuster.

Quillian, Lincoln, Devah Pager, Ole Hexel, and Arnfinn H. Midtbøen. 2017. "Meta-Analysis of Field Experiments Shows No Change in Racial Discrimination in Hiring over Time." *Proceedings of the National Academy of Sciences* 114(41):10870–75. doi: 10.1073/pnas.1706255114.

Rawls, J. 1971. *A Theory of Justice.* Cambridge, MA: Harvard University Press.

Rawls, John. 1999. *A Theory of Justice*, 2 edition. Cambridge, MA: Belknap Press: An Imprint of Harvard University Press.

Rector, Robert. 2014. *The War on Poverty: 50 Years of Failure. Commentary.* Washington, DC: The Heritage Foundation.

Reeves, Richard V. 2017. *Dream Hoarders: How the American Upper Middle Class Is Leaving Everyone Else in the Dust, Why That Is a Problem, and What to Do About It*. Washington, D.C: Brookings Institution Press.

Regnerus, M. 2015. "The Family as First Building Block." Pp. 49–66 in *The Thriving Society: On the Social Conditions of Human Flourishing*, edited by J. R. Stoner, Jr. and H. James. Princeton, NJ: Witherspoon Institute.

Ridley, M. 2020. *How Innovation Works and Why It Flourishes in Freedom*. New York: Harper.

Riddle, Travis, and Stacey Sinclair. 2019. "Racial Disparities in School-Based Disciplinary Actions Are Associated with County-Level Rates of Racial Bias." *Proceedings of the National Academy of Sciences* 116(17):8255–60. doi: 10.1073/pnas.1808307116.

RIP Medical Debt. N.d. Retrieved here: https://ripmedicaldebt.org/.

Robeyns, Ingrid. 2019. What, If Anything, Is Wrong With Extreme Wealth? *Journal of Human Development and Capabilities* 20(3): 251–66.

Robinson, D. L. 2006. "No Clear Evidence from Countries That Have Enforced the Wearing of Helmets." *British Medical Journal* 332(7543):722–5.

Roemer, John E. 1996. *Egalitarian Perspectives: Essays in Philosophical Economics*. Cambridge: Cambridge University Press.

Rose, D. C. 2011. *The Moral Foundation of Economic Behavior*. New York: Oxford University Press.

Rose, D. C. 2019. *Why Culture Matters Most*. New York: Oxford University Press.

Rosenberg, N. and L. E. Birdzell, Jr. 1986. *How the West Grew Rich: The Economic Transformation of the Industrial World*. New York: Basic Books.

Roser, M. 2017. "The Global Decline of Extreme Poverty—Was It Only China?" *Our World in Data*. Retrieved here: https://ourworldindata.org/the-global-decline-of-extreme-poverty-was-it-only-china/.

Roser, M. and E. Ortiz-Ospina. 2017. "Global Extreme Poverty." *Our World in Data*. Retrieved here: https://ourworldindata.org/extreme-poverty.

Rosling, H., O. Rosling, and A. R. Rönnlund. 2018. *Factfulness: Ten Reasons We're Wrong about the World—And Why Things Are Better than You Think*. New York: Flatiron Books.

Rothschild, N. 2021. "Young Dems More Likely to Despise the Other Party." *Axios*. Retrieved here: https://www.axios.com/poll-political-polarization-students-a31e9888-9987-4715-9a2e-b5c448ed3e5a.html.

Rothwell, Jonathan. 2019. *A Republic of Equals: A Manifesto for a Just Society*. Princeton, NJ: Princeton University Press.

Rothwell, Jonathan, and Douglas Massey. 2015. "Geographic Effects on Intergenerational Income Mobility." *Economic Geography* 91(1):83–106. doi: 10.1111/ecge.12072.

Rummel, R. J. 1997. *Death by Government*. New York: Routledge.

Rummel, R. J. 2007. *The Blue Book of Freedom: Ending Famine, Poverty, Democide, and War.* Nashville, TN: Cumberland House.

Scanlon, T. M. 2018. *Why Does Inequality Matter?* Oxford: Oxford University Press.

Schanzenbach, Diane Whitmore. 2013. *Strengthening SNAP for a More Food-Secure, Healthy America.* Discussion Paper. 2013–06. Washington, DC: The Brookings Institution.

Schanzenbach, Diane Whitmore. 2019. "Exploring Options to Improve the Supplemental Nutrition Assistance Program (SNAP):" *The ANNALS of the American Academy of Political and Social Science.* doi: 10.1177/0002716219882677.

Schanzenbach, Diane Whitmore, Lauren Bauer, and Greg Nantz. 2016. *Twelve Facts about Food Security and SNAP. Economic Facts.* Washington, DC: The Brookings Institution.

Scheidel, W. 2017. *The Great Leveler: Violence and the History of Inequality from the Stone Age to the Twenty-First Century.* Princeton, NJ: Princeton University Press.

Schor, Juliet B. 1999. *The Overspent American: Why We Want What We Don't Need.* 1st HarperPerennial Ed edition. New York: Harper Perennial.

Schuck, P. H. 2014. *Why Government Fails So Often: And How It Can Do Better.* Princeton, NJ: Princeton University Press.

Scott, D. R. 2019. "Would Your Mobile Phone Be Powerful Enough to Get You to the Moon?" *The Conversation.* Retrieved here: https://theconversation.com/would-your-mobile-phone-be-powerful-enough-to-get-you-to-the-moon-115933.

Scott, J. C. 1998. *Seeing Like a State: How Certain Schemes to Improve the Human Condition Have Failed.* New Haven, CT: Yale University Press.

Semega, J., M. Kollar, E. A. Shrider, and J. Creamer. 2020. "Income and Poverty in the United States: 2019." United States Census Bureau. Retrieved here: https://www.census.gov/library/publications/2020/demo/p60-270.html.

Semega, Jessica, Melissa Kollar, John Creamer, and Abinash Mohanty. 2019. *Income and Poverty in the United States: 2018.* P60–266. Washington, DC: US Census Bureau.

Semuels, Alana. 2015. "America's Shame: How U.S. Housing Policy Is Failing the Country's Poor." *The Atlantic,* June 24.

Semuels, Alana. 2016. "The Role of Highways in American Poverty." *The Atlantic,* March 18.

Sen, Amartya. 2011. "Equality of What?" Pp. 197–220 in *The Tanner Lectures on Human Values I,* edited by S. McMurrin. Cambridge: Cambridge University Press.

Shah, Anuj K., Jiaying Zhao, Sendhil Mullainathan, and Eldar Shafir. 2018. "Money in the Mental Lives of the Poor." *Social Cognition* 36(1):4–19. doi: 10.1521/soco.2018.36.1.4.

Shapiro, Isaac, Robert Greenstein, Danilo Trisi, and Bryann Dasilva. 2016. *It Pays to Work: Work Incentives and the Safety Net*. Center on Budget and Policy Priorities.

Shealy, J. E., R. J. Johnson, and C. F. Ettlinger. 2009. "Do Helmets Reduce Fatalities or Merely Alter the Patterns of Death?" Pp. 39–42 in *Skiing Trauma and Safety: 17th Volume*, edited by R. Johnson, J. Shealy, and M. Langran. West Conshohocken, PA: ASTM International.

Sheffield, R. and R. Rector. 2014. "The War on Poverty after 50 Years." Backgrounder No. 2955. Washington, DC: Heritage Foundation. Retrieved here: https://www.heritage.org/poverty-and-inequality/report/the-war-poverty-after-50-years.

Sherraden, Michael Wayne. 1991. *Assets and the Poor: A New American Welfare Policy*. Armonk, NY: M.E. Sharpe, Incorporated.

Shlaes, A. 2014. *Coolidge*. New York: Harper Perennial.

Shleifer, Andrei. 2004. "Does Competition Destroy Ethical Behavior?" *American Economic Review* 94(2):414–18. doi: 10.1257/0002828041301498.

Simmons, R. T. 2011. *Beyond Politics: The Roots of Government Failure*. Oakland, CA: The Independent Institute.

Singer, Peter. 2009. *The Life You Can Save: Acting Now to End World Poverty*. New York: Random House.

Singer, Peter. 2010. *The Life You Can Save: How to Do Your Part to End World Poverty*. Reprint edition. New York: Random House Trade Paperbacks.

Singer, Peter. 2015. *The Most Good You Can Do: How Effective Altruism Is Changing Ideas About Living Ethically*. New Haven, CT: Yale University Press.

Slavov, S. N. 2013. "Public versus Private Provision of Public Goods." Retrieved here: https://ssrn.com/abstract=2211590.

Slemrod, eds Joel. 2001. *Rethinking Estate and Gift Taxation*, edited by W. Gale, J. J. R. Hines, and J. Slemrod. Washington, DC: Brookings Institution Press.

Smith, A. 1981 (1776). *An Inquiry into the Nature and Causes of the Wealth of Nations*, edited by R. H. Campbell and A. S. Skinner. Indianapolis, IN: Liberty Fund.

Smith, A. 1982 (1759). *The Theory of Moral Sentiments*, edited by D. D. Raphael and A. L. Macfie. Indianapolis, IN: Liberty Fund.

Song, Jae, David J. Price, Fatih Guvenen, Nicholas Bloom, and Till von Wachter. 2019. "Firming Up Inequality." *The Quarterly Journal of Economics* 134(1):1–50. doi: 10.1093/qje/qjy025.

Sowell, T. 2020. *Charter Schools and Their Enemies*. New York: Basic Books.

Stevenson, B. and J. Wolfers. 2013. "Subjective Well-Being and Income: Is There Any Evidence of Satiation?" Brookings Institute. Retrieved here: https://www.brookings.edu/research/subjective-well%E2%80%90being-and-income-is-there-any-evidence-of-satiation/.

Stiglitz, Joseph E. 2012. *The Price of Inequality: How Today's Divided Society Endangers Our Future*. Reprint edition. New York: W. W. Norton & Company.

Stringham, E. P., ed. 2015. *Private Governance: Creating Order in Economic and Social Life*. New York: Oxford University Press.

Stromberg, Joseph. 2015. "The Real Story behind the Demise of America's Once-Mighty Streetcars." *Vox*. Retrieved August 1, 2019 (https://www.vox.com/2015/5/7/8562007/streetcar-history-demise).

Strully, Kate W., David H. Rehkopf, and Ziming Xuan. 2010. "Effects of Prenatal Poverty on Infant Health: State Earned Income Tax Credits and Birth Weight." *American Sociological Review* 75(4):534–62. doi: 10.1177/0003122410374086.

Strumpf, Erin. 2011. *Medicaid's Effect on Single Women's Labor Supply: Evidence from the Introduction of Medicaid*. SSRN Scholarly Paper. ID 1655955. Rochester, NY: Social Science Research Network.

Stutzer, A. and B. S. Frey. 2006. "Does Marriage Make People Happy, or Do Happy People Get Married?" *Journal of Socio-Economics* 35(2):326–47.

Sumner, W. G. 1992 (1883). "The Forgotten Man." Pp. 201–22 in *On Liberty, Society, and Politics: The Essential Essays of William Graham Sumner*, edited by R. C. Bannister. Indianapolis, IN: Liberty Fund.

Sunstein, C. R. 2011. *Going to Extremes: How Like Minds Unite and Divide*. New York: Oxford University Press.

Tanner, Michael D. 2018. *The Inclusive Economy: How to Bring Wealth to America's Poor*. Washington, DC: Cato Institute.

Taylor, R. S. 2017. *Exit Left: Markets and Mobility in Republican Thought*. New York: Oxford University Press.

Thaler, R. H. 2015. *Misbehaving: The Making of Behavioral Economics*. New York: Norton.

Thoma, M. 2015. "Why Social Insurance Is a Necessary Part of Capitalism." *The Fiscal Times*. Retrieved here: http://www.thefiscaltimes.com/Columns/2015/02/10/Why-Social-Insurance-Necessary-Part-Capitalism.

Thompson, Owen. 2017. "The Long-Term Health Impacts of Medicaid and CHIP." *Journal of Health Economics* 51:26–40. doi: 10.1016/j.jhealeco.2016.12.003.

Trisi, Danilo. 2016. "Safety Net's Anti-Poverty Effectiveness Has Grown Nearly Ten-Fold Since 1967." Center on Budget and Policy Priorities. Retrieved July 16, 2020 (https://www.cbpp.org/blog/safety-nets-anti-poverty-effectiveness-has-grown-nearly-ten-fold-since-1967).

Tullock, G., A. Seldon, and G. L. Brady. 2002. *Government Failure: A Primer in Public Choice*. Washington, DC: Cato Institute.

Tupy, M. L. 2017. "Things Are Looking Up by Any Measure." Washington, DC: HumanProgress.org. Retrieved here: https://humanprogress.org/article.php?p=774.

Tupy, Marian L. 2019. "America Is in the Grips of a Living Standards Myth." *CapX*. June 26. Retrieved here: https://capx.co/G3Z8I.

Urban Institute. 2020. "The Nonprofit Sector in Brief." Retrieved here: https://nccs.urban.org/project/nonprofit-sector-brief.

Van Zanden, J. L., J. Baten, M. M. d'Ercole, A. Rijpma, C. Smith, and M. Timmer, eds. 2014. *How Was Life? Global Well-Being since 1820*. Paris: Organization for Economic Cooperation and Development.

Varian, Hal. 1980. "Redistributive Taxation as Social Insurance." *Journal of Public Economics* 14(1):49–68.

Walmart. N.d. "Walmart Health." Retrieved here: https://one.walmart.com/content/usone/en_us/company/walmart-health.html.

Wamhoff, Steve. 2019. *Congress Should Reduce, Not Expand, Tax Breaks for Capital Gains*. Washington, DC: Institute on Taxation and Economic Policy.

Welch, Finis. 1999. "In Defense of Inequality." *American Economic Review* 89(2):1–17. doi: 10.1257/aer.89.2.1.

Whaples, R. 2015. "Skeptical Thoughts on a Taxpayer-Funded Basic Income Guarantee." *The Independent Review* 19(4): 531–36.

Whaples, R., ed. 2017. *Pope Francis and the Caring Society*. Oakland, CA: Independent Institute.

White, L. H. 2012. *The Class of Economic Ideas: The Great Policy Debates and Experiments of the Last Hundred Years*. New York: Cambridge University Press.

White, M. 2012. *The Great Big Book of Horrible Things: The Definitive Chronicle of History's 100 Worst Atrocities*. New York: Norton.

Whitehurst, Grover J., and Ellie Klein. 2015. *Do We Already Have Universal Preschool?* Washington, DC: Brookings Institution.

Wilde, G. J. S. 1998. "Risk Homeostasis Theory: An Overview." *Inquiry Prevention* 4:89–91.

Wilkinson, Richard, and Kate Pickett. 2011. *The Spirit Level: Why Greater Equality Makes Societies Stronger*. Reprint edition. New York, NY: Bloomsbury Publishing.

Williams, D. L. 2021. "Hobbes on Wealth, Poverty, and Economic Inequality." *Hobbes Studies* 34(1):9–57.

Wimer, Christopher, Liana Fox, Irwin Garfinkel, Neeraj Kaushal, and Jane Waldfogel. 2016. "Progress on Poverty? New Estimates of Historical Trends Using an Anchored Supplemental Poverty Measure." *Demography* 53(4):1207–18. doi: 10.1007/s13524-016-0485-7.

Wood, Michelle, Jennifer Turnham, and Gregory Mills. 2008. "Housing Affordability and Family Well-being: Results from the Housing Voucher Evaluation." *Housing Policy Debate* 19(2):367–412. doi: 10.1080/10511482.2008.9521639.

World Bank. 2015. "World Bank Forecasts Global Poverty to Fall Below 10% for First Time; Major Hurdles Remain in Goal to End Poverty by 2030." Retrieved here: http://www.worldbank.org/en/news/press-release/2015/10/04/world-bank-forecasts-global-poverty-to-fall-below-10-for-first-time-major-hurdles-remain-in-goal-to-end-poverty-by-2030.

Yunus, M. 2017. *A World of Three Zeros: The New Economics of Zero Poverty, Zero Unemployment, and Zero Net Carbon Emissions.* New York: Public Affairs.

Zewde, Naomi. 2020. "Universal Baby Bonds Reduce Black-White Wealth Inequality, Progressively Raise Net Worth of All Young Adults." *The Review of Black Political Economy* 47(1):3–19. doi: 10.1177/0034644619885321.

Zhao, M. 2019. "Solidarity, Fate-Sharing, and Community." *Philosopher's Imprint* 19(46): 1–13.

Zwolinski, Matt. 2017. "Libertarianism and the Welfare State." Pp. 323–41 in *The Routledge Handbook of Libertarianism*, edited by J. Brennan, B. van der Vossen, and D. Schmidtz. New York: Routledge.

Index

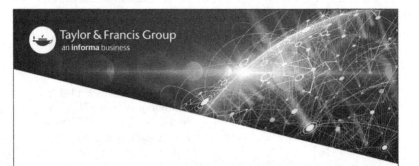

Printed in the United States
by Baker & Taylor Publisher Services